The Stars of Hollywood Remembered

The Stars of Hollywood Remembered

Career Biographies of 82 Actors and Actresses of the Golden Era, 1920s–1950s

J.G. ELLROD

McFarland & Company, Inc., Publishers

Jefferson, North Carolina, and London

Cover: Although stranded, Natalie Wood, Rosalind Russell and Karl Malden still see the bright side by singing in *Gypsy* (Warner Bros., 1962).

British Library Cataloguing-in-Publication data are available

Library of Congress Cataloguing-in-Publication Data

Ellrod, J. G., 1924–
     The stars of Hollywood remembered : career biographies of 82 actors and actresses of the golden era, 1920s–1950s / J. G. Ellrod.
         p.   cm.
     Includes filmographies.
     Includes bibliographical references and index.
     ISBN-13: 978-0-7864-0294-6 (softcover : 55# alkaline paper) ∞
     1. Motion picture actors and actresses — United States — Biography —
Dictionaries.   2. Motion picture actors and actresses — United
States — Credits.
PN1998.2.E46   1997
791.43'028'092273 — dc21
[B]   97-9338
                                                                                        CIP

Manufactured in the United States of America

McFarland & Company, Inc., Publishers
  Box 611, Jefferson, North Carolina 28640

Table of Contents

Preface

My introduction to the movies came when I was a youngster in Champaign-Urbana, Illinois, attending Saturday matinees and seeing Westerns and the weekly serials. As I grew older, these were replaced by films starring James Cagney, Will Rogers, Clark Gable, Claudette Colbert and Shirley Temple.

After moving to Chicago, I learned that the movie theaters in the neighborhood had double features. What a bargain — two films for the price of one! To top that, when my parents went to the movies they got free dishes.

A great adventure was to go downtown to the Loop theaters (such as the Chicago, RKO Palace, Oriental and State Lake) which had first-run features and vaudeville, too. Such stars as Jack Benny, Milton Berle, Eddie Cantor, the Marx Brothers and Edgar Bergen reigned supreme. Also gracing the stages were great orchestras like Fats Waller, Duke Ellington, Ted Lewis, Ben Bernie, Cab Calloway and Lawrence Welk, to name a few.

Next came an introduction to legitimate theater where screen personalities appeared in plays and musicals. Highlights were seeing Leslie Howard as Hamlet, Katharine Hepburn as Jane Eyre and Laurence Olivier with Vivien Leigh as the ill-fated Romeo and Juliet. In musical comedies and dramas, such as Al Jolson, Martha Raye, Bob Hope, Helen Morgan, Tallulah Bankhead, Constance Bennett, Miriam Hopkins and Lillian Gish appeared every year. Sonja Henie brought her ice follies on tour to the city. In the suburbs, Gloria Swanson, Ruth Chatterton and Conrad Nagel acted in the new summer stock theaters. Lucky me — the stars were not only on the silver screen but in person, too — and at each offering, you got a program which became a special souvenir.

We took a summer vacation trip to Los Angeles and that was like icing on the cake. At Grauman's Chinese Theatre we saw Janet Gaynor and Fredric March in *A Star Is Born*. Outside the theater after the film, I put my feet in the stars' footprints. One day we had lunch at the renowned Brown Derby. At the next booth sat Claude Rains and his party while across the room was Robert Montgomery. It was exciting to see these screen idols in person.

Family friends got us on the Paramount lot where I saw Cecil B. DeMille, Fredric March and Gary Cooper. I also got a glimpse of Carole Lombard and Marlene Dietrich. One evening we went to a sneak preview which turned out to be *Second Honeymoon* with Tyrone Power and Loretta Young. Another evening we went to the Biltmore Theater to see the stage play *Golden Boy* with Francis Lederer and Betty Furness. Then came an unexpected bonus — only two rows away from us in the audience were Joan Crawford and Franchot Tone.

No holiday in Los Angeles is complete without buying a map directing you to the homes of the stars, and we had one. A special treat was seeing Irene Dunne working in her garden. She looked up, smiled and continued her gardening.

Hollywood in those days was America's dream castle and its inhabitants were America's royalty. The glamour which surrounded the film industry in the golden years from the late 20s to the mid–50s has long since faded and will not come again. Still, we have the heritage of the "golden age" as seen through the showing of its films on television, video cassettes, at film society showings and film festivals throughout the world. The memory lingers on!

This is a sequel to my first book, *Hollywood Greats of the Golden Years*, which was printed in the fall of 1989. It contained 81 stars. The stars I selected for inclusion in that book were in my

opinion among the brightest, most beloved and most enduring. The one strict criterion observed in their selection was that they were no longer living as of the date of publication. In this book I have included stars who were no longer living as of September 1996; there are no actors or actresses repeated from my earlier book. I hope that you will find some of your favorites and enjoy the "golden years" of the movies.

J. G. Ellrod

Reference Works Consulted

Motion Picture Guide. Volumes I-IX. Evanston, Illinois. Cinebooks 1985-7
Movie Greats, the Players, Directors, Producers. New York: Garland, 1969
New York Times Directory of the Film. New York. Arno/Random House, 1983
Variety Film Review. Volumes 3-16. New York: Garland, 1983
Obituary notices from the following newspapers: *Miami Herald, New Orleans Times-Picayune, New York Times, Variety*

Abbreviation Key

AA   Allied Artists
ABF   Anglo British Films
ABP   Associated British Pathe
AE   AVCO Embassy
AFD   Associated Film Distributing Corp.
AFT   American Film Theatre
AFG   Associated General Films
AIP   American International Pictures
BIP   British International Pictures
BL   British Lion
BV   Buena Vista
Col.   Columbia Pictures
EFD   European Film Distributors
EL   Eagle-Lion
EMI   EMI Productions
GFD   General Film Distributors
GN   Grand National Pictures
Grade-AFD   Grade-Associated Film Distribution

IND   Independent Release
Int. Cinema   International Cinema
LFP   London Films
Lip.   Lippert Pictures
MGM   Metro-Golden-Mayer
Mon.   Monogram Pictures
NGP   National General Pictures
Par.   Paramount Pictures
PRC   Producers Releasing Corporation
PRO   Producers Releasing Organization
Rank   J. Arthur Rank
Rep.   Republic Pictures
RKO   RKO Radio Pictures
Telstar   3 Capitals — London
Tif.   Tiffany
20th   20th Century–Fox Film Corp.
UA   United Artists
Univ.   Universal Pictures, Universal-International
WB   Warner Brothers Pictures

The Stars of Hollywood Remembered

Brian Aherne (1902–1986)

Brian Aherne was born in King's Norton, England, and made his stage debut at the age of eight in a pantomime show with Noël Coward. He enrolled at Malvern College and studied architecture but returned to the stage when he was 20 and became a silent film favorite in England. In 1931 Aherne came to the U.S. to appear opposite Katharine Cornell in the play *The Barretts of Wimpole Street*. His first American film was *Song of Songs* opposite Marlene Dietrich. He appeared opposite Cornell on Broadway in *Romeo and Juliet, Saint Joan* and *Lucrece* and played Iago in Walter Huston's *Othello*. During World War II, *Wimpole Street* was revived and toured the world playing to servicemen. During his screen career he appeared opposite Joan Crawford, Rosalind Russell, Merle Oberon, Carole Lombard, Jeanette MacDonald, Rita Hayworth, Claudette Colbert and Bette Davis and made almost 40 films. In 1958 he returned to the stage in a U.S. touring production of *My Fair Lady*. His portrayal of Henry Higgins won rave reviews. His autobiography, *A Proper Job*, was published in 1969. His first marriage to Joan Fontaine in 1939 ended in divorce in 1945. His second wife (married 1946) was Eleanor Labrote. He died of heart failure in Venice, Florida.

Feature Sound Films

The Song of Songs (Par., 1933), *What Every Woman Knows* (MGM, 1934), *The Fountain* (RKO, 1934), *The Constant Nymph* (Fox, 1934), *Sylvia Scarlet* (RKO, 1935), *I Live My Life* (MGM, 1935), *Beloved Enemy* (UA, 1936), *The Great Garrick* (WB, 1937), *Merrily We Live* (MGM, 1938), *Captain Fury* (UA, 1939), *Juarez* (WB, 1939), *The Lady in Question* (Col., 1940), *Hired Wife* (Univ., 1940), *My Son, My Son* (UA, 1940), *The Man Who Lost Himself* (Univ., 1941), *Skylark* (Par., 1941), *Smilin' Through* (MGM, 1941), *My Sister Eileen* (Col., 1942), *Forever and a Day* (RKO, 1943), *A Night to Remember* (Col., 1943), *First Comes Courage* (Col., 1943), *What a Woman!* (Col., 1943), *The Locket* (RKO, 1946), *Smart Woman* (AA, 1948), *Angel on the Amazon* (Rep., 1948), *I Confess* (WB, 1953), *Titanic* (20th, 1953), *Prince Valiant* (20th, 1954), *A Bullet Is Waiting* (Col., 1954), *The Swan* (MGM, 1956), *The Best of Everything* (20th, 1959), *Susan Slade* (WB, 1961), *Sword of Lancelot* (Univ., 1963), *The Cavern* (20th, 1965), *Rosie!* (Univ., 1968), *Slipstreams* (Canadian, 1974)

Top: Brian Ahern, a sculptor, and Lionel Atwill, a rich patron of the arts, are both in love with Ahern's model (Marlene Dietrich) in *Song of Songs* (Paramount, 1933). *Bottom:* Brian Ahern is a writer of romantic novels who sacrifices most of his life for others and especially for his ungrateful son in *My Son, My Son* with Laraine Day and Leland Hodgson (United Artists, 1940).

Don Ameche (1908–1993)

Don Ameche, one of eight children, was born in Kenosha, Wisconsin. His father was the manager of a saloon. He attended Catholic boys' schools and Columbia (now Loras) College. Ameche later studied law at Marquette and Georgetown universities and at the University of Wisconsin but dropped out to join a stock company in Madison, Wisconsin. He appeared on Broadway in 1929, toured in vaudeville with Texas Guinan, and started his radio career in Chicago in 1930. Ameche soon became a leading radio actor, starring in *The First Nighter* and *Grand Hotel*. He married Honore Prendergast in 1932 and from this union came four boys and two girls. His radio fame led to a long-term contract with 20th Century–Fox in 1935. In 1944, after appearing in 30 Fox films, his contract expired and he began to free lance. Ameche had a pleasant singing voice and sang in many of his movie roles. On Broadway he appeared in the musicals *Silk Stockings* (1955) with music and lyrics by Cole Porter and *Goldilocks* (1958) with a Leroy Anderson score. While still in films and under contract to Fox, he appeared on *The Chase and Sanborn Hour* (radio) with Edgar Bergen and Charlie McCarthy. Later on radio and TV he co-starred with Frances Langford as *The Bickersons*. From 1961 to 1965 he was the ringmaster of NBC-TV's *International Showtime*. Ameche continued film work intermittently and his appearance on *Corrina, Corrina*, just before his death of prostate cancer in Scottsdale, Arizona, at 85.

Feature Films

Clive of India (UA, 1935), *Sins of Man* (20th, 1936), *Ramona* (20th, 1936), *Ladies in Love* (20th, 1936), *One in a Million* (20th, 1936), *Love Is News* (20th, 1937), *Fifty Roads to Town* (20th, 1937), *You Can't Have Everything* (20th, 1937), *Love Under Fire* (20th, 1937), *In Old Chicago* (20th, 1938), *Happy Landing* (20th, 1938), *Josette* (20th, 2938), *Alexander's Ragtime Band* (20th, 1938), *Gateway* (20th, 1938), *The Three Musketeers* (20th, 1939), *Midnight* (Par., 1939), *The Story of Alexander Graham Bell* (20th, 1939), *Hollywood Cavalcade* (20th, 1939), *Swanee River* (20th, 1939), *Little Old New York* (20th, 1939), *Lillian Russell* (20th, 1940), *Four Sons* (20th, 1940), *Down Argentine Way* (20th, 1940), *That Night in Rio* (20th, 1941), *Moon Over Miami* (20th, 1941), *Kiss the Boys Goodbye* (Par., 1941), *The Feminine Touch* (MGM, 1941), *Confirm or Deny* (20th, 1941), *The Magnificent Dope* (20th, 1942), *Girl Trouble* (20th, 1942), *Heaven Can Wait* (20th, 1943), *Happy Land* (20th, 1943), *Something to Shout About* (Col., 1943), *Wing and a Prayer* (20th, 1944), *Greenwich Village* (20th, 1944), *It's in the Bag!* (UA, 1945), *Guest Wife* (UA, 1945), *So Goes My Love* (Univ., 1946), *That's My Man* (Rep., 1947), *Sleep, My Love* (UA, 1948), *Slightly French* (Col., 1949), *A Fever in the Blood* (WB, 1961), *Rings Around the World* (Col., 1966), *Picture Mommy Dead* (Embassy, 1966), *The Boatniks* (BV, 1966), *Suppose They Gave a War and Nobody Came* (Cinerama, 1970), *Trading Places* (Par., 1983), *Cocoon* (20th, 1985), *Harry and the Hendersons* (Univ., 1987), *Coming to America* (Par., 1988), *Cocoon: The Return* (20th, 1988), *Things Change* (Col., 1988), *Oddball Hall* (Cannon, 1990), *Oscar* (BV, 1991), *Folks!* (20th, 1992), *Homeward Bound: The Incredible Journey* (voice only; BV, 1993), *Corrina, Corrina* (New Line Cinema, 1994)

Top: Don Ameche is the son of a Venezuelan rubber planter who comes to New York to negotiate a loan. Joan Bennett is the penniless heiress who rents her apartment to him and pretends to be the maid in *Girl Trouble* (20th Century–Fox, 1942). *Bottom:* Tyrone Power, Don Ameche and Alice Faye are reunited after their blockbuster *In Old Chicago* in the musical *Alexander's Ragtime Band* which included 28 Irving Berlin compositions (20th Century–Fox, 1938).

Eve Arden (1908–1990)

Eve Arden was born Eunice Quedens in Mill Valley, California. While attending high school, she appeared in school plays. She was interviewed by stage producer Henry Duffy who cast her in her first professional play. After 18 months in Duffy's employment she joined the Bandbox Repertory Theatre for a year. While she was appearing at the Pasadena Playhouse in Leonard Stillman's revue *Lo and Behold* with Tyrone Power, producer Lee Shubert hired her for Billie Burke's show *Ziegfeld Follies* in 1934. Next she appeared with Jimmy Savo in the Theatre Guild's *Parade*. Arden returned to co-star opposite Bob Hope in *Ziegfeld Follies* (1936 edition) with Fannie Brice and Josephine Baker. In 1937 she went back to California to do film work, appearing opposite Edward Everett Horton in *Oh, Doctor* and working steadily at various studios. She returned to Broadway opposite Jack Whiting in Jerome Kern and Oscar Hammerstein's *Very Warm for May* and Danny Kaye in Cole Porter's *Let's Face It*. Then she did more film assignments in Hollywood. In 1948 she debuted on CBS Radio in *Our Miss Brooks*. The show moved to television in 1952. It was a hit for four seasons and Arden won an Emmy for her starring role. She continued to appear in movies and on the stage, starring in the West Coast production of *Auntie Mame* and the national company of *Butterflies Are Free*. In Chicago she replaced Carol Channing in *Hello, Dolly*. She did a television sitcom, *The Mothers-in-Law* with Kaye Ballard and made other TV appearances. Her first husband was Ned Bergen (married 1939, divorced 1947). In 1951 she married actor Brooks West and the union lasted until his death in 1984. She died in Los Angeles of heart failure with two of her children at her bedside.

Feature Films

as Eunice Quedens: *Song of Love* (Col., 1929), *Dancing Lady* (MGM, 1933)
as Eve Arden: *Oh, Doctor* (Univ., 1937), *Stage Door* (RKO, 1937), *Cocoanut Grove* (Par., 1938), *Letter of Introduction* (Univ., 1938), *Having Wonderful Time* (RKO, 1938), *Women in the Wind* (WB, 1939), *Big Town Czar* (Univ., 1939), *The Forgotten Woman* (Univ., 1939), *Eternally Yours* (UA, 1939), *At the Circus* (MGM, 1939), *A Child Is Born* (WB, 1940), *Slightly Honorable* (UA, 1940), *Comrade X* (MGM, 1940), *No, No, Nanette* (RKO, 1940), *Ziegfeld Girl* (MGM, 1941), *That Uncertain Feeling* (UA, 1941), *She Couldn't Say No* (WB, 1941), *She Knew All the Answers* (Col., 1941), *San Antonio Rose* (Univ., 1941), *Sing for Your Supper* (Col., 1941), *Manpower* (WB, 1941), *Whistling in the Dark* (MGM, 1941), *Last of the Duanes* (20th, 1941), *Obliging Young Lady* (RKO, 1941), *Bedtime Story* (Col., 1941), *Hit Parade of 1943* (Rep., 1943), *Let's Face It* (Par., 1943), *Cover Girl* (Col., 1944), *The Doughgirls* (WB, 1944), *Pan Americana* (RKO, 1945), *Patrick the Great* (Univ., 1945), *Earl Carroll's Vanities* (Rep., 1945), *Mildred Pierce* (WB, 1945), *My Reputation* (WB, 1946), *The Kid from Brooklyn* (RKO, 1946), *Night and Day* (WB, 1946), *Song of Scheherazade* (Univ., 1947), *The Arnelo Affair* (MGM, 1947), *The Unfaithful* (WB, 1947), *The Voice of the Turtle* (WB, 1947), *One Touch of Venus* (Univ., 1948), *Whiplash* (WB, 1948), *My Dream Is Yours* (WB, 1949), *The Lady Takes a Sailor* (WB, 1949), *Paid in Full* (Par., 1950), *Curtain Call at Cactus Creek*

Top: Joan Crawford as *Mildred Pierce,* a housewife turned businesswoman who finds success but loses control of her daughter (played by Ann Blyth). Eve Arden remains her loyal friend and employee (Warner Brothers, 1945). *Bottom:* Arthur O'Connell is a legal researcher and Eve Arden is James Stewart's faithful secretary. They are trying to save an Army lieutenant accused of murder in *Anatomy of Murder* (Columbia, 1959).

(Univ., 1950), *Tea for Two* (WB, 1950), *Three Husbands* (UA, 1950), *Goodbye My Fancy* (WB, 1951), *We're Not Married* (20th, 1952), *The Lady Wants Mink* (Rep., 1953), *Our Miss Brooks* (WB, 1956), *Anatomy of a Murder* (Col., 1959), *Beauty Jungle* (Rank, 1966), *The Strongest Man in the World* (BV, 1975), *Grease* (Par., 1978), *Under the Rainbow* (Orion-WB, 1981), *Grease 2* (Par., 1982), *Pandemonium* (MGM/UA, 1982)

Jean Arthur (1900–1991)

Born Gladys Georgiana Green in 1900 in New York City, she was the daughter of a photographer. Her career began as a model. A Fox talent scout offered her a screen test which led to a Hollywood contract. She renamed herself Jean Arthur after Jeanne d'Arc and King Arthur. In 1923 she made her screen debut opposite John Gilbert in *Cameo Kirby*, directed by John Ford. Next Arthur appeared in low-budget westerns and short comedies with Charley Chase and Slim Summerville. In the late silent era she appeared with Buster Keaton, William Collier, Jr., Jack Mulhall and Monty Banks. She was signed by Paramount for her first sound film, *Warming Up* with Richard Dix. At that studio she appeared with Emil Jannings, William Powell and Clara Bow. Paramount lent her out for undistinguished pictures, and upon the completion of her contract she headed for Broadway where she appeared with Dorothy Gish, Osgood Perkins and J. Edward Bromberg in the highly successful *Foreign Affairs*. She turned down Hollywood offers and next appeared in another play, *The Man Who Reclaimed His Head* with Claude Rains as the leading man. Two more successful plays followed — *The Curtain Riser* and *The Bride of Torozho*. She then signed a long-term contract with Columbia. Under John Ford's direction in *The Whole Town's Talking* with Edward G. Robinson, Arthur became a star. Nevertheless, her studio lent her out at big fees for mediocre productions. Director Frank Capra requested her for the lead opposite Gary Cooper in *Mr. Deeds Goes to Town*. Again, she proved herself to be a lovely, poised and confident actress. She was loaned to Paramount for Cecil B. DeMille's *The Plainsman* and Preston Sturges' *Easy Living* and to United Artists for *History Is Made at Night*. Columbia chief Harry Cohn suspended her many times for her refusal to accept dull scripts. Still he took her back (if reluctantly) when Frank Capra and Howard Hawks requested her. When Arthur's contract expired, she returned to the stage in Garson Kanin's *Born Yesterday*. During tryouts she became ill and was replaced by Judy Holliday. In 1950 she starred in a successful revival of *Peter Pan*. She attended Stephens and Bennington colleges. This led to a teaching position at Vassar and North Carolina School of the Arts. She was married briefly to Julian Anker in 1928 and to Frank Ross from 1932 to 1947. At 90 she died of heart failure at her old-fashioned home on a cliff facing the ocean in Carmel, California.

Feature Sound Films

Easy Come, Easy Go (Par., 1928), *The Canary Murder Case* (Par., 1929), *The Mysterious Dr. Fu Manchu* (Par., 1929),

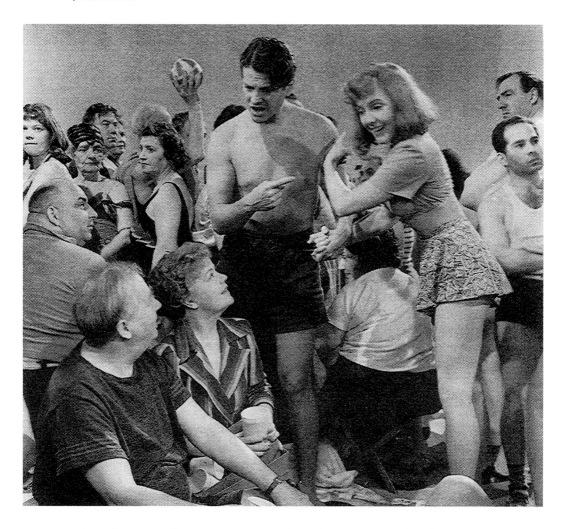

Charles Coburn, seated by Spring Byington, is the world's richest man. He infiltrates his own department store unknown to others to learn about the working conditions of his employees. Robert Cummings and Jean Arthur (standing) star in *The Devil and Miss Jones* (RKO, 1941).

The Greene Murder Case (Par., 1929), *The Saturday Night Kid* (Par., 1929), *Half Way to Heaven* (Par., 1929), *Street of Chance* (Par., 1930), *Young Eagles* (Par., 1930), *Paramount on Parade* (Par., 1930), *The Return of Dr. Fu Manchu* (Par., 1930), *Danger Lights* (RKO, 1930), *The Silver Horde* (RKO, 1930), *The Gang Buster* (Par., 1931), *Virtuous Husband* (Univ., 1931), *The Lawyer's Secret* (Par., 1931), *Ex-Bad Boy* (Univ., 1931), *Get That Venus* (Regent, 1933), *The Past of Mary Holmes* (RKO, 1933), *Whirlpool* (Col., 1934), *The Defense Rests* (Col., 1934), *Most Precious Thing in Life* (Col., 1934), *The Whole Town's Talking* (Col., 1935), *Public Hero Number One* (MGM, 1935), *Party Wire* (Col., 1935), *Diamond Jim* (Univ., 1935), *The Public Menace* (Col., 1935), *If You Could Only Cook* (Col., 1935), *Mr. Deeds Goes to Town* (Col., 1936), *The Ex-Mrs. Bradford* (RKO, 1936), *Adventure in Manhattan* (Col., 1936), *The Plainsman* (Par., 1936), *More Than a Secretary* (Col., 1936), *History Is Made at Night* (UA, 1937), *Easy Living* (Par., 1937), *You Can't Take It with*

Jean Arthur marries Melvyn Douglas after receiving word that her first husband, Fred MacMurray, has drowned when actually he has been rescued and returns in *Too Many Husbands* (Columbia, 1940).

You (Col., 1938), *Only Angels Have Wings* (Col., 1939), *Mr. Smith Goes to Washington* (Col., 1939), *Too Many Husbands* (Col., 1940), *Arizona* (Col., 1940), *The Devil and Miss Jones* (RKO, 1941), *The Talk of the Town* (Col., 1942), *The More the Merrier* (Col., 1943), *A Lady Takes a Chance* (RKO, 1943), *The Impatient Years* (Col., 1944), *A Foreign Affair* (Par., 1948), *Shane* (Par., 1953)

Lucille Ball (1911–1989)

Lucille Ball was born in Celeron, New York. She dropped out of high school, went to New York and worked briefly as a chorus dancer. Then she studied acting and modeling. As a model she graced many ads and became a top model for Hattie Carnegie's creations. She had to give up modeling for two years because she was suffering from rheumatoid arthritis. When she recovered she went back to modeling. That led to a Hollywood contract with Samuel Goldwyn as a Goldwyn Girl in his musicals. She played tiny roles for Goldwyn and also did two-reel comedies with Leon Errol and the Three Stooges. She signed a seven-year contract with RKO and made mostly mediocre films until

Richard Keith, Desi Arnaz, Lucille Ball, William Frawley and Vivian Vance in a scene from the television hit series *I Love Lucy.*

she was cast in *Stage Door* with Katharine Hepburn and Ginger Rogers in 1937. After that the studio cast her in better films. During the filming of *Too Many Girls* she met and married Desi Arnaz, who was appearing in the film. MGM bought out her contract from RKO. After that contract expired, Ball freelanced with Columbia, Universal, United Artists and Paramount. Then she toured for six successful months in the Elmer Rice play *Dream Girl.* She debuted on radio in the CBS series *My Favorite Husband* which scored high ratings. In 1950 she toured with Desi in an act which led to the television pilot of *I Love Lucy* for CBS. Cast as their neighbors in the show were William Frawley and Vivian Vance. The series was an instant hit, winning Emmys and many other awards. Lucille and Desi formed Desilu Productions and produced their own and other top TV shows. They also appeared together in two MGM films. They had two children, Lucie and Desi, Jr. After 20 years together, Lucy and Desi divorced. When she appeared in the Broadway musical *Wildcat,* she met comedian Gary Morton and married him in 1961. She returned to TV and made some films. She died at 75 after emergency open-heart surgery.

Feature Films

Broadway Thru a Keyhole (UA, 1933), *Roman Scandals* (UA, 1933), *Blood Money* (UA, 1933), *Moulin Rouge* (UA, 1934), *Nana* (UA, 1934), *Hold That Girl* (Fox, 1934), *Jealousy* (Col., 1934), *Fugitive Lady* (Col., 1934), *Men of the Night*

Lucille Ball is the wife of Bob Hope, a theatre critic. His review of his wife's new play leads to comic results in *Critic's Choice* (Warner Bros., 1961).

(Col., 1934), *Bottoms Up* (Fox, 1934), *Broadway Bill* (Col., 1934), *Bulldog Drummond Strikes Back* (UA, 1934), *Kid Millions* (UA, 1934), *Affairs of Cellini* (UA, 1934), *Roberta* (RKO, 1935), *Old Man Rhythm* (RKO, 1935), *Carnival* (Col., 1935), *I Dream Too Much* (RKO, 1935), *Top Hat* (RKO, 1935), *Chatterbox* (RKO, 1935), *Winterset* (RKO, 1936), *Follow the Fleet* (RKO, 1936), *The Farmer in the Dell* (RKO, 1936), *Bunker Bean* (RKO, 1936), *That Girl from Paris* (RKO, 1936), *Don't Tell the Wife* (RKO, 1937), *Stage Door* (RKO, 1937), *Joy of Living* (RKO, 1938), *Go Chase Yourself* (RKO, 1938), *Having Wonderful Time* (RKO, 1938), *The Affairs of Annabel* (RKO, 1938), *Room Service* (RKO, 1938), *Next Time I Marry* (RKO, 1938), *Annabel Takes a Tour* (RKO, 1938), *Beauty for the Asking*

(RKO, 1939), *Twelve Crowded Hours* (RKO, 1939), *Panama Lady* (RKO, 1939), *Five Came Back* (RKO, 1939), *That's Right, You're Wrong* (RKO, 1939), *The Marines Fly High* (RKO, 1940), *You Can't Fool Your Wife* (RKO, 1940), *Dance, Girl, Dance* (RKO, 1940), *Too Many Girls* (RKO, 1940), *A Girl, a Guy and a Gob* (RKO, 1940), *Look Who's Laughing* (RKO, 1941), *Valley of the Sun* (RKO, 1942), *The Big Street* (RKO, 1942), *Seven Days' Leave* (RKO, 1942), *DuBarry Was a Lady* (MGM, 1943), *Best Foot Forward* (MGM, 1943), *Thousands Cheer* (MGM, 1943), *Meet the People* (MGM, 1944), *Abbott and Costello in Hollywood* (MGM, 1945), *Without Love* (MGM, 1945), *Ziegfeld Follies of 1946* (MGM, 1946), *The Dark Corner* (20th, 1946), *Lover Come Back* (Univ., 1946), *Easy to Wed* (MGM, 1946), *Two Smart People* (MGM, 1946), *Lured* (UA, 1947), *Her Husband's Affairs* (Col., 1947), *Miss Grant Takes Richmond* (Col., 1949), *Sorrowful Jones* (Par., 1949), *Easy Living* (RKO, 1949), *Fancy Pants* (Par., 1950), *A Woman of Distinction* (unbilled guest appearance, Col., 1950), *The Fuller Brush Girl* (Col., 1950), *The Magic Carpet* (Col., 1951), *The Long, Long Trailer* (MGM, 1954), *Forever, Darling* (MGM, 1956), *The Facts of Life* (UA, 1960), *Critic's Choice* (WB, 1963), *A Guide for the Married Man* (20th, 1967), *Yours, Mine and Ours* (US, 1968), *Mame* (WB, 1974), *That's Entertainment* (MGM, 1974), *That's Entertainment III* (UA/MGM, 1994)

Anne Baxter (1923–1985)

The granddaughter of famed architect Frank Lloyd Wright, Anne Baxter was born in Michigan City, Indiana. Her family moved to New York and enrolled her in Theodora Irvine's School of the Theatre, which she attended from 1934 to 1936. She made her Broadway debut at age 13 in *Seen But Not Heard*. She then studied acting under Maria Ouspenskaya. More Broadway appearances followed. Then she worked in summer stock with the Cape Playhouse Stock Company in Dennis, Massachusetts. In 1940 she signed a movie contract with 20th Century–Fox. She appeared in many major films, including *The Magnificent Ambersons*, *Five Graves to Cairo* and *The Razor's Edge*, for which she won an Oscar for Best Supporting Actress of 1946. In 1950 she and Bette Davis appeared in *All About Eve*. For their roles in that film both actresses were nominated for Oscars. (The 1950 Oscar was awarded to Judy Holliday for *Born Yesterday*.) After Baxter's 20th Century–Fox contract ended, she freelanced at various studios. She returned to the stage and toured with Tyrone Power in *John Brown's Body*. Then she returned to Broadway in the ill-fated *The Square Root of Wonderful*. Next Baxter went on the London stage and was successful in *The Joshua Tree*. In between screen roles, she appeared on many television shows and replaced Bette Davis in the hit series *Hotel*. Her first marriage (1946) to John Hodiak ended in divorce after seven years. In 1960 she married Australian rancher Randolph Gault and gave up her career to live in Australia, but in 1970 the couple divorced. She next replaced Lauren Bacall in *Applause* (a musical stage version of *All About Eve)* and won raves from the critics in the starring role of Margo Channing. In 1977 she married investment broker David Klee. He died of a heart attack the same year. Baxter died in New York of a cerebral hemorrhage.

Top: Anne Baxter, a teacher in New London, Connecticut, is romanced by Tyrone Power, an officer at the submarine base, in *Crash Dive* (20th Century–Fox, 1943). *Bottom:* Gary Merrill is the successful Broadway director and Anne Baxter is the conniving and vicious user in *All About Eve* (20th Century–Fox, 1950).

Feature Films

20 Mule Team (MGM, 1940), *The Great Profile* (20th, 1940), *Charlie's Aunt* (20th, 1941), *Swamp Water* (20th, 1941), *The Magnificent Ambersons* (RKO, 1942),*The Pied Piper* (20th, 1942), *Crash Dive* (20th, 1943), *Five Graves to Cairo* (Par., 1943), *The North Star* (RKO, 1943), *The Sullivans* (20th, 1944), *The Eve of St. Mark* (20th, 1944), *Guest in the House* (UA, 1944), *Sunday Dinner for a Soldier* (20th, 1944), *A Royal Scandal* (20th, 1945), *Smoky* (20th, 1946), *Angel on My Shoulder* (UA, 1946), *The Razor's Edge* (20th, 1946), *Mother Wore Tights* (narrator, 20th, 1947), *Blaze of Noon* (Par., 1947), *Homecoming* (MGM, 1948), *The Luck of the Irish* (20th, 1948), *The Walls of Jericho* (20th, 1948), *Yellow Sky* (20th, 1949), *You're My Everything* (20th, 1949), *A Ticket to Tomahawk* (20th, 1950), *All About Eve* (20th, 1950), *Follow the Sun* (20th, 1951), *Outcasts of Poker Flat* (20th, 1952), *My Wife's Best Friend* (20th, 1952), *O. Henry's Full House* (20th, 1952), *Bedevilled* (MGM, 1955), *One Desire* (Univ., 1955), *The Spoilers* (Univ., 1955), *The Come-On* (AA, 1956), *The Ten Commandments* (Par., 1956), *Three Violent People* (Par., 1956), *Chase a Crooked Shadow* (WB, 1958), *Cimarron* (MGM, 1960), *Mix Me a Person* (Blackton, 1961), *Season of Passion* (UA, 1961), *Walk on the Wild Side* (Col., 1962), *The Family Jewels* (unbilled guest appearance, Par., 1965), *Tall Women* (AA, 1967), *The Busy Body* (Par., 1967), *Fool's Parade* (Col., 1971), *The Late Liz* (Gateway, 1971), *Jane Austin in Manhattan* (Contemporary, 1980)

Ralph Bellamy (1904–1991)

The son of an advertising executive, Ralph Bellamy was born in Chicago. At New Trier High School he was active in the drama department. When he graduated in 1922 he formed his own acting company, the North Shore Players, and toured the Midwest. Bellamy made his Broadway debut in 1929 in *Town Boy*. It was a flop but he received excellent reviews. He toured opposite Hope Williams in *Holiday* and Helen Hayes in *Coquette*. In 1931 he signed a two-year movie contract with Fox. When the contract ended, Bellamy accepted freelance jobs at various Hollywood studios. In 1937 he was nominated for Best Supporting Actor in Columbia's *The Awful Truth* with Irene Dunne and Cary Grant but lost the Oscar to Joseph Schildkraut in *The Life of Emile Zola*. He continued his screen work and did frequent radio appearances until 1943. He returned to Broadway opposite Shirley Booth in the hit play *Tomorrow the World*, which ran for 500 performances. Then he went back to Hollywood for three films, appearing opposite Anne Baxter, Deanna Durbin and Constance Moore. He then returned to Broadway in the hit *State of the Union* and appeared on television in the highly successful live series *Man Against Crime*. In 1949 he went back to Broadway in Sidney Kingsley's hit *Detective Story* (581 performances). He was vice-president of Actor's Equity (1949–52) and then became its president (1952–64). His greatest success on Broadway was his portrayal of Franklin Roosevelt in *Sunrise at Campobello* for which he won a Tony. He toured nationally in the play and repeated the role on film. In 1987 he was awarded an honorary Oscar for his "unique artistry and distinguished service to the profession of acting." Bellamy

Ralph Bellamy as Franklin D. Roosevelt is encouraged by his wife Eleanor (Greer Garson) not to give up his political aspirations in spite of being paralyzed in *Sunrise at Campobello* (Warner Bros., 1960).

was married to Alice Delbridge from 1922 until their divorce in 1930. In 1931 he married actress Catherine Willard. They had two children, Lynn and Willard, and divorced in 1945. He married organist Ethel Smith in 1945 and that union ended in divorce in 1947. His last marriage in 1949 to actors' agent Alice Murphy lasted until his death in 1991.

Feature Films

The Secret Six (MGM, 1931), *Magnificent Lie* (Par., 1931), *Surrender* (Fox, 1931), *West of Broadway* (MGM, 1932), *Forbidden* (Col., 1932), *Disorderly Conduct* (Fox, 1932), *Young America* (Fox, 1932), *The Woman in Room 13* (Fox, 1932), *Rebecca of Sunnybrook Farm* (Fox, 1932), *Almost Married* (Fox, 1932), *Wild Girl* (Fox, 1932), *Air Mail* (Univ., 1932), *Second Hand Wife* (Fox, 1933), *Parole Girl* (Col., 1933), *Destination Unknown* (Univ., 1933), *Picture Snatchers* (WB, 1933), *Below the Sea* (Col., 1933), *Narrow Corner* (WB, 1933), *Flying Devils* (RKO, 1933), *Headline Shooters* (RKO, 1933), *Ever in My Heart* (WB, 1933), *Blind Adventure* (RKO, 1933), *Ace of Aces* (RKO, 1933), *Spitfire* (RKO, 1934), *This Man Is Mine* (RKO, 1934), *Once to Every Woman* (Col., 1934), *Before Midnight* (Col., 1934), *One Is Guilty* (Col., 1934), *Girl in Danger* (Col., 1934), *Crime of Helen Stanley* (Col., 1934), *Woman in the Dark* (RKO, 1935), *Helldorado* (Fox, 1935), *Wedding Night* (UA, 1935), *Rendezvous at Midnight* (Univ., 1935), *Eight*

Billionaire commodity tycoons Don Ameche and Ralph Bellamy break in ghetto survivor Eddie Murphy on his prestige job with their brokerage firm in *Trading Places* (Paramount, 1983).

Bells (Col., 1935), *Air Hawks* (Col., 1935), *The Healer* (Mon., 1935), *Gigolette* (RKO, 1935), *Navy Wife* (Fox, 1935), *Hands Across the Table* (Par., 1935), *Dangerous Intrigue* (Col., 1936), *Roaming Lady* (Col., 1936), *Straight from the Shoulder* (Par., 1936), *The Final Hours* (Col., 1936), *Wild Brian Kent* (RKO, 1936), *The Man Who Lived Twice* (Col., 1936), *Counterfeit Lady* (Col., 1937), *Let's Get Married* (Col., 1937), *The Awful Truth* (Col., 1937), *The Crime of Dr. Hallett* (Univ., 1938), *Fools for Scandal* (WB, 1938), *Boy Meets Girl* (WB, 1938), *Carefree* (RKO, 1938), *Girls' School* (Col., 1938), *Trade Winds* (UA, 1938), *Let Us Live* (Col., 1939), *Smashing the Spy Ring* (Col., 1939), *Blind Alley* (Col., 1939), *Coast Guard* (Col., 1939), *His Girl Friday* (Col., 1940), *Flight Angels* (WB, 1940), *Brother Orchid* (WB, 1940), *Queen of the Mob* (Par., 1940), *Dance, Girl, Dance* (RKO, 1940), *Public Deb No. 1* (20th, 1940), *Ellery Queen, Master Detective* (Col., 1940), *Meet the Wildcat* (Univ., 1940), *Ellery Queen's Penthouse Mystery* (Col., 1941), *Footsteps in the Dark* (WB, 1941), *Affectionately Yours* (WB, 1941), *Ellery Queen and the Perfect Crime* (Col., 1941), *The Wolf Man* (Univ., 1941), *The Ghost of Frankenstein* (Univ., 1942), *Lady in a Jam* (Univ., 1942), *Men of Texas* (Univ., 1942), *The Great Impersonation* (Univ., 1942), *Stage Door Canteen* (UA, 1943), *Guest in the House* (UA, 1944), *Delightfully Dangerous* (UA, 1945), *Lady on a Train* (Univ., 1945), *The Court-Martial of Billy Mitchell* (WB, 1955), *Sunrise at Campobello* (WB, 1960), *The Professionals* (Col., 1966), *Rosemary's Baby* (Par., 1968), *Doctor's Wives* (Col., 1971), *Cancel My Reservation* (WB, 1972), *Oh,*

God! (WB, 1977), *Trading Places* (Par., 1983), *Amazon Women on the Moon* (Univ., 1987), *Disorderlies* (WB, 1987), *Coming to America* (Par., 1988), *The Good Mother* (Touchstone, 1988), *Pretty Woman* (Touchstone, 1990)

Joan Bennett (1910–1990)

Joan Bennett was born in Palisades, New Jersey, the daughter of actor Richard Bennett and actress Adriene Morrison. Her sisters were Barbara and Constance. She attended boarding schools in Connecticut and a finishing school in Versailles, France, before making her stage debut with her father on Broadway in *Jarnegan* (1928). She appeared in a few films made in New York and then went to Hollywood. She became a star when she appeared opposite Ronald Colman in *Bulldog Drummond.* She was typed as a blonde ingenue opposite George Arliss, John Barrymore and Joe E. Brown. Next she signed a two-year contract with Fox and appeared opposite such actors as Edmund Lowe, Warner Baxter, Lew Ayres, Spencer Tracy, John Boles, Charles Farrell and Ralph Bellamy. When her contract ended she was signed to appear in *Little Woman* at RKO. Independent producer Walter Wagner signed her to a contract, gave her starring roles and also loaned her to other studios. In 1938 she became a brunette with a striking resemblance to Hedy Lamarr for her role in *Trade Winds.* (She remained a brunette for the remainder of her career.) After returning to the stage in the touring company of *Stage Door*, she went back to Hollywood. With Fritz Lang she formed her own producing company and appeared opposite Edward G. Robinson in two successful films. On loan she appeared in films opposite James Mason, Gregory Peck, Robert Preston, Paul Henried, Paul Douglas, Humphrey Bogart and Robert Cummings. She returned to the theater and appeared opposite Donald Cook in many touring plays. In 1968 she began work in the TV "gothic soap opera" *Dark Shadows.* She married four times — John Fox (1926–28), Gene Markey (1932–37), Walter Wanger (1940–62) and David Wilde (1978–90). She died in White Plains, New York, of a heart attack.

Feature Films

Power (Pathe, 1928), *Bulldog Drummond* (UA, 1929), *Three Live Ghosts* (UA, 1929), *Disraeli* (WB, 1929), *Mississippi Gambler* (Univ., 1929), *Puttin' on the Ritz* (UA, 1930), *Crazy That Way* (Fox, 1930), *Moby Dick* (WB, 1930), *Maybe It's Love* (WB, 1930), *Scotland Yard* (Fox, 1930), *Many a Slip* (Univ., 1931) *Doctors' Wives* (Fox, 1931), *Hush Money* (Fox, 1931), *She Wanted a Millionaire* (Fox, 1932), *The Trial of Vivienne Ware* (Fox, 1932), *Weekends Only* (Fox, 1932), *Wild Girl* (Fox, 1932), *Me and My Gal* (Fox, 1932), *Arizona to Broadway* (Fox, 1933), *Little Women* (RKO, 1933), *The Pursuit of Happiness* (Par., 1934), *The Man Who Reclaimed His Head* (Univ., 1935), *Private Worlds* (Par., 1935), *Mississippi* (Par., 1935), *Two for Tonight* (Par., 1935), *The Man Who Broke the Bank at Monte Carlo* (Fox, 1935), *She Couldn't Take It* (Col., 1935), *13 Hours by Air* (Par., 1936), *Big Brown Eyes* (Par., 1936), *Two in a Crowd* (Univ., 1936), *Wedding Present* (Par., 1936), *Vogues of 1938* (UA, 1937), *I Met My Love Again* (UA, 1938), *The Texans* (Par., 1938), *Artists and Models Abroad* (Par., 1938), *Trade Winds* (UA, 1938),

Top: Spencer Tracy, the *Father of the Bride,* with his wife, Joan Bennett, toast their newlywed daughter (Elizabeth Taylor) and the groom (Dan Taylor) (MGM, 1950). *Bottom:* Gail Patrick and Joan Bennett are sisters who fall in love with a showboat singer (Bing Crosby) in *Mississippi* (Paramount, 1935).

The Man in the Iron Mask (UA, 1939), *The Housekeeper's Daughter* (UA, 1939), *Green Hell* (Univ., 1940), *The House Across the Bay* (UA, 1940), *The Man I Married* (20th, 1940), *The Son of Monte Cristo* (UA, 1940), *She Knew All the Answers* (Col., 1941), *Man Hunt* (20th, 1941), *Wild Geese Calling* (20th, 1941), *Confirm or Deny* (20th, 1941), *Twin Beds* (UA, 1942), *The Wife Takes a Flyer* (Col., 1942), *Margin for Error* (20th, 1943), *Woman in the Window* (RKO, 1944), *Nob Hill* (20th, 1945), *Scarlet Street* (Univ., 1945), *Col. Effingham's Raid* (20th, 1946), *The Macomber Affair* (UA, 1947), *Woman on the Beach* (RKO, 1947), *The Secret Beyond the Door* (Univ., 1948), *Hollow Triumph* (*The Scar*) (EL, 1948), *The Reckless Moment* (Col., 1940), *Father of the Bride* (MGM, 1950), *For Heaven's Sake* (20th, 1950), *Father's Little Dividend* (MGM, 1951), *The Guy Who Came Back* (20th, 1951), *Highway Dragnet* (AA, 1954), *We're No Angels* (Par., 1955), *There's Always Tomorrow* (Univ., 1956), *Navy Wife* (AA, 1956), *Desire in the Dust* (20th, 1960), *House of Dark Shadows* (MGM, 1970), *Suspiria* (Italy, 1977)

Joan Blondell (1909–1979)

Born in New York City to vaudeville troupers, she became part of their act and spent her childhood touring the U.S., Europe, China and Australia. When she was 17 she joined a stock company in Dallas and appeared in its productions until she won the Miss Dallas beauty contest. She then went to New York and appeared in *Tarnished*, *The Trial of Mary Dugan* and *Ziegfeld Follies*. She was cast opposite James Cagney in *Maggie the Magnificent* and *Penny Arcade*. Warner Brothers bought the rights to *Penny Arcade*, renamed it *Sinner's Holiday* and hired Cagney and Blondell to repeat their stage roles in the movie. It was so successful that both were signed to long-term contracts. Blondell was one of Warners' busiest actresses. She worked 52 weeks a year instead of the customary 40 and made as many as 10 films per year. In 1939 she began to freelance at United Artists, Columbia, Universal, MGM, Republic and 20th Century–Fox. After entertaining the troops in World War II, she returned to Broadway to star in *The Naked Genius*, written by Gypsy Rose Lee and produced by Mike Todd. Between screen appearances she contin-

ued to tour in plays. In 1951 she was nominated for an Oscar for her performance in *The Blue Veil*. In addition to her successful film and stage career she authored the best seller *Center Door Fancy*. She was married three times, to cameraman George Barnes (1933–35), Dick Powell (1936–45) and Mike Todd (1947–50).

Feature Films

Office Wife (WB, 1930), *Sinner's Holiday* (WB, 1930), *Illicit* (WB, 1931), *Millie* (RKO, 1931), *My Past* (WB, 1931), *Big Business Girl* (WB, 1931), *Public Enemy* (WB, 1931), *God's Gift to Women* (WB, 1931), *Other Men's Women* (WB, 1931), *The Reckless Hour* (WB, 1931), *Night Nurse* (WB, 1931), *Blonde Crazy* (WB, 1931), *The Greeks Had a Word for Them* (UA, 1932), *Union Depot* (WB, 1932), *The Crowd Roars* (WB, 1932), *Famous Ferguson Case* (WB, 1932), *Make Me a Star* (Par., 1932), *Miss Pinkerton* (WB, 1932), *Big City Blues* (WB, 1932), *Three on a Match* (WB, 1932), *Central Park* (WB, 1932), *Lawyer Man* (WB, 1932),

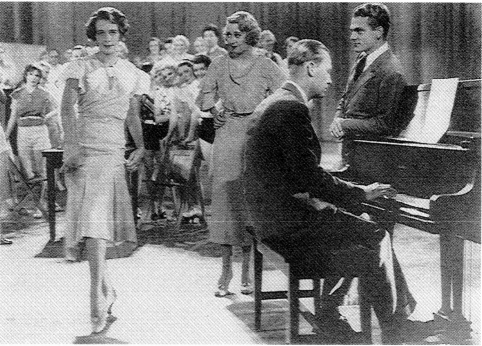

Top: Joan Blondell, a Hollywood *Stand-In,* is hired by Leslie Howard to be his secretary. Together they save a Hollywood studio from ruin (United Artists, 1937). *Bottom:* Ruby Keeler demonstrates a dance number to Joan Blondell and James Cagney as Lee Moran plays the piano in *Footlight Parade* (Warner Bros., 1933).

Broadway Bad (Fox, 1933), *Blondie Johnson* (WB, 1933), *Gold Diggers of 1933* (WB, 1933), *Goodbye Again* (WB, 1933), *Footlight Parade* (WB, 1933), *Havana Widows* (WB, 1933), *Convention City* (WB, 1933), *I've Got Your Number* (WB, 1934), *Smarty* (WB, 1934), *He Was Her Man* (WB, 1934), *Dames* (WB, 1934), *Kansas City Princess* (WB, 1934), *Traveling Saleslady* (WB, 1935), *Broadway Gondolier* (WB, 1935), *We're in the Money* (WB, 1935), *Miss Pacific Fleet* (WB, 1935), *Colleen* (WB, 1936), *Sons o' Guns* (WB, 1936), *Bullets or Ballots* (WB, 1936), *Stage Struck* (WB, 1936), *Three Men on a Horse* (WB, 1936), *Gold Diggers of 1937* (WB, 1936), *The King and the Chorus Girls* (WB, 1937), *Back in Circulation* (WB, 1937), *Perfect Specimen* (WB, 1937), *Stand-In* (UA, 1937), *There's Always a Woman* (Col., 1938), *Off the Record* (WB, 1939), *East Side of Heaven* (Univ., 1939), *The Kid from Kokomo* (WB, 1939), *Good Girls Go to Paris* (Col., 1939), *The Amazing Mr. Williams* (Col., 1939), *Two Girls on Broadway* (MGM, 1940), *I Want a Divorce* (Par., 1940), *Topper Returns* (UA, 1941), *Model Wife* (Univ., 1941), *Three Girls About Town* (Col., 1941), *Lady for a Night* (Rep., 1941), *Cry Havoc* (MGM, 1943), *A Tree Grows in Brooklyn* (20th, 1945), *Don Juan Quilligan* (20th, 1945), *Adventure* (MGM, 1945), *The Corpse Came C.O.D.* (Col., 1947), *Nightmare Alley* (20th, 1947), *Christmas Eve* (UA, 1947), *For Heaven's Sake* (20th, 1950), *The Blue Veil* (RKO, 1951), *The Opposite Sex* (MGM, 1956), *Lizzie* (MGM, 1957), *This Could Be the Night* (MGM, 1957), *Desk Set* (20th, 1957), *Will Success Spoil Rock Hunter?* (20th, 1957), *Angel Baby* (AA, 1961), *Advance to the Rear* (MGM, 1964), *The Cincinnati Kid* (MGM, 1965), *Ride Beyond Vengeance* (Col., 1966), *Paradise Road* (Sagas, 1966), *Waterhole #3* (Par., 1967), *Kona Coast* (WB-7 Arts, 1968), *Stay Away, Joe* (MGM, 1968), *Big Daddy* (Sagas, 1969), *The Phynx* (WB, 1970), *Support Your Local Gunfighter* (UA, 1971), *Won Ton Ton, the Dog Who Saved Hollywood* (Par., 1976), *Opening Night* (Faces, 1977), *The Glove* (Pro International, 1978), *Grease* (Par., 1978), *The Champ* (MGM-UA, 1979), *The Woman Inside* (20th, 1981)

Virginia Bruce (1910–1982)

Virginia Bruce was born in Minneapolis and grew up in Fargo, North Dakota. She went to Los Angeles in 1929 to attend UCLA but was spotted by a Paramount scout and signed to a contract. At Paramount she was given minor roles. When her contract ended in 1931, she signed with MGM where she was cast in leads. When she married silent screen idol John Gilbert in 1932, she retired briefly from the screen, but returned after their divorce in 1934. In 1936 she married film director J. Walter Rubin. She was widowed when he died in 1942. While under contract to MGM, Bruce appeared opposite Robert Taylor, Spencer Tracy, Robert Montgomery, William Powell, Nelson Eddy and Melvyn Douglas. After the MGM contract expired she freelanced at many studios. In her last film, *Strangers When We Meet* (1960), she played Kim Novak's mother. She died of natural causes in 1982 at the age of 72.

Feature Films

Woman Trap (Par., 1929), *Why Bring That Up?* (Par., 1929), *The Love Parade*

Surrounded by members of their opera company, Virginia Bruce and Lawrence Tibbett rehearse in *Metropolitan* (Fox, 1935).

(Par., 1929), *Lilies of the Field* (Par., 1930), *Only the Brave* (Par., 1930), *Slightly Scarlet* (Par., 1930), *Paramount on Parade* (Par., 1930), *Young Eagles* (Par., 1930), *The Love Parade* (Par., 1930), *Safety in Numbers* (Par., 1930), *Social Lion* (Par., 1930), *Hell Divers* (MGM, 1931), *Are You Listening?* (MGM, 1932), *The Wet Parade* (MGM, 1932), *Sky Bride* (Par., 1932), *The Miracle Man* (Par., 1932), *Winner Take All* (WB, 1932), *Downstairs* (MGM, 1932), *Kongo* (MGM, 1932), *A Scarlet Week-end* (MGM, 1932), *Jane Eyre* (Mon., 1934), *The Mighty Barnum* (UA, 1934), *Dangerous Corner* (RKO, 1934), *Times Square Lady* (MGM, 1935), *Society Doctor* (MGM, 1935), *Shadow of a Doubt* (MGM, 1935), *Let 'Em Have It* (UA, 1935), *Escapade* (MGM, 1935), *Here Comes the Band* (MGM, 1935), *The Murder Man* (MGM, 1935), *Metropolitan* (20th, 1935), *The Garden Murder Case* (MGM, 1936), *The Great Ziegfeld* (MGM, 1936), *Born to Dance* (MGM, 1936), *Women of Glamour* (Col., 1937), *When Love is Young* (Univ., 1937), *Between Two Women* (MGM, 1937), *Wife, Doctor and Nurse* (20th, 1937), *The First Hundred Years* (MGM, 1938), *Arsene Lupin Returns* (MGM, 1938), *Bad Man of Brimstone* (MGM, 1938), *Yellow Jack* (MGM, 1938), *Woman Against Woman* (MGM, 1938), *There's That Woman Again* (Col., 1938), *There Goes My Heart* (UA, 1938), *Let Freedom Ring* (MGM, 1939), *Society Lawyer* (MGM, 1939), *Stronger Than Desire* (MGM, 1939), *Flight Angels* (WB, 1940),

Warren William escorts a fabulous jewel from New York to Europe. On board an ocean liner en route he meets passenger Virginia Bruce and jewel thief Melvyn Douglas in *Arsene Lupin Returns* (MGM, 1938).

The Man Who Talked Too Much (WB, 1940), *Hired Wife* (Univ., 1940), *The Invisible Woman* (Univ., 1941), *Adventure in Washington* (Col., 1941), *Butch Minds the Baby* (Univ., 1942), *Pardon My Sarong* (Univ., 1942), *Careful, Soft Shoulders* (20th, 1942), *Brazil* (Rep., 1944), *Action in Arabia* (RKO, 1944), *Love, Honor and Goodbye* (Rep., 1945), *The Night Has a Thousand Eyes* (Par., 1948), *State Dept. File 649* (Film Classics, 1949), *The Reluctant Bride* (Gaumont-British, 1952), *Istanbul* (Turkish, 1953), *Three Grooms for a Bride* (20th, 1957), *Strangers When We Meet* (Col., 1960)

Yul Brynner (1915–1985)

Yul Brynner was born Taidje Khan in Sakhalin, an island north of Japan, to a Mongolian father and a gypsy mother who died during his birth. His father, a mining engineer, changed the family name to Brynner. He spent part of his childhood in China. As a youth he moved to France, where he was a cabaret singer and a circus performer. He studied philosophy at the Sorbonne, then moved

Yul Brynner as the king of Siam in *The King and I* (20th Century–Fox, 1956).

to London and studied acting under Michael Chekhov. In 1940 he came to the U.S. with the Chekhov Company and appeared briefly in the play *Twelfth Night.* Then he returned to London, where he appeared in other stage productions. During World War II he worked as a French-speaking radio announcer and commentator for the U.S. Office of War Information. After the war, Brynner was cast opposite Mary Martin in *Lute Song* on Broadway, and after its run he toured with that production opposite Dolly Haas in the Martin role. He next worked for NBC television as an actor and director. Brynner made his film debut as the villain in *Port of New York* (1949). Richard Rodgers and Oscar Hammerstein cast him in the stage musical *The King and I* opposite Gertrude Lawrence and he won a Tony for his performance. When the film version was made, he repeated his role as the gruff and stubborn monarch of Siam. It won him as Oscar. He then went on to star in many Hollywood and international films. In 1975 he returned to the theater in *Odyssey.* It was a big grosser on its national tour but failed on Broadway. The 1977 stage revival of *The King and I* was so successful that it toured for years and "The King" chalked up almost 5,000 performances. He died in New York at Cornell Medical Center of lung cancer at the age of 70.

Feature Films

Port of New York (EL, 1949), *The King and I* (20th, 1956), *The Ten Commandments* (Par., 1956), *Anastasia* (20th,

The Sound and the Fury, William Faulkner's novel about decadence in the South, is brought to life by Joanne Woodward, Ethel Waters and Yul Brynner (20th Century–Fox, 1959).

1956), *The Brothers Karamazov* (MGM, 1958), *The Buccaneer* (Par., 1958), *The Journey* (MGM, 1959), *The Sound and the Fury* (20th, 1959), *Solomon and Sheba* (UA, 1959), *Once More with Feeling* (Col., 1960), *The Magnificent Seven* (UA, 1960), *Surprise Package* (Col., 1960), *Escape from Zahrain* (Par., 1962), *Taras Bulba* (UA, 1962), *Kings of the Sun* (UA, 1964), *The Saboteur — Code Name Morituri* (20th, 1965), *Cast a Giant Shadow* (UA, 1966), *Is Paris Burning?* (Par., 1966), *Return of the Seven* (UA, 1966), *The Poppy Is Also a Flower* (1966), *Triple Cross* (WB, 1967), *The Double Man* (WB-7 Arts, 1967), *The Long Duel* (Rank, 1967), *Villa Rides* (Par., 1968), *The Picasso Summer* (CBS Films, 1968), *The File of the Golden Goose* (UA, 1969), *Madwoman of Chaillot* (WB, 1969), *Bounty Hunters* (Cinematographia, 1972), *The Magic Christian* (Commonwealth, 1970), *Adios Sabata* (UA, 1971), *Battle of Neretva* (AIP, 1971), *Light at the Edge of the World* (NGP, 1971), *Romance of a Horse Thief* (AA, 1971), *Fuzz* (UA, 1972), *The Serpent* (La Boetie, 1973), *Westworld* (MGM, 1973), *The Ultimate Warrior* (WB, 1975), *Futureworld* (AIP, 1976), *Death Rage* (S.J. International, 1978)

George Burns and Walter Matthau are a reunited vaudeville team with a love-hate relationship in *The Sunshine Boys* (United Artists, 1975).

George Burns (1896–1996)

George Burns was born on the lower east side of Manhattan, the ninth of twelve children. At age seven he was performing in the Pee-Wee Quartet and at age thirteen he and a friend opened B-B's College of Dancing. Next came vaudeville where he toiled unsuccessfully for years until he met Gracie Allen in 1922 in Newark. He persuaded her to join him and they formed the comedy team of Burns and Allen. She was born in San Francisco, the daughter of vaudevillians, and she began performing on stage as a child. In their act she originally played the straight man, but, seeing that she was a natural comedienne, Burns rewrote the act to give his partner most of the laughs. In 1926 they were married between shows in Cleveland where their successful act "Lamb Chops" earned them a six-year contract on the Keith theater circuit. They made their debut on radio while playing the Palladium in London. Their radio show on NBC lasted from 1932 to 1950. During that time, they appeared in successful movies playing themselves. In 1958, Allen retired and Burns continued working in television. In 1960, he teamed up with Carol Channing for nightclub appearances. Allen died in 1964 and Burns fell into involuntary semi-retirement. That ended in 1975 when he was

George Burns and Samuel S. Hinds listen as Gracie Allen tells that she and George have rights to a television device her uncle invented in *The Big Broadcast of 1936* (Paramount, 1935).

cast as the aging vaudevillian in the movie version of Neil Simon's *The Sunshine Boys* and won an Academy Award for Best Supporting Actor. Success followed with other films, television and nightclub appearances. He was the author of ten books and in 1990 he won a Grammy for the best spoken recording, *Gracie: A Love Story.* He was honored in 1988 for lifetime achievement by the John F. Kennedy Center for the Performing Arts. He died at the age of 100 at his Beverly Hills home.

Feature Films

The Big Broadcast (Par., 1932), *International House* (Par., 1933), *College Humor* (Par., 1933), *Six of a Kind* (Par., 1934), *We're Not Dressing* (Par., 1934), *Many Happy Returns* (Par., 1934), *Love in Bloom* (Par., 1935), *Here Comes Cookie* (Par., 1935), *Big Broadcast of 1936* (Par., 1935), *Big Broadcast of 1937* (Par., 1936), *College Holiday* (Par., 1936), *A Damsel in Distress* (RKO, 1937), *College Swing* (Par., 1938, *Honolulu* (MGM, 1939), *The Solid Gold Cadillac* (voice only; Col., 1956), *The Sunshine Boys* (UA, 1975), *Oh, God!* (WB, 1977), *Sgt. Pepper's Lonely Hearts Club Band* (Univ., 1978), *Movie Movie* (WB, 1978), *Going in Style* (WB, 1979), *Just You and Me, Kid* (Col., 1979), *Oh, God! Book II* (WB, 1980), *Oh, God! You Devil!* (WB, 1984), *18 Again* (New World, 1988)

Richard Burton is *Doctor Faustus* (adapted from Christopher Marlowe's 16th-century play) who sells his soul to the devil (Columbia, 1967).

Richard Burton (1925–1984)

Richard Burton was born Richard Walter Jenkins, Jr., in Pontrhydyfen, South Wales. He was one of 13 children of a coal-mining family and the only one to attend a university. When he entered Oxford at 16, teacher Richard Burton gave him acting lessons and helped him eliminate his decided Welsh accent. He took his stage name as a tribute to Burton. After Oxford, he enlisted in the Royal Air Force and trained as a navigator. Upon his discharge, he joined the Hugh Beaumont Stock Company and appeared in six plays. In 1948 he made his film debut. After several appearances on the London stage Burton gained stardom in *The Lady's Not for Burning* which was brought to Broadway and received critical acclaim. He returned to England to do more films and stage work before going to Hollywood to appear opposite Olivia de Havilland in Daphne du Maurier's *My Cousin Rachel*. At London's Old Vic he appeared in many Shakespeare plays and received acclaim. He returned to Broadway to appear opposite Dorothy McGuire in *Legends of Lovers* and *Time Remembered* with Helen Hayes and Susan Strasberg. In 1960 he got his first Tony as King Arthur in *Camelot* opposite Julie Andrews. Continuing his success in films and on stage, he also made several appearances on TV. Burton won his second Tony in the Broadway production of

Richard Burton is a history professor married to a shrew (Elizabeth Taylor). They are shown with their guests George Segal and Sandy Dennis in *Who's Afraid of Virginia Woolf?* (Warner Bros., 1966).

Equus and in 1964 he made theatrical history by appearing in the longest consecutive run of *Hamlet* on Broadway. He was nominated seven times for an Oscar but never won. He was married five times. His three ex-wives were Sybil Williams, Elizabeth Taylor (married twice) and Susan Hunt. At his death from a cerebral hemorrhage, he was married to Sally Hay.

Feature Films

The Last Days of Dolwyn (London Films, 1948), *Now Barabbas Was a Robber* (WB, 1949), *Waterfront* (GFD, 1950), *Green Grow the Rushes* (1951), *The Woman with No Name* (Rank, 1952), *My Cousin Rachel* (20th, 1952), *The Rains of Ranchipur* (20th, 1955), *Alexander the Great* (UA, 1956), *Sea Wife* (20th, 1957), *Bitter Victory* (Col., 1958), *Look Back in Anger* (WB, 1959), *Bramble Bush* (WB, 1960), *Ice Palace* (WB, 1960), *A Midsummer Night's Dream* (narrator: Czechoslovakian-British, 1961), *The Longest Day* (20th, 1962), *Cleopatra* (20th, 1963), *The V.I.P.s* (MGM, 1963), *Becket* (Par., 1964), *The Night of the Iguana* (MGM, 1964), *Hamlet* (WB, 1964), *Zulu* (narrator; 1964), *The Sandpiper* (MGM, 1965), *What's New Pussycat?* (UA, 1965)*, *The Spy Who Came In from the Cold* (Par.,

1966), *Who's Afraid of Virginia Woolf?* (WB, 1966), *The Comedians* (1967), *The Taming of the Shrew* (Col., 1967), *Dr. Faustus* (Col., 1968), *Boom* (Univ., 1968), *Candy* (Cinerama, 1968), *Where Eagles Dare* (MGM, 1968), *Anne of the Thousand Days* (Univ., 1969), *Staircase* (20th, 1969), *Raid on Rommel* (Univ., 1971), *Villain* (MGM, 1971), *The Assassination of Trotsky* (Cinerama, 1972), *Bluebeard* (Cinerama, 1972), *Hammersmith Is Out* (Cinerama, 1972), *Massacre in Rome* (NGP, 1973), *Under Milk Wood* (Altura, 1973), *The Klansman* (Par., 1974), *The Voyage* (Seven Pine Productions, 1974), *Equus* (UA, 1977), *Exorcist: The Heretic* (WB, 1977), *Breakthrough* (WB, 1978), *Medusa Touch* (WB, 1978), *Wild Geese* (AA, 1978), *Circle of Two* (Film Consortium, 1980), *Absolution* (Enterprise Pictures, 1981), *Wagner* (BIP, 1983), *1984* (BIP, 1984)

*Unbilled guest appearance

Maurice Chevalier (1888–1972)

Maurice Chevalier was born in the Menilmontant quarter of Paris. At the age of 12, he ran away from home and took odd jobs doing manual labor. Soon he began appearing in cafes as a singer and comedian. For a time Chevalier was in vaudeville and then danced at the Folies Bergère with the famed Mistinguett as his partner. The appearances led to roles in French movies. While serving in World War I, he was wounded, captured and put in a prisoner-of-war camp where he learned to speak English. After the war he appeared in a 1919 London revue. Then he went back to Paris and starred for three seasons at the Casino de Paris. In 1921 Chevalier formed his own film company and made five successful films under the direction of Henri Diamant-Berger. He next appeared on the Paris stage in a successful two-year run of *Dede*. In 1926 he married dancer Yvonne Vallee. They divorced in 1935. He came to the U.S. when Jesse Lasky, vice-president of Paramount, signed him to a contract. In Hollywood he was cast as a debonair sophisticate and enjoyed a great success starring opposite Jeanette MacDonald, Claudette Colbert, Frances Dee and Miriam Hopkins. However, his appeal (and consequently the box-office receipts) waned after several years and when his Paramount contract expired, he went to MGM. Because of artistic differences with MGM his contract was dissolved by mutual consent. He returned to France and continued with his screen career there and in England. Following World War II he opened his one-man show in London. After its successful run he took it to New York and then toured with it all over the world. He continued to make occasional films and TV appearances. In 1958 Chevalier was presented with a special Oscar for his contribution of more than half of a century to the world of entertainment. After publishing his memoirs, he died in Paris at the age of 83.

English-Language Sound Feature Films

Innocents of Paris (Par., 1929), *The Love Parade* (Par., 1929), *Paramount on Parade* (Par., 1930), *The Big Pond* (Par., 1930), *The Playboy of Paris* (Par., 1930), *The Smiling Lieutenant* (Par., 1931), *One Hour with You* (Par., 1932), *Make Me a Star* (Par., 1932)*, *Love Me Tonight* (Par.,

Haley Mills and Michael Anderson begin a search for their father with the help of Maurice Chevalier. Wilfrid Hyde-White looks on in *The Search of the Castaways* (BV, 1962).

1932), *A Bedtime Story* (Par., 1933), *The Way to Love* (Par., 1933), *The Merry Widow* (MGM, 1934), *Folies Bergère* (UA, 1935), *The Beloved Vagabond* (Col., 1937), *Love in the Afternoon* (AA, 1957), *Gigi* (MGM, 1958), *Count Your Blessings* (MGM, 1959), *A Breath of Scandal* (Par., 1960), *Can-Can* (20th, 1960), *Pepe* (Col., 1960), *Fanny* (WB, 1961), *Jessica* (UA, 1962), *In Search of the Castaways* (BV,

Maurice Chevalier is a wealthy baron who hires a performer from the *Folies Bergère* to impersonate him and Merle Oberon is the baron's wife (Fox, 1935).

1962), *A New Kind of Love* (Par., 1963), *Panic Button* (Gorton Associates, 1964), *I'd Rather Be Rich* (Univ., 1964), *Mon-keys, Go Home!* (BV, 1967), *The Aristocats* (voice only; BV, 1970)

*Unbilled guest appearance

Claudette Colbert (1903–1996)

Claudette Colbert was born in Paris and came to the United States at the age of six with her parents. They settled in New York where she graduated from Washington Irving High. At the Art Students' League Colbert studied dress design as she hoped to make that her career. At an afternoon tea party, she met playwright Ann Morrison who gave her a small role in her play *The Wild Westcotts* in 1923. Broadway producer Al Woods put her under contract and over the next few years she appeared in the plays *We've Got the Money, The Cat Came Back, A*

Ronald Colman is a member of the French Foreign Legion and Claudette Colbert is a camp follower in *Under Two Flags* (20th Century–Fox, 1936).

Kiss in a Taxi, The Ghost Train and *The Barker.* She became a Broadway star opposite Walter Huston in *The Barker* and went to London in that production. Upon her return to New York, Colbert made the silent film *For the Love of Mike* under Frank Capra's direction. Eugene O'Neill's *Dynamo* marked her return to the stage. Then Paramount signed her to a contract assigning her to films shot in Astoria Studio in Queens. She often worked in films by day and in the theater

On a train to Hollywood, authoress Claudette Colbert meets John Wayne. She wants him to play the lead in her book's screen adaptation in *Without Reservations* with Don DeFore (RKO, 1946).

at night. Colbert moved to California and appeared opposite such stars as Fredric March, Herbert Marshall, Gary Cooper, Clive Brooks, Charles Boyer and George M. Cohan. Because she demanded better vehicles, she was loaned out to Columbia Pictures, then a minor studio, for a starring role in *It Happened One Night*, directed by Frank Capra. (The role had been turned down by Myrna Loy, Constance Bennett and Miriam Hopkins.) Her co-star was Clark

Gable, on loan to Columbia from MGM, also as a punishment. This film swept all the major Academy Awards: Best Picture, Oscars for both Colbert and Gable, Capra for Best Director and Robert Ruskin for Best Screenplay. In 1935 Colbert was sixth among the top ten box-office stars. A year later her brother and manager Charles negotiated a seven-year contract with Paramount. By 1938 she was Hollywood's top paid star, earning more than four hundred thousand dollars a year. Her film career, (which included two other Oscar nominations) flourished until 1955. In 1956 she returned to Broadway, replacing Margaret Sullavan in *Janus*. She and Charles Boyer appeared in the hit *Marriage-Go-Round*, followed by such plays as *Julia, Jake and Uncle Joe* (1961), *The Irregular Verb to Love* (1963), *The Kingfisher* (1978) opposite Rex Harrison, *A Talent for Murder* (1981) opposite Jean-Pierre Aumont and *Aren't We All* (1985), again opposite Harrison. She appeared frequently in special television plays such as *Blithe Spirit* and *The Two Mrs. Greenvilles*. In 1989 she was honored by the Film Society of Lincoln Center and the Kennedy Center for Performing Arts.

Her first husband was actor-director Norman Foster (1928–35). After her divorce from Foster she married Dr. Joel Freeman, who died in 1968. She moved to Barbados where she lived for many years, and died there of stroke complications at the age of 92.

Sound Feature Films

The Hole in the Wall (Par., 1929), *The Lady Lies* (Par., 1929), *Manslaughter* (Par., 1930), *The Big Pond* (Par., 1930), *Young Man of Manhattan* (Par., 1930), *The Smiling Lieutenant* (Par., 1930), *Honor Among Lovers* (Par., 1931), *Secrets of a Secretary* (Par., 1931), *His Woman* (Par., 1931), *The Wiser Sex* (Par., 1932), *Make Me a Star* (Par., 1932)*, *Misleading Lady* (Par., 1932), *Man from Yesterday* (Par., 1932), *Phantom President* (Par., 1932), *The Sign of the Cross* (Par., 1932), *Tonight Is Ours* (Par., 1933), *I Cover the Waterfront* (UA, 1933), *Three-Cornered Moon* (Par., 1933), *Torch Singer* (Par., 1933), *Four Frightened People* (Par., 1934), *It Happened One Night* (Col., 1934), *Cleopatra* (Par., 1934), *Imitation of Life* (Univ., 1934), *The Gilded Lily* (Par., 1935), *Private Worlds* (Par., 1935), *She Married Her Boss* (Col., 1935), *The Bride Comes Home* (Par., 1935), *Under Two Flags* (20th, 1936), *Main of Salem* (Par., 1937), *I Met Him in Paris* (Par., 1937), *Tovarich* (WB, 1937), *Bluebeard's Eighth Wife* (Par., 1938), *Zaza* (Par., 1939), *Midnight* (Par., 1939), *It's a Wonderful World* (MGM, 1939), *Drums Along the Mohawk* (20th, 1939), *Boom Town* (MGM, 1940), *Arise, My Love* (Par., 1940), *Skylark* (Par., 1941), *The Palm Beach Story* (Par., 1942), *Remember the Day* (20th, 1942), *No Time for Love* (Par., 1943), *So Proudly We Hail* (Par., 1943), *Since You Went Away* (UA, 1944), *Practically Yours* (Par., 1944), *Guest Wife* (UA, 1945), *Without Reservations* (RKO, 1946), *Tomorrow Is Forever* (RKO, 1946), *The Secret Heart* (MGM, 1946), *The Egg and I* (Univ., 1947), *Sleep, My Love* (UA, 1948), *Family Honeymoon* (Univ., 1948), *Bride for Sale* (RKO, 1949), *Three Came Home* (20th, 1950), *The Secret Fury* (RKO, 1950), *Thunder on the Hill* (Univ., 1951), *Let's Make It Legal* (20th, 1951), *Outpost in Malaya* (UA, 1952), *Texas Lady* (RKO, 1955), *Parrish* (WB, 1961)

*Unbilled guest appearance

Ethel Barrymore views the *Portrait of Jennie* and tells the artist (Joseph Cotten) that his painting will establish his artistic reputation (Selznick, 1948).

Joseph Cotten (1905–1994)

Joseph Cotten was born in Petersburg, Virginia, and studied for the stage at the Hickman School of Expression in Washington, D.C. His first job was as a paint salesman. He moved to Miami and started the Top Salad Company, which failed. He joined the *Miami Herald* as an ad salesman and then wrote dramatic criticism.

Cotten went to New York with a letter of introduction to Broadway producer David Belasco, who cast him in *Dancing Partner*. Roles in *Absent Father*, *Accent on Youth*, and *The Postman Always Rings*

Twice followed. He next appeared in Orson Welles' Mercury Theatre productions of *Julius Caesar* and *The Shoemaker's Holiday*. Then he appeared opposite Katharine Hepburn on Broadway and on tour in *The Philadelphia Story*. Cotten followed Welles to Hollywood and co-starred in his productions *Citizen Kane*, *The Magnificent Ambersons* and *Journey Into Fear*. His role opposite Merle Oberon in *Lydia* established him as a romantic leading man. He signed a long-term contract with David O. Selznick and appeared in

Joseph Cotten is an American engineer hunted by Nazi agents in Turkey. He takes a freighter to escape. Aboard are two mysterious men (Herbert Drake and Bill Roberts) and Dolores Del Rio in *Journey Into Fear* (RKO, 1942).

Alfred Hitchcock's suspenseful *Shadow of a Doubt*. He was cast opposite Jennifer Jones in *Love Letters, Duel in the Sun* and *Portrait of Jennie. Jennie* brought him the Venice Film Festival Award for best actor. In subsequent films he appeared opposite Ingrid Bergman, Ginger Rogers, Loretta Young, Bette Davis, Joan Fontaine, Barbara Stanwyck, Deanna Durbin, Ava Gardner, Marilyn Monroe and Olivia de Havilland.

Cotten's first wife died in 1960. He then married actress Patricia Medina. She was at his bedside when he died of pneumonia at their home in Westwood, California, at the age of 88.

Feature Films

Citizen Kane (RKO, 1941), *Lydia* (UA, 1941), *The Magnificent Ambersons* (RKO, 1942), *Journey Into Fear* (RKO, 1942), *Shadow of a Doubt* (Univ., 1943), *Hers to Hold* (Univ., 1943), *Gaslight* (MGM, 1944), *Since You Went Away* (UA, 1944), *I'll Be Seeing You* (UA, 1944), *Love Letters* (Par., 1945), *Duel in the Sun* (Selznick, 1946), *The Farmer's Daughter* (RKO, 1947), *Portrait of Jennie* (Selznick, 1948), *Under Capricorn* (WB, 1949), *Beyond the Forest* (WB, 1949), *The Third Man* (Selznick, 1950), *Walk Softly, Stranger* (RKO, 1950), *Two Flags West* (20th, 1950), *September Affair* (Par., 1950), *Half*

Angel (20th, 1951), *Peking Express* (Par., 1951), *The Man with a Cloak* (MGM, 1951), *Untamed Frontier* (Univ., 1952), *The Steel Trap* (20th, 1952), *Niagara* (20th, 1953), *Blueprint for Murder* (20th, 1953), *Special Delivery* (Col., 1955), *The Bottom of the Bottle* (20th, 1956), *The Killer Is Loose* (UA, 1956), *The Halliday Brand* (UA, 1957), *Touch of Evil* (Univ., 1958)*, *From the Earth to the Moon* (WB, 1958), *The Angel Wore Red* (MGM, 1960), *The Last Sunset* (Univ., 1961), *Hush...Hush, Sweet Charlotte* (20th, 1965), *The Great Sioux Massacre* (Col., 1965), *The Oscar* (Par., 1966), *The Tramplers* (Embassy, 1966), *The Money Trap* (MGM, 1966), *Brighty of the Grand Canyon* (Feature Film Corp. of America, 1967), *The Diamond Spy* (Embassy, 1967), *Jack of Diamonds* (MGM, 1967), *Some May Live* (RKO, 1967), *The Hellbenders* (Embassy, 1967), *Days of Fire* (Italian, 1968), *Petulia* (WB, 1968), *Latitude Zero* (NGP, 1969), *The Grasshopper* (NGP, 1970), *Tora! Tora! Tora!* (20th, 1970), *The Abominable Dr. Phibes* (AIP, 1971), *Lady Frankenstein* (New World, 1971), *Baron Blood* (AIP, 1972), *Doomsday Voyage* (Futurama International, 1973), *Soylent Green* (MGM, 1973), *Airport '77* (Univ., 1977), *Twilight's Last Gleaming* (AA, 1977), *Caravans* (Univ., 1978), *Screamers* (New World, 1978), *Guyana, Cult of the Damned* (Univ., 1980), *The Hearse* (Merimark/Crown, 1980), *Heaven's Gate* (UA, 1980), *Survivor* (Ginnane, 1980)

*Unbilled guest appearance

Broderick Crawford (1911–1985)

Born in Philadelphia, he was the son of vaudevillian Lester Crawford and comedienne Helen Broderick. As a child and teenager, Crawford performed in vaudeville and on radio. He made his stage debut in London in 1932 and first appeared on Broadway in 1935 when he was 24. His performance resulted in a contract with Samuel Goldwyn. After minor roles in movies, he returned to Broadway and won critics' acclaim as Lennie in John Steinbeck's *Of Mice and Men*. After its run, Crawford went back to Hollywood. After the war, he was cast as politician Willie Stark (a thinly disguised portrayal of Louisiana governor Huey Long) in director Robert Rossen's *All the King's Men*. For that performance he was awarded both an Oscar and the New York Film Critics' Award in 1949. Columbia cast him in disappointing films until he was cast opposite Judy Holliday in the now-classic comedy *Born Yesterday*. When his contract with Columbia ended, he freelanced at various studios. From 1955 to 1959 he starred in the TV series *Highway Patrol* as Chief Dan Matthews. Two more successful series followed: He was a dock detective in *King of Diamonds* and a gruff doctor in *The Interns*. He died at 74 from complications following a stroke.

Feature Films

Woman Chases Man (UA, 1937), *Submarine D-1* (WB, 1937), *Start Cheering* (Col., 1938), *Sudden Money* (Par., 1939), *Ambush* (Par., 1939), *Undercover Doctor* (Par., 1939), *Beau Geste* (Par., 1939), *Eternally Yours* (UA, 1939), *Island of Lost Men* (Par., 1939), *The Real Glory* (UA, 1939), *Slightly Honorable* (UA, 1940), *I*

Robert Greenleaf, an upstanding judge, confronts Broderick Crawford, a notorious politician who ruins the judge's career, as Anne Seymour, William Bruce, John Ireland and Ralph Dumke witness the scene in *All the King's Men* (Columbia, 1949).

Can't Give You Anything But Love, Baby (Univ., 1940), *When the Daltons Rode* (Univ., 1940), *Seven Sinners* (Univ., 1940), *Trail of the Vigilantes* (Univ., 1940), *Texas Rangers Ride Again* (Par., 1940), *The Black Cat* (Univ., 1941), *Tight Shoes* (Univ., 1941), *Badlands of Dakota* (Univ., 1941), *South of Tahiti* (Univ., 1941), *North of the Klondike* (Univ., 1942), *Larceny, Inc.* (WB, 1942), *Butch Minds the Baby* (Univ., 1942), *Broadway* (Univ., 1942), *Men of Texas* (Univ., 1942), *Sin Town* (Univ., 1942), *The Runaround* (Univ., 1946), *Black Angel* (Univ., 1946), *Slave Girl* (Univ., 1947), *The Flame* (Rep., 1947), *The Time of Your Life* (UA, 1948), *Sealed Verdict* (Par., 1948), *Bad Men of Tombstone* (AA, 1948), *A Kiss in the Dark* (WB, 1949), *Night*

Unto Night (WB, 1949), *Anna Lucasta* (Col., 1949), *All the King's Men* (Col., 1949), *Cargo to Capetown* (Col., 1950), *Convicted* (Col., 1950), *Born Yesterday* (Col., 1950), *The Mob* (Col., 1951), *Scandal Sheet* (Col., 1952), *Lone Star* (MGM, 1952), *Stop, You're Killing Me* (WB, 1952), *Last of the Comanches* (Col., 1952), *Night People* (20th, 1954), *Down Three Dark Streets* (UA, 1954), *Human Desire* (Col., 1954), *New York Confidential* (WB, 1955), *Big House, U.S.A.* (UA, 1955), *Not as a Stranger* (UA, 1955), *The Fastest Gun Alive* (MGM, 1956), *Between Heaven and Hell* (20th, 1956), *The Decks Ran Red* (MGM, 1958), *Convicts 4* (AA, 1962), *The Castillian* (WB, 1963), *Square of Violence* (MGM, 1963), *A House Is Not a Home* (Embassy, 1964), *Up from the Beach*

John Ireland is the captain of an oil tanker and Broderick Crawford is the ship's engineer who disagrees with orders in *Cargo to Capetown* (Columbia, 1950).

(20th, 1965), *The Oscar* (Par., 1966), *Kid Rodelo* (Par., 1966), *The Texican* (Col., 1966), *Red Tomahawk* (Par., 1967), *The Vulture* (Par., 1967), *Hell's Bloody Devils* (*The Fakers*) (Independent International, 1970), *The Candidate* (WB, 1972), *Embassy* (Hemdale, 1972), *Terror in the Wax Museum* (Cinerama, 1972), *Won Ton Ton, the Dog Who Saved Hollywood* (Par., 1976), *The Private Files of Edgar Hoover* (AIP, 1978), *Little Romance* (Orion, 1979), *Harlequin* (Hemdale, 1980), *There Goes the Bride* (Vanguard, 1980), *Liar's Moon* (Crown International, 1982)

Olivia de Havilland is a European princess whose uncle brings her to America to find a suitable husband. She begins to learn about America with Robert Cummings in Frank Puglis' diner in *Princess O'Rourke* (Warner Bros., 1943).

Robert Cummings (1910–1990)

Born in Joplin, Missouri, Cummings studied engineering and business before turning to the theater. He began his acting career in England and passed himself off as Blade Stanhope-Conway. When he returned to the U.S. he worked as a straight man for Milton Berle and appeared with Fannie Brice and Eve Arden in *Ziegfeld Follies* (1934 edition) under the name of Brice Hutchins. He was signed by Paramount and had a successful film career, appearing with Dorothy Lamour, Hedy Lamarr, Doris Day, Jean Arthur, Margaret Sullavan, Joan Bennett, Deanna Durbin, Barbara Stanwyck, Shirley MacLaine, Loretta Young, Grace Kelly and Leslie Caron. Most of Cummings' films were light comedies, but he played some serious roles such as *Kings Row* and two Alfred Hitchcock thrillers. In 1952-53 he appeared on NBC's hit series *My Hero* and he won an Emmy in 1954 for *Twelve Angry Men*. *The Bob Cummings Show* ran from 1955 to 1959 on NBC. He appeared in a revived series called *The New Bob Cummings Show* from 1955 to 1959. He also starred opposite Julie Newmar in *My Living Doll* on CBS in 1964 and 1965. After retiring from show business, Cummings

Betty Grable plays a showgirl with a friend who witnesses a murder. They flee to a college town and meet Robert Cummings, a student who has put off graduating for 17 years so that his inheritance money will keep coming in *How to Be Very, Very Popular* (20th Century–Fox, 1955).

authored the book *How to Stay Young and Vital.* He died in Woodland Hills of kidney failure and pneumonia. He suffered from Parkinson's disease. He was survived by his fifth wife, Janie.

Feature Films

The Virginia Judge (Par., 1935), *So Red the Rose* (Par., 1935), *Millions in the Air* (Par., 1935), *Forgotten Faces* (Par., 1936), *Desert Gold* (Par., 1936), *Arizona Mahoney* (Par., 1936), *Border Flight* (Par., 1936), *Three Cheers for Love* (Par., 1936), *Hollywood Boulevard* (Par., 1936), *The Accusing Finger* (Par., 1936), *Hideaway Girl* (Par., 1937), *Last Train from Madrid* (Par., 1937), *Souls at Sea* (Par., 1937), *Wells Fargo* (Par., 1937), *College Swing* (Par., 1938), *You and Me* (Par., 1938), *The Texans* (Par., 1938), *Touchdown Army* (Par., 1938), *I Stand Accused* (Rep., 1938), *Three Smart Girls Grow Up* (Univ., 1939), *The Under-Pup* (Univ., 1939), *Rio* (Univ., 1939), *Everything Happens at Night* (20th, 1939), *Charlie McCarthy, Detective* (Univ., 1939), *And One Was Beautiful* (MGM, 1940), *Private Affairs* (Univ., 1940), *Spring Parade* (Univ., 1940), *One Night in the Tropics* (Univ., 1941), *Free and Easy* (MGM, 1941), *The Devil and Miss Jones* (RKO, 1941), *Moon Over Miami* (20th, 1941), *It Started with Eve* (Univ., 1941), *Kings Row* (WB, 1942), *Saboteur* (Univ., 1942), *Between Us Girls*

(Univ., 1942), *Forever and a Day* (RKO, 1943), *Princess O'Rourke* (WB, 1943), *Flesh and Fantasy* (Univ., 1942), *You Came Along* (Par., 1945), *The Bride Wore Boots* (Par., 1946), *The Chase* (UA, 1946), *Heaven Only Knows* (UA, 1947), *The Lost Moment* (Univ., 1947), *Sleep, My Love* (UA, 1948), *Let's Live a Little* (EL, 1948), *The Accused* (Par., 1948), *Free for All* (Univ., 1949), *Tell It to the Judge* (Col., 1949), *Reign of Terror* (UA, 1949), *Paid in Full* (Par., 1950), *The Petty Girl* (Col., 1950), *For Heaven's Sake* (20th, 1950), *The Barefoot Mailman* (Col., 1951), *The First Time* (Col., 1952), *Marry Me Again* (RKO, 1953), *Lucky Me* (WB, 1954), *Dial M for Murder* (WB, 1954), *How to Be Very, Very Popular* (20th, 1955), *My Geisha* (Par., 1962), *Beach Party* (AIP, 1963), *What a Way to Go!* (20th, 1964), *The Carpetbaggers* (Par., 1964), *Promise Her Anything* (Par., 1966), *Stagecoach* (20th, 1966), *Five Golden Dragons* (WB, 1967)

Bette Davis (1908–1989)

Born in Lowell, Massachusetts, Bette Davis was determined to be an actress. In New York she was rejected as a student by Eva La Gallienne, but enrolled in John Murray Anderson's drama school and studied acting under him. She obtained a job with a Rochester stock company only to be fired by its director, George Cukor. Then she joined Providence Playhouse in New York's Greenwich Village, playing various roles there and on tour. Her performances in two Broadway successes—*Solid South* and *Broken Dishes*—led to a movie contract at Universal. It was not a successful association. After appearing in six forgettable films, she was ready to leave Hollywood, but actor George Arliss requested her for a role in Warner Brothers' *The Man Who Played God*. She was placed under contract and that movie was the beginning of her legendary career. However, Warners cast her in several mediocre films from 1932 to 1935. She fought to be lent to RKO in order to play Mildred in *Of Human Bondage*, the role which made her a star. Upon her return to Warners, she was again given mostly inferior material but won an Oscar for *Dangerous*. After that award she had a legal battle with the studio for better quality films and won another Oscar for *Jezebel*. In 1949 she asked for a release from her contract with Warner Brothers and freelanced at various studios. She scored a triumph in 1950 as Margo Channing in *All About Eve* for 20th Century–Fox. A return to the stage included roles in the musical revue *Two's Company*, *An Evening with Carol Sandburg* and Tennessee Williams' *Night of the Iguana*. Her film career was revitalized by her performance in *What Ever Happened to Baby Jane?* with Joan Crawford. She appeared in television movies and won an Emmy. Davis married her high school sweetheart Ham Nelson, a nightclub orchestra leader, in 1932. She divorced him in 1936. In 1940 she married aircraft engineer Arthur Farnsworth. He died in 1943. Two years later she married William Grant Sherry, an artist, and their daughter Barbara Davis (B.D.) was born in 1947. This union ended in divorce in 1950. Then she married actor Gary Merrill. They settled in Maine and adopted two children, Margot and Michael. This marriage also ended in

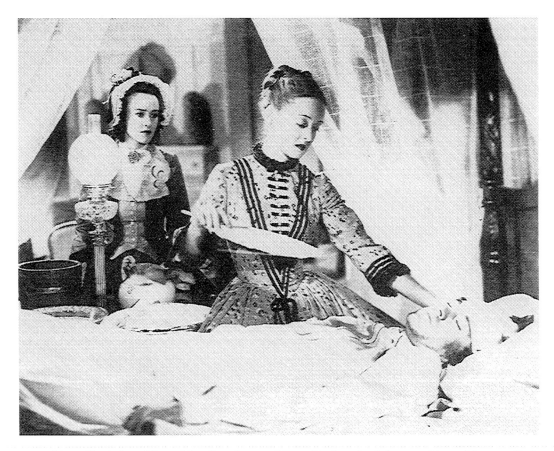

Henry Fonda is stricken with yellow fever and Bette Davis as *Jezebel* nurses him as Margaret Lindsay observes passively (Warner Bros., 1938).

divorce in 1960. While returning from Spain where she had been honored at the San Sebastian Film Festival, Davis died of cancer at the age of 81.

Feature Films

Bad Sister (Univ., 1931), *Seed* (Univ., 1931), *Waterloo Bridge* (Univ., 1931), *Way Back Home* (RKO, 1932), *The Menace* (Col., 1932), *Hell's House* (Capital Film Exchange, 1932), *The Man Who Played God* (WB, 1932), *The Rich Are Always with Us* (WB, 1932), *The Dark Horse* (WB, 1932), *Cabin in the Cotton* (WB, 1932), *Three on a Match* (WB, 1932), *20,000 Years in Sing Sing* (WB, 1933), *Parachute Jumper* (WB, 1933), *The Working Man* (WB, 1933), *Ex-Lady* (WB, 1933), *Bureau of Missing Persons* (WB, 1933), *Fashions of 1934* (WB, 1934), *Jimmy the Gent* (WB, 1934), *Fog Over Frisco* (WB, 1934), *Of Human Bondage* (RKO, 1934), *Housewife* (WB, 1934), *Bordertown* (WB, 1935), *The Girl from Tenth Avenue* (WB, 1935), *Front Page Woman* (WB, 1935), *Special Agent* (WB, 1935), *Dangerous* (WB, 1935), *The Petrified Forest* (WB, 1936), *The Golden Arrow* (WB, 1936), *Satan Met a Lady* (WB, 1936), *Marked Woman* (WB, 1937), *Kid Galahad* (WB, 1937), *That Certain Woman* (WB, 1937), *It's Love I'm After* (WB, 1937), *Jezebel* (WB, 1938), *The Sisters* (WB, 1938), *Dark Victory* (WB, 1939), *Juarez*

Joan Crawford and Bette Davis starred in the superb gothic horror film that revitalized their careers — *What Ever Happened to Baby Jane?* (Warner Bros., 1962).

(WB, 1939), *The Old Maid* (WB, 1939), *The Private Lives of Elizabeth and Essex* (WB, 1939), *All This and Heaven Too* (WB, 1940), *The Letter* (WB, 1940), *The Bride Came C.O.D.* (WB, 1941), *The Little Foxes* (RKO, 1941), *The Man Who Came to Dinner* (WB, 1941), *In This Our Life* (WB, 1942), *Now, Voyager* (WB, 1942), *Watch on the Rhine* (WB, 1943), *Thank Your Lucky Stars* (WB, 1943), *Old Acquaintance* (WB, 1943), *Mr. Skeffington* (WB, 1944), *Hollywood Canteen* (WB, 1944), *The Corn Is Green* (WB, 1945), *A Stolen Life* (WB, 1946), *Deception* (WB, 1947), *Winter Meeting* (WB, 1948), *June Bride* (WB, 1948), *Beyond the Forest* (WB, 1949), *All About Eve* (20th, 1950), *Payment on Demand* (RKO, 1951), *Another Man's Poison* (UA, 1951), *Phone Call from a Stranger* (20th, 1952), *The Star* (20th, 1953), *The Virgin Queen* (20th, 1955), *Storm Center* (Col., 1956), *The Catered Affair* (MGM, 1956), *John Paul Jones* (WB, 1959), *The Scapegoat* (MGM, 1959), *A Pocketful of Miracles* (UA, 1961), *What Ever Happened to Baby Jane?* (WB, 1962), *Dead Ringer* (WB, 1964), *The Empty Canvas* (Embassy, 1964), *Where Love Has Gone* (Par., 1964), *Hush...Hush, Sweet Charlotte* (20th, 1965), *The Nanny* (20th, 1965), *The Anniversary* (20th, 1968), *Connecting Rooms* (Telstar-London, 1971), *Bunny O'Hare* (AIP, 1971), *The Scientific Cardplayer* (Dino de Laurentiis-Italy, 1972), *Burnt Offerings* (UA, 1976), *Death on the Nile* (Par., 1978), *Return from Witch Mountain* (BV, 1978), *The Watcher in the Woods* (BV, 1980), *The Whales of August* (Alive Films, 1987), *Wicked Stepmother* (MGM/UA, 1989)

Frank Sinatra, Peter Lawford, Dean Martin and Sammy Davis, Jr., are soldiers at a Western outpost who encounter Indian warrior Mountain Hawk (played by Henry Silva) in *Sergeants 3* (United Artists, 1962).

Sammy Davis, Jr. (1925–1990)

Davis was born to vaudeville hoofer Sammy Davis, Sr., and Chorine "Baby" Sanchez, who came from Puerto Rico. They performed with an adopted uncle, Will Mastin, in his act *Holiday in Dixieland*, which played major vaudeville circuits. By the time Sammy was four years old he was a full-fledged entertainer in "Will Mastin's Gang," being featured as "Little Sammy." In 1933 he made several Vitaphone shorts with Ethel Waters and Lita Grey Chaplin. He then went on to establish himself as a night club entertainer and recording star before he was drafted into the Army in 1943. Davis was assigned to Special Services to put on camp shows. After his discharge, he toured with the Martin Trio with Mickey Rooney. Then he

played Manhattan's Capitol Theatre with Frank Sinatra. Next came TV guest appearances on Ed Sullivan's *Toast of the Town*, *Colgate Comedy Hour* and as a summer replacement for the *Colgate* show. In 1956-57 he appeared on Broadway in the successful musical *Mr. Wonderful*. He continued his career with more films, dramatic roles on TV in many series and many top recordings. Then he returned to Broadway to star in the musical version of *Golden Boy* directed by Arthur Penn. Between movies and television appearances, he did live concerts. His last concert was with Frank Sinatra and Liza Minnelli in 1988-89. He was the author of three memoirs: *Yes, I Can*, *Hollywood in a Suitcase* and *Why Me?* He was married three

Sammy Davis, Jr., and Peter Lawford are part of a group using its military knowledge to rob five Las Vegas casinos in *Oceans Eleven* (Warner Bros., 1960).

times — Loray White (1958–59), May Britt (1960–67) and Altovise Gore (1970–90). Davis died in Beverly Hills of throat cancer at the age of 64.

Feature Films

Anna Lucasta (UA, 1958), *Porgy and Bess* (Col., 1959), *Ocean's 11* (WB, 1960), *Pepe* (Col., 1960), *Sergeants 3* (UA, 1962), *Convicts 4* (AA, 1962), *Johnny Cool* (UA, 1963), *Robin and the 7 Hoods* (WB, 1964), *Nightmare in the Sun* (Zodiac, 1965), *A Man Called Adam* (Embassy, 1966), *Salt and Pepper* (UA, 1966), *Sweet Charity* (Univ., 1969), *One More Time* (UA, 1970), *Save the Children* (1973), *Sammy Stops the World* (Special Events Entertainment, 1978), *The Cannonball Run* (20th, 1981), *Heidi's Song* (Par., 1982), *Three Penny Opera* (French/German, 1983), *Cannonball Run II* (20th, 1984), *That's Dancing!* (MGM, 1985), *The Perils of P.K.* (Independent, 1986), *Moon Over Parador* (Univ., 1988), *Tap* (Tri-Star, 1989)

Dolores Del Rio (1905–1983)

Dolores Del Rio was born in Durango, Mexico. Her father was a bank manager and she was educated in convents. At 16 she married Jaime Del Rio. While visiting Mexico City, film director Edwin Carewe cast her in a

Henry Fonda as *The Fugitive*, a saintly priest who is hunted in a country that has outlawed the clergy. Dolores Del Rio is the Mexican woman who befriends him (RKO, 1947).

Gene Raymond, a bandleader, takes Dolores Del Rio by plane to the location of his current engagement. Wallace MacDonald stands by in *Flying Down to Rio* (RKO, 1933).

silent film he was making and put her under special contract. She soon became a successful silent screen star and made a successful transition to the talkies. After the death of her first husband, she married Cedric Gibbons in 1930. They divorced in 1941. She returned to Mexico in 1943 and made very successful films under the direction of Emilio Fernandez. When John Ford made *The Fugitive* in Mexico, she was cast in the film. She also made movies in Argentina and Spain. Occasionally she returned to the U.S. for film and television work. She married Lewis J. Riley and they lived in a suburb outside Mexico City. During her later years she was active in many charity affairs. She died at the age of 77 of natural causes.

English-Language Feature Films

Evangeline (UA, 1929), *The Bad One* (UA, 1930), *Girl of the Rio* (RKO, 1932), *Bird of Paradise* (RKO, 1932), *Flying Down to Rio* (RKO, 1933), *Wonder Bar* (RKO, 1934), *Madame Du Barry* (WB, 1934), *In Caliente* (WB, 1935), *I Live for Love* (WB, 1935), *Widow from Monte Carlo* (WB, 1935), *Accused* (UA, 1936), *Devil's Playground* (Col., 1937), *Lancer Spy* (20th, 1937), *International Settlement* (20th, 1938), *The Man from Dakota* (MGM, 1940), *Journey into Fear* (RKO, 1942), *The Fugitive* (RKO, 1947), *Flaming Star* (20th, 1960), *Cheyenne Autumn* (WB, 1964), *More Than a Miracle* (MGM, 1967), *Children of Sanchez* (AA, 1978)

Amidst political unrest rebels attack the *Shanghai Express*. Anna May Wong and Marlene Dietrich are taken as hostages (Paramount, 1932).

Marlene Dietrich (1901–1992)

Born Maria Magdalene Dietrich to an upper-class Berlin family, Dietrich studied violin and played in a theater orchestra until a hand injury ended her aspirations as a violinist. She then became a stage and screen actress and contracted her two given names to Marlene. In 1924 she married Rudolf Sieber, a Czech, who worked in films. Their marriage produced one child, Maria Riva, and lasted until Sieber's death in 1976, although they lived apart for many years. Josef von Sternberg cast her in the German film *The Blue Angel* opposite Emil Jannings. Her performance made

her a star. With a Paramount contract she came to the U.S. and made films with von Sternberg as her director. Paramount ended the Sternberg-Dietrich partnership in 1935 because of poor box office receipts. She continued her film career working with other directors, and when her contract ended she was off the screen for two years. Her return in *Destry Rides Again* opposite James Stewart revitalized her career. She became a U.S. citizen in 1939. During World War II she sold war bonds, entertained troops in battle zones (the South Pacific, North Africa, Italy and Germany) and was awarded the

Marlene Dietrich is a nightclub singer who is drawn to Legionnaire Gary Cooper in *Morocco* (Paramount, 1930).

Medal of Freedom and named a Chevalier of the French Legion of Honor. After the war she returned to films. In 1954 she started giving cabaret performances in which she sang some of her "trademark" songs from her hit movies. She continued her cabaret act (with variations) for over two decades, earning universal acclaim in her world tours. In the mid 1970s she stopped performing and became a recluse in her Paris apartment. She authored two books—*Marlene Dietrich's ABC* and *Marlene*. At the age of 90 she died of natural causes in Paris and was buried next to her mother's grave in Berlin, as she had requested.

English-Language Feature Films

The Blue Angel (Par., 1930), *Morocco* (Par., 1930), *Dishonored* (Par., 1931), *Shanghai Express* (Par., 1932), *Blonde Venus* (Par., 1932), *The Song of Songs* (Par., 1933), *The Scarlet Empress* (Par., 1934), *The Devil Is a Woman* (Par., 1935), *Desire* (Par., 1936), *The Garden of Allah* (UA, 1936), *Knight Without Armour* (UA, 1937), *Angel* (Par., 1937), *Destry Rides Again* (Univ., 1939) *Seven Sinners* (Univ., 1940), *The Flame of New Orleans* (Univ., 1941), *Manpower* (WB, 1941), *The Lady Is Willing* (Col., 1942), *The Spoilers* (Univ., 1942), *Pittsburgh* (Univ., 1942) *Follow the Boys* (Par., 1948), *Jigsaw* (UA, 1949)*, *Stage Fright* (WB, 1950), *No Highway in the Sky* (20th, 1951), *Rancho*

Notorious (RKO, 1952), *Around the World in 80 Days* (UA, 1956), *The Monte Carlo Story* (UA, 1957), *Witness for the Prosecution* (UA, 1957), *Touch of Evil* (Univ., 1958)*, *Judgment at Nuremberg* (UA, 1961), *The Black Fox* (narrator; Capri, 1963), *Paris When It Sizzles* (Par., 1964)*, *Just a Gigolo* (UA, 1979), *Marlene* (voice only; European, 1984)

*Unbilled guest appearance

Irene Dunne (1901–1990)

Born the daughter of a government official in Louisville, Kentucky, Dunne was educated at the Loretta Academy. She studied voice at a conservatory in Indianapolis and won a scholarship to the Chicago Musical College. After graduation she went to New York and won the lead in a touring company of *Irene*. Her successful Broadway debut in 1923's *Clinging Vine* led to appearances in six hit musicals through 1929 with such stars as Eddie Foy, Jr., Beatrice Lillie and Clifton Webb. Producer Florins Ziegfeld cast her as Magnolia in the Chicago company of *Show Boat*, which ran there for more than a year. RKO signed Dunne to a seven-year contract and she became an international star in her third film, *Cimarron* which won an Oscar for Best Picture. Dunne was nominated for Best Actress. After she concluded her RKO contract she freelanced, working for Columbia, Paramount, Universal, Warner Brothers, 20th Century–Fox and RKO. She was nominated for an Oscar five times but never won, and in 1952 she retired from the screen. She did some television work but tired of show business and turned her interests to politics and business interests. In 1957 President Eisenhower appointed her a delegate to the U.N. General Assembly. For two years in this position she promoted better international understanding. Dunne's marriage to Dr. Francis Griffin lasted 38 years. After his death in 1965, she made only infrequent public appearances. At the 1967 Academy Awards she was presented an Oscar and in 1975 she was honored at the Los Angeles International Film Exposition. She was long active in raising money for charities, especially St. John's Hospital in Santa Monica. In 1985 Dunne was one of the recipients of honors at the Kennedy Center in Washington. She died of heart failure at her home in the Holmby Hills section of Los Angeles.

Feature Films

Leathernecking (RKO, 1930), *Bachelor Apartment* (RKO, 1931), *Cimarron* (RKO, 1931), *Great Lover* (MGM, 1931), *Consolation Marriage* (RKO, 1931), *Symphony of Six Million* (RKO, 1932), *Thirteen Women* (RKO, 1932), *Back Street* (Univ., 1932), *Secret of Madame Blanche* (MGM, 1933), *No Other Woman* (RKO, 1933), *Silver Cord* (RKO, 1933), *Ann Vickers* (RKO, 1933), *If I Were Free* (RKO, 1933), *This Man Is Mine* (RKO, 1934), *Stingaree* (RKO, 1934), *Age of Innocence* (RKO, 1934), *Roberta* (RKO, 1935), *Sweet Adeline* (WB, 1935), *Magnificent Obsession* (Univ., 1935), *Show Boat* (Univ., 1936), *Theodora Goes Wild* (Col., 1936), *High, Wide and Handsome* (Par., 1937), *The Awful Truth* (Col., 1937), *Joy of Living* (RKO, 1938), *Love Affair* (RKO, 1939), *Everything's on Ice* (RKO, 1939),

Top: Cary Grant, Ralph Bellamy and Irene Dunne were the stars of *The Awful Truth* which became the epitome of the screwball comedies of the 1930's (Columbia, 1937). *Bottom:* Robert Montgomery, Preston Foster and Irene Dunne in the romantic comedy *Unfinished Business.* The stars try to mend a marriage that has hit the rocks (Universal, 1941).

Invitation to Happiness (Par., 1939), *When Tomorrow Comes* (Par., 1939), *My Favorite Wife* (RKO, 1940), *Penny Serenade* (Col., 1941), *Unfinished Business* (Univ., 1941), *Lady in a Jam* (Univ., 1942), *A Guy Named Joe* (MGM, 1943), *The White Cliffs of Dover* (MGM, 1944), *Together Again* (Col., 1944), *Over 21* (Col., 1945), *Anna and the King of Siam* (20th, 1946), *Life with Father* (WB, 1947), *I Remember Mama* (RKO, 1948), *Never a Dull Moment* (RKO, 1950), *The Mudlark* (20th, 1950), *It Grows on Trees* (Univ., 1952)

Madge Evans (1909–1981)

Madge Evans was born in Manhattan and at the age of five was one of the first professional child models. This led her to the theater and silent films at a very early age. After appearing in many silents her stage experience enabled her to make a successful transition to sound movies. In her early contract days at MGM she appeared opposite Clark Gable, Ramon Novarro, John Gilbert, William Haines and Robert Montgomery. On loan to other studios she appeared in hit films with Al Jolson, Warner Baxter, Richard Dix, Charles Farrell, James Cagney and Fred MacMurray. Returning to her home lot (MGM), she appeared opposite Spencer Tracy, John Barrymore, Robert Young, Lee Tracy, Brian Aherne, Paul Lukas, Franchot Tone, Chester Morris, Edmund Lowe and Bing Crosby. In 1939 she married successful playwright Sidney Kingsley and shortly afterward returned to the Broadway theater and stock. She appeared in many successful plays including Phillip Barry's *Here Come the Clowns* and her husband's *The Patriots*. She appeared on *Lux Radio Theatre* and was also seen on television. She died of cancer at her home in Oakland, New Jersey, with her husband at her side in 1981.

Sound Feature Films

Sporting Blood (MGM, 1931), *Son of India* (MGM, 1931), *Guilty Hands* (MGM, 1931), *Heartbreak* (Fox, 1931), *West of Broadway* (MGM, 1932), *Are You Listening* (MGM, 1932), *Lovers Courageous* (MGM, 1932), *The Greeks Had a Word for Them* (UA, 1932), *Huddle* (MGM, 1932), *Fast Life* (MGM, 1932), *Hell Below* (MGM, 1933), *Hallelujah, I'm a Bum* (UA, 1933), *Made on Broadway* (MGM, 1933), *Dinner at Eight* (MGM, 1933), *The Nuisance* (MGM, 1933), *Mayor of Hell* (WB, 1933), *Broadway to Hollywood* (MGM, 1933), *Beauty for Sale* (MGM, 1933), *Day of Reckoning* (MGM, 1933), *Fugitive Lovers* (MGM, 1934), *The Show-Off* (MGM, 1934), *Stand Up and Cheer* (Fox, 1934), *Death on the Diamond* (MGM, 1934), *Grand Canary* (Fox, 1934), *Paris Interlude* (MGM, 1934), *What Every Woman Knows* (MGM, 1934), *Helldorado* (Fox, 1935), *David Copperfield* (MGM, 1935), *Age of Indiscretion* (MGM, 1935), *Transatlantic Tunnel* (Gaumont-British, 1935), *Calm Yourself* (MGM, 1935), *Men Without Names* (Par., 1935), *Moonlight Murder* (MGM, 1936), *Exclusive Story* (MGM, 1936), *Piccadilly Jim* (MGM, 1936), *Pennies from Heaven* (Col., 1936), *Espionage* (MGM, 1937), *The Thirteenth Chair* (MGM, 1937), *Sinners in Paradise* (Univ., 1938), *Army Girl* (Rep., 1938)

Top: James Cagney is appointed deputy inspector of a state reform school. Frankie Darro is being treated by Madge Evans in *The Mayor of Hell* (Warner Bros., 1933). *Bottom:* Marie Dressler is one of the many guests for *Dinner at Eight* with Madge Evans as the daughter of the hostess (MGM, 1933).

Silent film audiences were thrilled by the teaming of Greta Garbo and John Gilbert in three success-ful MGM productions. Their only sound film together was *Queen Christina* (MGM, 1933).

Greta Garbo (1905–1990)

Garbo was born Greta Gustafson, the daughter of a laborer, in Sodra, Sweden. Her first job was as a helper in a men's barber shop. Then she worked in a department store, a job which led to advertising modeling. She won a scholarship to the Royal Stockholm Theatre School and while there she was recommended to movie director Maurice Stiller for the lead in his 1924 film *The Atonement of Greta Berling*. The actress then changed her name and was known from then on as Greta Garbo. Louis B. Mayer was impressed with Stiller's work and wanted to put him under contract, but he refused unless Mayer would do the same for his protégé, Garbo. Two separate contracts were signed. However, Stiller was dropped from MGM. (He then went to Paramount where he directed three films before returning to Sweden, where he died in 1928.)

At MGM, Garbo was cast opposite Ricardo Cortez in *The Torrent*, the role which made her a star. Through 1929 she appeared in ten silent films which were big box office around the world. She continued her successful career until 1941 and the ill-fated *Two-Faced Woman*. Then she retired. For two years in succession (1935 and 1936) she won the New York Film Critics Award for Best Actress but the Oscar eluded her. In 1955, a special Oscar was awarded her for "a series

Greta Garbo is Alexandre Dumas' tragic heroine *Camille*. Ely Malyon is her servant. She sacrifices her own happiness in order to prove her love for Robert Taylor (MGM, 1937).

of luminous and unforgettable performances." Garbo never married and called herself "a wanderer." In keeping with the sobriquet she traveled extensively. For over 40 years she lived in a Manhattan apartment on East 52nd Street. In 1951 she became an American citizen. She died at the age of 84 at New York Hospital.

Feature Sound Films

Anna Christie (MGM, 1930), *Romance* (MGM, 1930), *Inspiration* (MGM, 1931), *Susan Lennox — Her Fall and Rise* (MGM, 1931), *Mata Hari* (MGM, 1931), *Grand Hotel* (MGM, 1932), *As You Desire Me* (MGM, 1932), *Queen Christina* (MGM, 1933), *The Painted Veil* (MGM, 1934), *Anna Karenina* (MGM, 1935), *Camille* (MGM, 1936), *Conquest* (MGM, 1937), *Ninotchka* (MGM, 1939), *Two-Faced Woman* (MGM, 1941)

Mel Ferrer as King Arthur and Ava Gardner as Queen Guinevere are the legendary sixth-century monarchs in *Knights of the Round Table* (MGM, 1953).

Ava Gardner (1922–1990)

Ava Gardner was born in Grafton, a community outside Smithfield, North Carolina, to Jonas Bailey Gardner, a tobacco and cotton farmer, and Mary Elizabeth Gardner. Her father died when she was 16 and her mother then managed

Top: Richard Burton is a defrocked Episcopalian minister who earns his living as a tour guide in Mexico. Ava Gardner is the owner of a seedy hotel in *The Night of the Iguana* (Seven Arts/MGM, 1964). *Bottom:* Anthony Quinn's control of his territory is threatened when new settlers like Ava Gardner and Howard Keel fight back for their rights and Robert Taylor joins them in *Ride Vaquero!* (MGM, 1953).

a boarding house. In high school Gardner took commercial courses and then attended Atlantic College in Wilson, North Carolina, for one year. When she was 18 she went to New York to visit her sister Beatrice. Her brother-in-law Larry Tarr, a commercial photographer, took pictures of her and sent them to Metro-Golden-Mayer. The result was a seven-year contract with that studio. MGM groomed her for stardom for a period of five years. During that time she had brief marriages to Mickey Rooney and Artie Shaw. On loan to Universal in *The Killers* opposite Burt Lancaster, she became a star. In 1951 she married Frank Sinatra but they were divorced in 1957 after many bitter public quarrels. In 1958 Gardner left MGM and became an independent actress, accepting roles in films that were mostly European-made. For over 30 years the actress made London her home. She died at her home in London's Kensington section of pneumonia. At her request, the 67-year-old Gardner was buried beside her parents in North Carolina.

Feature Films

We Were Dancing (MGM, 1942), *Joe Smith, American* (MGM, 1942), *Sunday Punch* (MGM, 1942), *This Time for Keeps* (MGM, 1942), *Calling Dr. Gillespie* (MGM, 1942), *Kid Glove Killer* (MGM, 1942), *Reunion in France* (MGM, 1942), *Pilot No. 5* (MGM, 1943), *Hitler's Madman* (MGM, 1943), *Ghosts on the Loose* (Mon., 1943), *DuBarry Was a Lady* (MGM, 1943), *Young Ideas* (MGM, 1943), *Lost Angel* (MGM, 1943), *Swing Fever* (MGM, 1944), *Music for Millions* (MGM, 1944), *Three Men in White* (MGM, 1944), *Blonde Fever* (MGM, 1944), *Maisie Goes to Reno* (MGM, 1944), *Two Girls and a Sailor* (MGM, 1944), *She Went to the Races* (MGM, 1945), *Whistle Stop* (UA, 1946), *One Touch of Venus* (Univ., 1948), *The Great Sinner* (MGM, 1949), *East Side, West Wide* (MGM, 1949), *The Bribe* (MGM, 1949), *My Forbidden Past* (RKO, 1951), *Show Boat* (MGM, 1951), *Pandora and the Flying Dutchman* (MGM, 1951), *Lone Star* (MGM, 1952), *The Snows of Kilimanjaro* (20th, 1952), *Ride Vaquero!* (MGM, 1953), *The Band Wagon* (MGM, 1953)*, *Mogambo* (MGM, 1953), *Knights of the Round Table* (MGM, 1953), *The Barefoot Contessa* (UA, 1954), *Bhowani Junction* (MGM, 1956), *The Little Hut* (MGM, 1957), *The Sun Also Rises* (20th, 1957), *The Naked Maja* (UA, 1959), *On the Beach* (UA, 1959), *The Angel Wore Red* (MGM, 1960), *55 Days at Peking* (AA, 1963), *Seven Days in May* (Par., 1964), *The Night of the Iguana* (MGM, 1964), *The Bible* (20th, 1966), *Mayerling* (MGM, 1968), *The Devil's Widow* (BIP, 1971), *The Life and Times of Judge Roy Bean* (First Artists, 1972), *Earthquake* (Univ., 1974), *Permission to Kill* (AE, 1975), *The Blue Bird* (20th, 1976), *The Cassandra Crossing* (AGF, 1977), *The Sentinel* (Univ., 1977), *City on Fire* (Astral/AE, 1979), *The Kidnapping of the President* (Crown International, 1980), *Priest of Love* (Filmways, 1981)

*Unbilled guest appearance

Greer Garson (1903–1996)

Greer Garson was born in County Down, Northern Ireland. She studied to be a teacher on a scholarship at the University of London and won honors in

Greer Garson, a beautiful but reserved librarian, meets Clark Gable, a roughneck seaman, in a San Francisco library in *Adventure* (MGM, 1945).

French, 18th-century literature and secretarial courses. She obtained a position as a market researcher in a London firm but gave it up to study acting with the Birmingham Repertory Theatre for two years. In 1934 she made her London debut at Regent's Park Open Air Theatre. On the London stage she was praised for

At a ball Frieda Inescort and Laurence Olivier are bumped by Vernon Downing as he dances with Greer Garson in the superior adaptation of Jane Austen's novel *Pride and Prejudice* (MGM, 1940).

her talent, drive and professionalism even though the plays themselves were weak. While in London, Louis B. Mayer, the head of Metro-Goldwyn-Mayer, saw Garson on stage and signed her to a Hollywood contract. Director Sam Wood cast her opposite Robert Donat in *Goodbye, Mr. Chips*. It brought Garson the first of seven Academy Award nominations in a career that included fewer than 30 films. She won an Oscar in 1942 for her performance in *Mrs. Miniver*. After her contract with MGM ended, she appeared on television in *Reunion in Vienna* and *The Little Foxes*. She replaced Rosalind Russell in the highly successful Broadway play *Auntie Mame* and then played Eleanor Roosevelt in the film *Sun-*

rise at Campobello, which was her final Oscar nomination. She was first married to Edward A. Snelson, a British civil servant (1933 to 1937). In 1943 she married actor Richard Ney and they divorced in 1947. She married Texas oil and real estate magnate Col. E.E. (Buddy) Fogelson in 1949 and that union lasted until his death in 1987. She enjoyed her retirement and was known for her charitable endeavors. She died of heart failure at Presbyterian Hospital in Dallas at the age of 92.

Feature Films

Goodbye, Mr. Chips (MGM, 1939), *Remember?* (MGM, 1939), *Pride and*

Prejudice (MGM, 1940), *Blossoms in the Dust* (MGM, 1941), *When Ladies Meet* (MGM, 1941), *Mrs. Miniver* (MGM, 1942), *Random Harvest* (MGM, 1942), *The Youngest Profession* (MGM, 1943), *Madame Curie* (MGM, 1943), *Mrs. Parkington* (MGM, 1944), *Valley of Decision* (MGM, 1945), *Adventure* (MGM, 1945), *Desire Me* (MGM, 1947), *Julia Misbehaves* (MGM, 1948), *That Forsyte Woman* (MGM, 1949), *The Miniver Story* (MGM, 1950), *The Law and the Lady* (MGM, 1951), *Julius Caesar* (MGM, 1953), *Scandal at Scourie* (MGM, 1953), *Her Twelve Men* (MGM, 1954), *Strange Lady in Town* (WB, 1955), *Pepe* (Col., 1960), *Sunrise at Campobello* (WB, 1960), *The Singing Nun* (MGM, 1966), *The Happiest Millionaire* (BV, 1967)

Lillian Gish (1893–1993)

Lillian Gish was born in Springfield, Ohio. When she was still a little girl, her parents moved to Baltimore where her father abandoned his wife and two daughters. Mrs. Gish with her two girls moved to New York City where she worked in a department store and took in boarders. One boarder, Alice Miles, persuaded Mrs. Gish to let her take Lillian with her for an acting role in a touring play. At the age of five, Lillian made her stage debut at a salary of ten dollars a week in *The Convict's Stripes*. Her younger sister Dorothy and their mother joined another touring group and began their stage careers. In 1909 they went to see fellow stage actress Gladys Smith (later known as Mary Pickford) at the Biograph Film Studio in Manhattan, where Gladys worked in films for D.W. Griffith. Smith introduced the Gish sisters to Griffith and in a few hours the sisters started their film careers. Lillian not only acted before the camera, she edited film, set up lights, selected costumes and directed two films. For more than a decade, Gish and Griffith collaborated on short films and later she starred in his critically acclaimed full-length films such as *Birth of a Nation*, *Way Down East*, *Orphans of the Storm* and *Hearts of the World*. After an amicable parting from Griffith, Gish made the successful films *The White Sister* and *Romola*—both directed by Henry King—at Inspiration Pictures. Next she moved to MGM where she had direct control of her films and produced such classics as *La Bohème* and *The Scarlet Letter*. Although they were successes, Gish left the studio and signed with United Artists. She made her sound debut in *One Romantic Night*, based on Ferenc Molnar's play *The Swan*, and followed it with *His Double Life* opposite Roland Young. Both films were successful but Gish did not care for sound films and asked for a release. She returned to the theater and Broadway in *Uncle Vanya*. Next she played opposite John Gielgud in *Hamlet*, followed by an appearance with Judith Anderson. In Chicago she appeared in *Life with Father*, which ran there for 66 weeks. Between her stage roles she made some films and appeared on choice television programs. In 1970, the Academy of Motion Picture Arts and Sciences presented Gish with a career achievement award. In 1982 she was honored by the Kennedy Center and in 1984 she received the American Film Institute's Lifetime Achievement tribute. | Gish was never married. She died in her

Ronald Colman is an Italian army officer in World War I. He is engaged to Lillian Gish who is reported killed in action. She becomes a nun in *The White Sister* (MGM, 1923).

Lauren Bacall is the activities director and Lillian Gish is the spinster business affairs director at a psychiatric clinic in *The Cobweb* (MGM, 1955).

sleep at age 99 in her New York apartment.

Sound Feature Films

One Romantic Night (UA, 1930), *His Double Life* (Par., 1933), *Commandos Strike at Dawn* (Col., 1942), *Top Man* (Univ., 1943), *Miss Susie Slagle's* (Par., 1945), *Duel in the Sun* (Selznick, 1946), *Portrait of Jennie* (Selznick, 1948), *The Cobweb* (MGM, 1955), *The Night of the Hunter* (UA, 1955), *Orders to Kill* (United Motion Picture Organization, 1958), *The Unforgiven* (UA, 1960), *Follow Me, Boys* (BV, 1966), *Warning Shot* (Par., 1967), *The Comedians* (MGM, 1967), *A Wedding* (20th, 1978), *Sweet Liberty* (Univ., 1986), *The Whales of August* (Alive Films, 1987)

Jackie Gleason (1916–1987)

Born in the Bushwick section of Brooklyn, Jackie Gleason started playing local nightclubs in his early twenties. At one of these club engagements he was seen by studio mogul Jack L. Warner, who signed him to a movie contract in

Mike Henry as Junior and Jackie Gleason as Sheriff Buford T. Justice pursue the wanted Bandit in *Smokey and the Bandit II* (Universal, 1980).

1941. Gleason stayed in Hollywood for two years and then returned to New York where he appeared on Broadway in numerous musicals. He won a Tony for his performance in *Take Me Along*. Gleason starred in the NBC TV series *The Life of Riley*, which was cancelled after 26 weeks even though it won an Emmy. For the following two years he appeared as host of *Cavalcade* for the Dumont TV Network and then signed with CBS. At CBS Gleason played Ralph Kramden in the highly successful show *The Honeymooners*. His sidekick, Art Carney, played Ed Norton and Audrey Meadows played Ralph's wife, Alice Kramden, in this half-hour series. Next came *The Jackie Gleason Show*, a weekly Saturday night production with Norton continuing his co-starring role. It was the second-highest rated series on television (behind *I Love Lucy*). In 1966 the show moved to Miami Beach, where it was produced until 1970. Gleason then made guest appearances and appeared on specials as well as television movies. He died of cancer at 71 at his Lauderhill, Florida, home with his wife Marilyn at his side.

Feature Films

Navy Blues (WB, 1941), *All Through the Night* (WB, 1942), *Orchestra Wives* (20th, 1942), *Springtime in the Rockies* (20th, 1942), *Tramp, Tramp, Tramp* (Col., 1942), *The Desert Hawk* (Univ., 1950),

Art Carney as Ed Norton, Jackie Gleason as Ralph Kramden and Audrey Meadows as Ralph's faithful wife in *The Honeymooners* which became one of television's greatest hit series.

The Hustler (20th, 1961), *Gigot* (20th, 1962), *Requiem for a Heavyweight* (Col., 1962), *Papa's Delicate Condition* (Par., 1963), *Soldier in the Rain* (AA, 1963), *Skidoo* (Par., 1968), *Don't Drink the Water* (AE, 1969), *How to Commit Marriage* (Cinerama, 1969), *How Do I Love Thee?* (Cinerama, 1970), *Mister Billion* (20th, 1977), *Smokey and the Bandit* (Univ., 1977), *Smokey and the Bandit II* (Univ., 1980), *The Toy* (Col., 1982), *Smokey and the Bandit 3* (Univ., 1983), *The Sting II* (Univ., 1983), *Nothing in Common* (Col., 1986)

In a nightclub powder room Phyllis Povah and Paulette Goddard listen to Mary Boland tell Norma Shearer the latest gossip in *The Women* (MGM, 1939).

Paulette Goddard (1905–1990)

Born Paulette Goddard Levee in Whitestone Landing, New York, she made her Broadway debut as a Ziegfeld Girl in the 1926 production *No Fooling*. She married Edgar James in 1931 and they divorced the same year. She went to Hollywood and worked first as an extra at the Hal Roach Studio and later as a Goldwyn Girl in the Eddie Cantor film *The Kid from Spain*. In 1933 Goddard secretly married Charlie Chaplin and appeared opposite him in *Modern Times* and *The Great Dictator*. She made one film for David O. Selznick and two at Metro-Goldwyn-Mayer before signing a contract with Paramount. Goddard divorced Chaplin in 1942 and married Burgess Meredith in 1944. That union lasted until 1950. On television she appeared on such programs as *Ford Theatre* and episodes of *On Trial* and *Adventures in Paradise*. In 1958 she married writer Erich Maria Remarque and moved to Switzerland with him but maintained a residence in New York. She appeared at Dublin's Abbey Theatre in *Winterset*, on Broadway and on the road in *Caesar and Cleopatra* opposite Sir Cedric Hardwicke, and made a successful road tour of *Waltz of the Toreadors*. Remarque died in 1970.

Northwest Mounted Police is set in 1885 at the time of the Riel Rebellion in Canada. Cecil B. DeMille cast Gary Cooper as a Texas Ranger and Paulette Goddard as the half-breed Louvette (Paramount, 1940).

In 1972 Goddard appeared in the telefilm *The Snoop Sisters*. At the age of 84 she died at her villa in Ronco, Switzerland, of natural causes.

Feature Films

The Girl Habit (Par., 1931), *The Mouthpiece* (WB, 1932), *Pack Up Your Troubles* (MGM, 1932), *The Kid from Spain* (UA,

1932), *Modern Times* (UA, 1936), *The Young in Heart* (UA, 1938), *Dramatic School* (MGM, 1938), *The Women* (MGM, 1939), *The Cat and the Canary* (Par., 1939), *The Ghost Breakers* (Par., 1940), *The Great Dictator* (UA, 1940), *North West Mounted Police* (Par., 1940), *Second Chorus* (Par., 1940), *Pot o' Gold* (UA, 1941), *Nothing But the Truth* (Par., 1941), *Hold Back the Dawn* (Par., 1941), *The Lady Has Plans* (Par., 1942), *Reap the Wild Wind* (Par., 1942), *The Forest Rangers* (Par., 1942), *Star Spangled Rhythm* (Par., 1942), *The Crystal Ball* (UA, 1943), *So Proudly We Hail!* (Par., 1943), *Standing Room Only* (Par., 1944), *I Love a Soldier* (Par., 1944), *Duffy's Tavern* (Par., 1945), *Kitty* (Par., 1945), *The Diary of a Chambermaid* (UA, 1946), *Suddenly It's Spring* (Par., 1947), *Variety Girl* (Par., 1947), *Unconquered* (Par., 1947), *An Ideal Husband* (20th, 1948), *On Our Merry Way* (UA, 1948), *Hazard* (Par., 1948), *Bride of Vengeance* (Par., 1949), *Anna Lucasta* (Col., 1949), *The Torch* (EL, 1950), *Babes in Baghdad* (UA, 1952), *Vice Squad* (UA, 1953), *Paris Model* (Col., 1953), *Sins of Jezebel* (Lip., 1953), *Charge of the Lancers* (Col., 1954), *The Unholy Four* (Lip., 1954), *Time of Indifference* (Continental, 1965)

Rex Harrison (1908–1990)

Born Reginald Carey Harrison on March 5, 1908, in Huxton, England, he was educated at Liverpool College. He made his stage debut at the Liverpool Repertory Theatre in 1924 and worked there for three years before touring the provinces in various plays. In 1930 he made his London debut in *Getting George Married*. He began acting in films as well as doing many stage roles in the West End.

In 1936 Harrison became a star in Terence Rattigan's play *French Without Tears* in which he played the leading role for over a year. He concentrated on his film career in England until 1942, when he served in the Royal Air Force until 1944. Upon his release, he signed a Hollywood contract with 20th Century–Fox and made several top films before returning to the Broadway stage. He won his first Tony for his portrayal of Henry VIII in *Anne of the Thousand Days* (1949). More film work in Hollywood and England followed in between successful stage appearances. In 1956 he made theater history with *My Fair Lady*, a musical adaptation of Shaw's *Pygmalion* in which he starred as Henry Higgins. For his interpretation he won another Tony. He was nominated for an Oscar in 1963 as Julius Caesar in *Cleopatra*. He repeated his Henry Higgins role for film in 1964 and won an Oscar. In 1965 he received the Order of Merit from Italy for his portrayal of Pope Julius II in the film *The Agony and the Ecstasy*. His career spanned 65 years in the theater, films and television. Harrison was married to Marjorie Noel Thomas (1931–42), Lilli Palmer (1943–57), Kay Kendall (1957–59), Rachel Roberts (1962–71), Elizabeth Harris (1972–77) and Mercia Tinker (1982–90). In 1989 he was knighted and made his last stage appearance in a revival of Somerset Maugham's *The Circle* on Broadway with Glynis Johns and Stewart Granger. Harrison died at the age of 82 of pancreatic cancer at his Manhattan home.

Audrey Hepburn as Eliza Doolittle, the guttersnipe turned into a lady by linguist Rex Harrison in *My Fair Lady* (Warner Bros., 1964).

Feature Films

Get Your Man (British, 1929), *The Great Game* (Gaumont-British, 1930), *School for Scandal* (Albion Films, 1930), *Leave It to Blanche* (First National-British, 1934), *All at Sea* (British, 1935), *Men Are Not Gods* (London Films, 1936), *Storm in a Teacup* (London Films, 1937), *School for Husbands* (Richard Wainwright, 1937),

Kay Kendall and Rex Harrison play a married couple. John Saxon is an American musician and Sandra Dee is Harrison's daughter by a former marriage in the delightful comedy *The Reluctant Debutante* (MGM, 1958).

St. Martin's Lane (Par., 1938), *The Citadel* (MGM, 1938), *Over the Moon* (London Films, 1939), *Ten Days in Paris* (Col., 1939), *The Silent Battle* (Mon., 1939), *Night Train to Munich* (Gaumont-British, 1940), *Major Barbara* (UA, 1941), *Journey Together* (English Films, Inc., 1944), *I Live in Grosvenor Square* (*A Yank in London*) (Associated British, 1945), *Blithe Spirit* (Two Cities, 1945), *The Rake's Progress* (Individual Pictures, 1945), *Anna and the King of Siam* (20th,

1946), *The Ghost and Mrs. Muir* (20th, 1947), *The Foxes of Harrow* (20th, 1947), *Escape* (20th, 1948), *Unfaithfully Yours* (20th, 1948), *The Long Dark Hall* (UA, 1951), *The Four Poster* (Col., 1952), *Main Street to Broadway* (MGM, 1953), *King Richard and the Crusaders* (WB, 1954), *The Constant Husband* (London Films, 1955), *The Reluctant Debutante* (MGM, 1958), *Midnight Lace* (Univ., 1960), *The Happy Thieves* (UA, 1962), *Cleopatra* (20th, 1963), *My Fair Lady* (WB, 1964), *The Yellow Rolls-Royce* (MGM, 1965), *The Agony and the Ecstasy* (20th, 1965), *The Honey Pot* (UA, 1967), *Dr. Dolittle* (20th, 1967), *A Flea in Her Ear* (20th, 1968), *Staircase* (20th, 1969), *Behind the Iron Mask* (Col., 1977), *Crossed Swords* (WB, 1978), *Ashanti* (Col., 1979), *A Time to Die* (Almi, 1983)

Helen Hayes (1900–1993)

Helen Hayes was born Helen Hayes Brown in Washington, D.C., to a traveling salesman and a stock company actress. At the age of five she made her professional debut at the National Theatre. Four years later she made her Broadway debut as Little Mimi in Lew Field's production of *Old Dutch*. As a child and a young woman Hayes toured, playing one-night stands. On Broadway she scored a hit in Booth Tarkington's *Clarence* (1919), followed by *Bab* (1920), *To the Ladies* (1922) and *Dancing Mothers* (1925), all great light-comedy successes. She starred in Shaw's *Caeser and Cleopatra*, followed by James Barrie's *What Every Woman Knows*. In 1928 she met writer Charles MacArthur and they were married. The couple bought a home in the Hudson River town of Nyack, about 25 miles from Broadway. They lived there until MacArthur's death in 1956, and she remained there until her own death. She signed a contract with MGM in 1931 and won an Oscar for her first film. In 1935 she returned to the theater in Maxwell Anderson's *Mary of Scotland*. Then came her greatest success with Laurence Housman's *Victoria Regina* opposite Vincent Price. More successful plays followed —

Candle in the Wind, *Harriet* and *Happy Birthday*, which won her a Tony. More hits followed and she earned the title of "First Lady of the American Theater." She returned now and then to films and won an Oscar for her performance in *Airport*. She did television work and won an Emmy. Her memoir *On Reflection* was published in 1968. She collaborated with Katharine Hatch on her autobiography *My Life in Three Acts* (1990). Her only daughter, Mary MacArthur, died of polio in 1949. Hayes died of heart failure and is survived by her son, actor James MacArthur.

Sound Feature Films

The Sin of Madelon Claudet (MGM, 1931), *Arrowsmith* (UA, 1931), *A Farewell to Arms* (Par., 1932), *The Son-Daughter* (MGM, 1933), *The White Sister* (MGM, 1933), *Another Language* (MGM, 1933), *Night Flight* (MGM, 1933), *What Every Woman Knows* (MGM, 1934), *Crime Without Passion* (Par., 1934)*, *Vanessa, Her Love Story* (MGM, 1935), *Stage Door Canteen* (UA, 1943), *My Son John* (Par., 1952), *Main Street to Broadway* (MGM, 1953), *Let's Make Up* (1954), *Anastasia*

Top: Gary Cooper is an American adventurer serving in the Italian Ambulance Corps. Helen Hayes is an English nurse and Adolphe Menjou is a medical doctor in *A Farewell to Arms* (Paramount, 1932). *Bottom:* Whit Bissell, a passenger, drinks with Helen Hayes, a stowaway, as Van Heflin plans to blow up the in-flight in *Airport* (Universal, 1970).

(20th, 1956), *Third Man on the Mountain* (BV, 1959)*, *Airport* (Univ., 1970), *Herbie Rides Again* (BV, 1974), *One of Our Dinosaurs Is Missing* (BV, 1976), *Candleshoe* (BV, 1978).

*Unbilled guest appearance

Louis Hayward (1909–1985)

He was born in Johannesburg, South Africa. After the death of his father, a mining engineer, Hayward was raised in London by his mother. He also spent time in France, where he was sent to school. He became interested in the theater in England and joined a touring company. Then he managed a London nightclub before making his West End debut in *Dracula*. He appeared in such hit plays as *The Vinegar Tree, Another Language, Conversation Piece* and *The Ringer* and also played in British films. He made his Broadway debut in 1934 in *Point Valaine*, for which he won the New York Critics Award. Then he went to Hollywood to appear in films. The day before Pearl Harbor, Hayward became a naturalized U.S. citizen. He joined the Marine Corps, served three years during World War II and was awarded the Bronze Star. After the war he returned to films and was one of the first stars to get a percentage from the profits of his films. In 1954 Hayward starred in the successful television series *The Lone Wolf* and later appeared in two more series, *The Pursuers* and *The Survivors*, in the '60s. He was married to Ida Lupino (1939–45), Peggy Morrow (1946–50) and June Blanchard (1950), who survived him. He died at his home in Palm Springs, California, of lung cancer at the age of 75.

Feature Films

Self-Made Lady (UA, 1932), *Chelsea* (Par., 1933), *Sorrell and Son* (UA, 1934), *The Flame Within* (MGM, 1935), *A Feather in Her Hat* (Col., 1935), *Absolute Quiet* (MGM, 1936), *Trouble for Two* (MGM, 1936), *Anthony Adverse* (WB, 1936), *The Luckiest Girl in the World* (Univ., 1936), *The Woman I Love* (RKO, 1937), *Condemned Women* (RKO, 1938), *Midnight Intruder* (Univ., 1938), *The Saint in New York* (RKO, 1938), *The Rage of Paris* (Univ., 1938), *The Duke of West Point* (UA, 1938), *The Man in the Iron Mask* (UA, 1939), *My Son, My Son* (UA, 1940), *Dance, Girl, Dance* (RKO, 1940), *The Son of Monte Cristo* (UA, 1940), *Ladies in Retirement* (Col., 1941), *The Magnificent Ambersons* (RKO, 1942), *And Then There Were None* (20th, 1945), *Young Widow* (UA, 1946), *The Strange Woman* (UA, 1946), *The Return of Monte Cristo* (Col., 1946), *Repeat Performance* (EL, 1947), *Ruthless* (EL, 1948), *The Black Arrow* (Col., 1948), *Walk a Crooked Mile* (Col., 1948), *The Pirates of Capri* (Film Classics, 1949), *House by the River* (Rep., 1950), *Fortunes of Captain Blood* (Col., 1950), *The Lady and the Bandit* (Col., 1951), *The Son of Dr. Jekyll* (Col., 1951), *Lady in the Iron Mask* (20th, 1952), *Captain Pirate* (Col., 1952), *The Royal African Rifles* (AA, 1953), *The Saint's Girl Friday* (RKO, 1954), *Duffy of San Quentin* (WB, 1954), *The Search for Bridey Murphy* (Par., 1956), *Chuka* (Par., 1967), *The Christmas Kid* (PRO, 1967), *Electric Man* (PRO, 1967), *The Phynx* (Cinerama, 1970), *Terror in the Wax Museum* (Cinerama, 1973)

Top: Louis Hayward plays the twin brothers and Joan Bennett is Maria Theresa in the Alexandre Dumas classic *The Man in the Iron Mask* (United Artists, 1939). *Bottom:* Louis Hayward, Roland Young, Walter Huston, June Duprez and Barry Fitzgerald (seated) are some of the guests invited to a deserted island in Agatha Christie's classic whodunit *And Then There Were None* (20th Century–Fox, 1945).

Richard Crenna pretends to be a friend of Audrey Hepburn's husband and tries to trick the blind woman into believing her husband is a killer in *Wait Until Dark* (Warner Bros., 1967).

Audrey Hepburn (1929–1993)

Audrey Hepburn was born in Brussels, Belgium. Her father, J.A. Hepburn-Ruston, was a banker of English-Irish ancestry and her mother, Ella van Heemstra, was a Dutch baroness. When her parents divorced she attended a private girls' school outside London and later moved with her mother to Holland. There she endured the harsh winter of 1944-45 under Nazi occupation with little to eat. One of the organizations which eventually brought help was UNICEF.

After the war Hepburn returned to London on a ballet scholarship and became a fashion model. Then she studied acting. After minor jobs in stage musicals, she came to the attention of film producers who cast her in supporting movie roles. French author Colette met Hepburn during the filming of *Monte Carlo Baby* in 1951 and insisted that she play the part of "Gigi" when the novel was adapted to the stage. The play took her to Broadway where she became a star. She toured key U.S. cities in *Gigi*. For her first American film, *Roman Holiday* (1953), she won an Oscar. She would be nominated four more times in coming years. In 1954 she returned to Broadway in *Online* and won a Tony for her performance. She married Mel Ferrer in 1954 and in 1960 they had a son, Sean. She

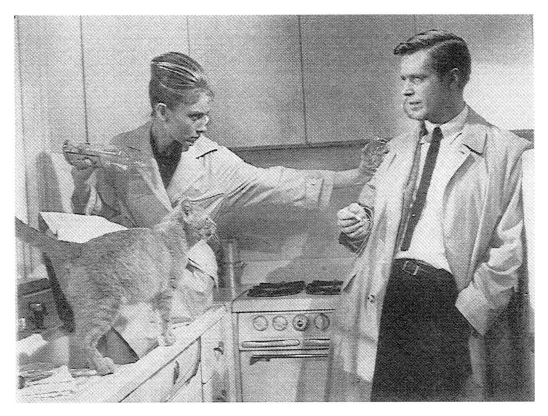

Audrey Hepburn portrays Holly Golightly in *Breakfast at Tiffany's,* based on a Truman Capote novella. George Peppard is the upstairs neighbor who falls in love with his intriguing neighbor (Paramount, 1961).

continued her film career and divorced Ferrer in 1968. She then married Andrea Dotti, an Italian psychiatrist. The couple had a son, Luca, born in 1970. The marriage ended in 1980. On TV she appeared in *Mayerling, Love Among Thieves* and *Gardens of the World.*

Hepburn became a goodwill ambassador for UNICEF in 1986 and devoted seven years to that cause. The Academy of Motion Picture Arts and Sciences awarded her the Jean Hersholt Humanitarian Award for her work with that organization. In 1991 she received a special tribute from the Film Society of Lincoln Center. She died of colon cancer at her home on Lake Geneva in Switzerland with her companion, Robert Wolders, at her bedside.

English-Language Feature Films

One Wild Oat (Eros Films, 1951), *Young Wives' Tale* (AA, 1951), *Laughter in Paradise* (Stratford, 1951), *The Lavender Hill Mob* (Univ., 1951), *Monte Carlo Baby* (GFD, 1952), *The Secret People* (Lip., 1952), *Roman Holiday* (Par., 1953), *Sabrina* (Par., 1954), *War and Peace* (Par., 1956), *Funny Face* (Par., 1957), *Love in the Afternoon* (AA, 1957), *The Nun's Story* (WB, 1959), *Green Mansions* (MGM, 1959), *The Unforgiven* (UA, 1960), *Breakfast at Tiffany's* (Par., 1961), *The Children's Hour* (UA, 1962), *Charade* (Univ., 1963), *Paris When It Sizzles* (Par., 1964), *My Fair Lady* (WB, 1964), *How to Steal a Million* (20th, 1966), *Two for the Road* (20th, 1967), *Wait Until Dark* (WB,

1967), *Robin and Marian* (Col., 1976), *Bloodline* (Par., 1979), *They All Laughed* (Independent, 1981), *Always* (MGM/UA, 1989)

William Holden (1918–1981)

William Holden was born in O'Fallon, Illinois. At the age of four he moved with his family to Monrovia, California. In high school he was interested in athletics, and while a student at South Pasadena Junior College he competed in the Golden Gloves competition. Holden was acting in a student production when he was spotted by a Paramount talent scout, tested and signed to a film contract. After two films on the Paramount lot, he was borrowed by Columbia for the lead in *Golden Boy* opposite Barbara Stanwyck. The role made him a star. Before enlisting in the Army, he made films for Paramount and Columbia (which shared his contract). He spent over three years in service during World War II and achieved the rank of lieutenant in the Army Air Corps. After the war he continued his screen career at Paramount and Columbia with permission to do films at other studios. In 1953 he won an Oscar for his performance in *Stalag 17* in which he portrayed a cynical prisoner-of-war in a German camp. With his film earnings he founded Mount Kenya Safari Club outside Nairobi in Kenya and made films in Europe. On television he appeared in the 1974 mini-series *The Blue Knight* and won an Emmy. He married actress Brenda Marshall in 1941. They had two sons before they divorced in 1971. He died in Santa Monica at age 63.

Feature Films

Prison Farm (Par., 1938), *Million Dollar Legs* (Par., 1939), *Golden Boy* (Col., 1939), *Invisible Stripes* (WB, 1940), *Our Town* (UA, 1940), *Those Were the Days* (Par., 1940), *Arizona* (Col., 1940), *I Wanted Wings* (Par., 1941), *Texas* (Col., 1941), *The Fleet's In* (Par., 1942), *The Remarkable Andrew* (Par., 1942), *Meet the Stewarts* (Col., 1942), *Young and Willing* (UA, 1943), *Blaze of Noon* (Par., 1947), *Dear Ruth* (Par., 1947), *Variety Girl* (Par., 1947), *Rachel and the Stranger* (RKO, 1948), *Apartment for Peggy* (20th, 1948), *The Man from Colorado* (Col., 1948), *The Dark Past* (Col., 1949), *Streets of Laredo* (Par., 1949), *Miss Grant Takes Richmond* (Col., 1949), *Dear Wife* (Par., 1949), *Father Is a Bachelor* (Col., 1950), *Force of Arms* (WB, 1951), *Submarine Command* (Par., 1951), *Boots Malone* (Col., 1952), *The Turning Point* (Par., 1952), *Stalag 17* (Par., 1953), *The Moon Is Blue* (UA, 1953), *Forever Female* (Par., 1953), *Escape from Fort Bravo* (MGM, 1953), *Executive Suite* (MGM, 1954), *Sabrina* (Par., 1954), *The Country Girl* (Par., 1954), *The Bridges at Toko-Ri* (Par., 1954), *Love Is a Many-Splendored Thing* (20th, 1955), *Picnic* (Col., 1955), *The Proud and the Profane* (Par., 1956), *Toward the Unknown* (WB, 1956), *The Bridge on the River Kwai* (Col., 1957), *The Key* (Col., 1958), *The Horse Soldiers* (UA, 1959), *The World of Suzie Wong* (Par., 1960), *Satan Never Sleeps* (20th, 1962), *The Counterfeit Traitor* (Par., 1962), *The Lion* (20th, 1962), *Paris When It Sizzles* (Par., 1964), *The*

Top: Ginger Rogers is a successful actress and William Holden is a supermarket employee who has written his first play which Paul Douglas plans to produce in *Forever Female* (Paramount, 1953). *Bottom:* Bing Crosby is an alcoholic has-been actor. Grace Kelly is his loyal wife and William Holden plays the director who gives Crosby a chance for a comeback in *The Country Girl* (Paramount, 1954).

Seventh Dawn (UA, 1964), *Alvarez Kelly* (Col., 1966), *Casino Royale* (Col., 1967), *The Devil's Brigade* (UA, 1968), *Christmas Tree* (Continental, 1969), *The Wild Bunch* (WB, 1969), *Wild Rovers* (MGM, 1971), *The Revengers* (NGP, 1972), *Breezy* (Univ., 1973), *Open Season* (Col., 1974), *The Towering Inferno* (20th-WB, 1974), *Network* (MGM/UA, 1976), *Damien — Omen II* (20th, 1978), *Fedora* (UA, 1978), *Ashanti* (Col., 1979), *Earthling* (Filmways, 1980), *When Time Ran Out* (WB, 1980), *S.O.B.* (Par., 1981)

Rock Hudson (1925–1985)

Rock Hudson was born Roy Scherer in Winnetka, Illinois, but changed his name legally when his mother remarried. After graduating from New Trier High School, he was drafted into the navy. After his discharge he held odd jobs in Winnetka and Los Angeles. He came to the attention of agent Henry Wilson who secured a Universal contract for him. At Universal Hudson played secondary roles while he was groomed for stardom. When he was cast opposite Jane Wyman, Hudson became a major star. After making more films at his home studio, he was borrowed to appear in George Stevens' *Giant* opposite Elizabeth Taylor and James Dean. It was a box office hit. His marriage to Phyllis Gates ended in divorce in less than three years. He co-starred with Doris Day in three comedy films which were box office hits. Next he turned to television and was successful in the series *McMillan and Wife* with Susan Saint John, which ran from 1971 to 1977. He made his stage debut in Los Angeles opposite Carol Burnett in *I Do, I Do* and appeared in the touring production of *On the Twentieth Century*. At the age of 59, Rock Hudson died of AIDS.

Feature Films

Fighter Squadron (WB, 1948), *Undertow* (Univ., 1949), *I Was a Shoplifter* (Univ., 1950), *One Way Street* (Univ., 1950), *Winchester '73* (Univ., 1950), *Peggy* (Univ., 1950), *The Desert Hawk* (Univ., 1950), *The Fat Man* (Univ., 1951), *Air Cadet* (Univ., 1951), *Tomahawk* (Univ., 1951), *Iron Man* (Univ., 1951), *Bright Victory* (Univ., 1951), *Bend of the River* (Univ., 1952), *Here Come the Nelsons* (Univ., 1952), *Scarlet Angel* (Univ., 1952), *Has Anybody Seen My Gal* (Univ., 1952), *Horizons West* (Univ., 1952), *The Lawless Breed* (Univ., 1952), *Seminole* (Univ., 1953), *Sea Devils* (RKO, 1953), *Gun Fury* (Col., 1953), *The Golden Blade* (Univ., 1953), *Back to God's Country* (Univ., 1953), *Taza, Son of Cochise* (Univ., 1954), *Magnificent Obsession* (Univ., 1954), *Bengal Brigade* (Univ., 1954), *Captain Lightfoot* (Univ., 1955), *One Desire* (Univ., 1955), *All That Heaven Allows* (Univ., 1955), *Never Say Goodbye* (Univ., 1956), *Giant* (WB, 1956), *Battle Hymn* (Univ., 1956), *Written on the Wind* (Univ., 1956), *Four Girls in Town* (Univ., 1956), *Something of Value* (MGM, 1957), *The Tarnished Angels* (Univ., 1957), *A Farewell to Arms* (20th, 1957), *Twilight for the Gods* (Univ., 1958), *This Earth Is Mine* (Univ., 1959), *Pillow Talk* (Univ., 1959), *The Last Sunset* (Univ., 1961), *Come September*

Elizabeth Taylor is the headstrong, spoiled rich girl from Virginia who falls in love with Rock Hudson. He marries her and takes her to his Texas ranch, Reata, in *Giant*, based on the Edna Ferber novel (Warner Bros., 1956).

Doris Day and Rock Hudson are co-starred for the third time as a happy married couple who become estranged through a misunderstanding which is solved before the happy fadeout. *Send Me No Flowers* (Universal, 1964).

(Univ., 1961), *Lover, Come Back* (Univ., 1961), *The Spiral Road* (Univ., 1962), *A Gathering of Eagles* (Univ., 1963), *Man's Favorite Sport?* (Univ., 1964) *Send Me No Flowers* (Univ., 1964), *Strange Bedfellows* (Univ., 1964), *A Very Special Favor* (Univ., 1965), *Blindfold* (Univ., 1966), *Seconds* (Par., 1966), *Tobruk* (Univ., 1967), *Ice Station Zebra* (MGM, 1968), *The Quiet Couple* (CBS Films, 1968), *The Undefeated* (20th, 1969), *The Hornet's Nest* (UA, 1969), *Darling Lili* (Par., 1970), *Pretty Maids All in a Row* (MGM, 1971), *Showdown* (Univ., 1972), *Embryo* (Cine Arts, 1975), *Avalanche* (New World, 1978), *The Mirror Crack'd* (EMI, 1980), *The Ambassador* (Cannon, 1984)

Danny Kaye (1913–1987)

Danny Kaye was born in Brooklyn and began his career as a singer, dancer and comedian at summer resorts in the Catskills. He moved on to nightclub work with his wife Sylvia Fine, who wrote songs and special material for him. In 1940 he appeared with Gertrude Lawrence in *Lady in the Dark* and in 1941 he was the star of the hit Broadway musical *Let's Face It.*

Kaye went to Hollywood under contract to Samuel Goldwyn and became a top film star. In 1954 he received a special Oscar for his talent and services to the Academy and the motion picture industry. Another Oscar was awarded to him in 1982 for his charity work, especially UNICEF. Among his other awards were two Emmies for appearances on television. Queen Margrethe of Denmark

Top: Danny Kaye plays an American nightclub entertainer. He is hired to impersonate a famed French aviator whose wife is Gene Tierney in *On the Riviera* (20th Century–Fox, 1951). *Bottom:* Bing Crosby, Vera-Ellen, Rosemary Clooney and Danny Kaye sing Irving Berlin songs as they put on a show to save a friend's resort hotel in *White Christmas* (Paramount, 1954).

knighted him in 1983 for his portrayal of the Danish author Hans Christian Andersen in the 1951 Hollywood musical of the same name. The citation called him "the Pied Piper to the children of the world." He died at the age of 74 of a heart attack.

Feature Films

Up in Arms (RKO, 1944), *Wonder Man* (RKO, 1945), *The Kid from Brooklyn* (RKO, 1946), *The Secret Life of Walter* *Mitty* (RKO, 1947), *A Song Is Born* (RKO, 1948), *The Inspector General* (WB, 1949), *It's a Great Feeling* (WB, 1949), *On the Riviera* (20th, 1951), *Hans Christian Andersen* (RKO, 1952), *Knock on Wood* (Par., 1954), *White Christmas* (Par., 1954), *The Court Jester* (Par., 1956), *Merry Andrew* (MGM, 1958), *Me and the Colonel* (Col., 1958), *The Five Pennies* (Par., 1959), *On the Double* (Par., 1961), *The Man from the Diners Club* (Col., 1963), *The Madwoman of Chaillot* (WB-7 Arts, 1969)

Ruby Keeler (1909–1993)

Ruby Keeler was born in Halifax, Nova Scotia, and moved to New York City with her family when she was four years old. After studying dance as a child, she lied her way into the chorus of George M Cohan's *The Rise of Rosie O'Reilly* by saying she was 16 when she was only 14. For the next few years she danced in speak easies, including Texas Guinan's famous El Fey Club. Earl Lindsay, a stage director, cast her in the Broadway revue *Bye, Bye, Bonnie*, which won her good notices. Keeler next appeared opposite Bob Hope in *Lucky*. Florenz Ziegfeld saw her and offered her a role opposite Eddie Cantor in *Whoopee*, which she accepted. She met Al Jolson and after a whirlwind courtship they were secretly married in 1928 in Port Chester, New York. Keeler left the Cantor show during the out-of-town tryouts at Jolson's request. A year later she was cast in George Gershwin's *Show Girl* but stayed only one month, again acceding to her husband's wishes. While Jolson was in Hollywood making a film, Darryl Zanuck tested Keeler and cast her as the ingenue in the now-classic musical *42nd Street*. A cycle of lavish Busby Berkeley musicals starring Keeler followed. She was earning $4,000 a week, an enormous sum during the depths of the Depression. She and Jolson appeared together in one musical film. In 1935 they adopted a baby boy. Jolson had a dispute with Warner Brothers and he left the studio, taking Keeler with him. She signed with RKO and was cast in *Mother Carey's Chickens* which Katharine Hepburn had refused to do. Keeler separated from Jolson in 1940 and divorced him, gaining custody of their son, Al, Jr. In 1941 she made one film for Columbia, married real estate broker John Lowe, and gave up her film career. She raised Al, Jr., and had three daughters (Kathleen, Christine and Theresa) and a boy named John, Jr. After her husband's death in 1969, theatrical producer Harry Rigby contacted her for the lead role in a revival of the 1925 musical *No, No, Nanette*. Busby Berkeley was artistic supervisor. The show was a hit and ran for over two years on Broadway. She also toured with *Nanette*. Keeler

Una Merkle, Ruby Keeler and Ginger Rogers try out for the chorus in *42nd Street* by revealing their legs to the director (Warner Bros., 1933).

Dick Powell and Ruby Keeler (sitting on the car) wave to the other cadets and their brides in *Flirtation Walk* (Warner Bros., 1934).

appeared briefly in television and toured in summer stock in *Bell, Book and Candle*. She died at her home in Palm Springs, California, of cancer at the age of 82.

Feature Films

42nd Street (WB, 1933), *Gold Diggers of 1933* (WB, 1933), *Footlight Parade* (WB, 1933), *Dames* (WB, 1934), *Flirtation Walk* (WB, 1934), *Go Into Your Dance* (WB, 1935), *Shipmates Forever* (WB, 1935), *Colleen* (WB, 1936), *Ready, Willing and Able* (WB, 1937), *Mother Carey's Chickens* (RKO, 1938), *Sweetheart of the Campus* (Col., 1941), *The Phynx* (Cinema Organization, 1970)*

*Guest appearance

Gene Kelly (1912–1996)

Born in Pittsburgh, Gene Kelly and his four siblings took music and dancing lessons at the insistence of their mother. In his high school years, Kelly continued his dancing lessons while also playing on the football and hockey teams. He attended Pennsylvania State University and then transferred to the University of

Georges Guetary, Oscar Levant and Gene Kelly are close friends in Paris following World War II in *An American in Paris* (MGM, 1951).

Pittsburgh, where he received his degree in economics in 1933. Because of the Depression, jobs were scarce and he worked in a dancing school partly owned by his mother. In 1934 Kelly and his brother Fred performed at the Chicago World's Fair, returning home to work in the dance studio there. In 1938 he went to New York. His first job was in the hit musical *Leave It to Me* which starred William Gaxton, Victor Moore and Sophie Tucker and featured Mary Martin. The following season he appeared in the successful musical *One for the Money* and received excellent reviews. Next Kelly won critical acclaim as the comic hoofer in William Saroyan's play *The Time of Your Life*. In 1940 his role as the lead in the Rodgers and Hart hit musical *Pal Joey* made him a star. While appearing in *Pal Joey* he also choreographed the hit musical *Best Foot Forward*. Kelly signed a Hollywood contract with David O. Selznick and was lent to Metro-Goldwyn-Mayer for the film *For Me and My Gal* opposite Judy Garland. MGM bought his contract from Selznick and cast Kelly in minor parts. Columbia borrowed him to appear opposite Rita Hayworth in *Cover Girl*. As a team, Hayworth and Kelly advanced the use of movie song-and-dance numbers that evolve naturally from plot and action. In 1944 he joined the navy. Upon his release, Kelly returned to MGM where he soared to new heights as an actor, dancer and choreographer until 1957. Now a freelancer, he continued acting in films as well as directing and producing. He appeared on television in musical specials. In 1944 he received the National Medal of Arts in a ceremony at the

Gene Kelly on loan from MGM to Columbia became a star playing opposite Rita Hayworth in *Cover Girl* (Columbia, 1944).

White House. Kelly married Betsy Blair in 1940 and they were divorced in 1957. They had one daughter, Kerry. In 1960 he married Jeanne Coyne and they had two children, Timothy and Bridget. Mrs. Kelly died in 1973. In 1990 Kelly married Patricia Ward. At the age of 83 he died at his home in Beverly Hills from stroke complications.

Feature Films

For Me and My Gal (MGM, 1942), *Pilot No. 5* (MGM, 1943), *DuBarry Was a Lady* (MGM, 1943), *Thousands Cheer* (MGM, 1943), *The Cross of Lorraine* (MGM, 1943), *Cover Girl* (Col., 1944), *Christmas Holiday* (Univ., 1944), *Anchors Aweigh* (MGM, 1945), *Ziegfeld Follies of 1946* (MGM, 1946), *Living in a Big Way* (MGM, 1947), *The Pirate* (MGM, 1948), *The Three Musketeers* (MGM, 1948), *Words and Music* (MGM, 1948), *Take Me Out to the Ball Game* (MGM, 1949), *On the Town* (MGM, 1949), *The Black Hand* (MGM, 1950), *Summer Stock* (MGM, 1950), *An American in Paris* (MGM, 1951), *It's a Big Country* (MGM, 1951), *Singin' in the Rain* (MGM, 1952), *The Devil Makes Three* (MGM, 1952), *Love Is Better Than Ever* (MGM, 1952), *Brigadoon* (MGM, 1954), *Crest of the Wave* (MGM, 1954), *Deep in My Heart* (MGM, 1954), *It's Always Fair Weather*

(MGM, 1955), *Invitation to the Dance* (MGM, 1956), *The Happy Road* (MGM, 1957), *Les Girls* (MGM, 1957), *Marjorie Morningstar* (WB, 1958), *Inherit the Wind* (UA, 1960), *Let's Make Love* (20th, 1960), *What a Way to Go!* (20th, 1964), *The Young Girls of Rochefort* (WB-7 Arts, 1967), *Forty Carats* (Col., 1973), *That's Entertainment* (MGM, 1974), *That's Entertainment Part II* (MGM, 1976), *Viva Knievel!* (WB, 1977), *Xanadu* (Univ., 1980), *That's Dancing* (MGM, 1985), *That's Entertainment Part III* (MGM/UA, 1994)

Patsy Kelly (1910–1981)

Patsy Kelly was born in Brooklyn. A talented tap dancer as a child, she became a tap dance teacher in her teens. She toured in vaudeville as a dancer and comedienne in sketches before appearing at the Palace with Frank Fay as his partner in a headliner act. Going on to Broadway, she appeared in *Earl Carroll's Sketchbook* with Eddie Cantor, *Earl Carroll's Vanities* with Jack Benny, *Wonder Bar* with Al Jolson and *Flying Colors* with Clifton Webb.

Hal Roach brought her to Hollywood where she made over 50 comedy shorts with Thelma Todd, Pert Kelton and Lyda Roberti. In 1933 she made her feature film debut in *Going Hollywood* with Bing Crosby and continued in films until 1943. Following a tour of *Dear Charles* with Tallulah Bankhead, she was absent from show business until 1960 when she went back to films.

Her appearance in *No, No Nanette* marked her return to Broadway and she won a Tony. In 1973 she last appeared on Broadway with Debbie Reynolds in *Irene*. She did film and television work in Hollywood until her death at 71 of bronchial pneumonia.

Feature Films

Going Hollywood (MGM, 1933), *Countess of Monte Cristo* (Univ., 1934), *Party's Over* (Col., 1934), *The Girl from Missouri* (MGM, 1934), *Transatlantic Merry-Go-Round* (UA, 1934), *Go Into Your Dance* (WB, 1935), *Every Night at Eight* (Par., 1935), *Page Miss Glory* (WB, 1935), *Thanks a Million* (20th, 1935), *Kelly the Second* (MGM, 1936), *Private Number* (20th, 1936), *Sing, Baby, Sing* (20th, 1936), *Pigskin Parade* (20th, 1936), *Nobody's Baby* (MGM, 1937), *Pick a Star* (MGM, 1937), *Wake Up and Live* (20th, 1937), *Ever Since Eve* (WB, 1937), *Merrily We Live* (MGM, 1938), *There Goes My Heart* (UA, 1938), *The Cowboy and the Lady* (UA, 1938), *The Gorilla* (20th, 1939), *Hit Parade of 1941* (Rep., 1940), *Road Show* (UA, 1941), *Topper Returns* (UA, 1941), *Broadway Limited* (UA, 1941), *Playmates* (RKO, 1941), *Sing Your Worries Away* (RKO, 1942), *In Old California* (Rep., 1942), *My Son the Hero* (PRC, 1943), *Ladies' Day* (RKO, 1943), *Danger! Women at Work* (PRC, 1943), *Please Don't Eat the Daisies* (MGM, 1960), *The Crowded Sky* (WB, 1960), *The Naked Kiss* (AA, 1964), *The Ghost in the Invisible Bikini* (AIP, 1966), *C'mon, Let's Live a Little* (Par., 1967), *Rosemary's Baby* (Par., 1968), *The Phynx* (Cinerama, 1970), *Freaky Friday* (BV, 1976), *North Avenue Irregulars* (BV, 1979)

Top: Alice Faye, having lost her job as a singer in a nightclub, is helped by Patsy Kelly and Gregory Ratoff in *Sing, Baby, Sing* (20th Century–Fox). *Bottom:* Frances Langford, Alice Faye and Patsy Kelly, a singing trio, call themselves *The Swanee Sisters.* They work for bandleader George Raft on his radio show *Every Night at Eight* (Paramount, 1935).

Joel McCrea is cast as a successful Hollywood director of fluff movies. He dons hobo clothes with actress Veronica Lake to get background material on poverty for a serious film he wishes to do. His studio declines to produce in *Sullivan's Travels* (Paramount, 1941).

Veronica Lake (1919–1973)

Veronica Lake was born in Brooklyn. When she was twelve, her father died and she relocated with her mother to Miami. After graduating from high school, Lake moved to California and studied acting at Bliss-Hayden Dramatic School. Her appearance in several plays led to a screen test and small roles. Producer Arthur Hornblow, Jr., of Paramount cast her in *I Wanted Wings*, which made her a star. Her "peek-a-boo" hairstyle (hair falling over one eye) became a national fad. She scored another hit in her second film, the satire *Sullivan's Travels*, with Preston Sturges as director

and Joel McCrea as her co-star. Paramount teamed her with Alan Ladd and the combination proved to be a big success with movie fans. They made several films together. During World War II, the government asked Lake to stop wearing her hair long because women working in war plants were catching their hair in machines. She complied by wearing it in a knot when she played a nurse in *So Proudly We Hail*. When her Paramount contract expired, she toured in such plays as *The Voice of the Turtle*, *The Little Hut* and the Off Broadway revival of *Best Foot Forward*. She made one more

Conductor Pat O'Malley accepts money from killer Phillip Raven (played by Alan Ladd) as Veronica Lake is attracted to him in *This Gun for Hire* (Paramount, 1942).

film before writing her autobiography, *Veronica*. Then she went to England and did stage work, most notably *A Streetcar Named Desire* opposite Ty Hardin. Returning to the States, she did more stock work before dying of acute hepatitis in 1973.

Feature Films

as **Constance Keane:** *All Women Have Secrets* (Par., 1939), *Sorority House* (RKO, 1939), *Forty Little Mothers* (MGM, 1940) as **Veronica Lake:** *I Wanted Wings* (Par., 1941), *Sullivan's Travels* (Par., 1941), *Hold Back the Dawn* (Par., 1941)*, *This Gun for Hire* (Par., 1942), *Star Spangled Rhythm* (Par., 1942), *So Proudly We Hail* (Par., 1943), *The Hour Before the Dawn* (Par., 1944), *Bring on the Girls* (Par., 1945), *Out of This World* (Par., 1945), *Duffy's Tavern* (Par., 1945), *Hold That Blonde* (Par., 1945), *Miss Susie Slagle's* (Par., 1945), *The Blue Dahlia* (Par., 1946), *Ramrod* (UA, 1947), *Variety Girl* (Par., 1947), *The Sainted Sisters* (Par., 1948), Saigon (Par., 1948), *Isn't It Romantic?* (Par., 1948), *Slattery's Hurricane* (20th, 1949), *Stronghold* (Lip., 1952), *Footsteps in the Snow* (Evergreen Film, 1966), *Flesh Feast* (Cine World Corporation, 1970)

*Unbilled guest appearance

Dorothy Lamour's film debut as a *Jungle Princess* opposite Ray Milland, an adventurer shipwrecked on a South Seas island (Par., 1936).

Dorothy Lamour (1914–1996)

Dorothy Lamour, the daughter of Walton Staton and Carmen Louise LaPorte, was born in New Orleans. Her father was a waiter and her mother, who soon divorced him, worked as a waitress. Dorothy never finished high school. In 1931 she won the Miss New Orleans beauty contest and she and her mother moved to Chicago where Miss Lamour worked as an elevator operator at Marshall Field Department Store. She auditioned as a vocalist with Herbie Kay, a band leader who had a national radio show, and he hired her. After working with the Kay group she moved to Manhattan, where Rudy Vallee helped her to get a job singing at El Morocco nightclub. Later she worked at One Fifth Avenue, a cabaret. This led to a Para-mount contract in 1935 which renamed her Dorothy Lamour. Her first marriage to Herbie Kay ended in divorce. She met her second husband, William Ross Howard III, in 1943 while she was on a war bond tour. She is credited for selling $300 million in war bonds on tours for which she received a citation from the Treasury Department. She spent many hours working at the Hollywood Canteen where she cheered up the GI's by talking and dancing with them. After she retired from films she and her husband lived in Baltimore with their two sons. She was active in various causes for many years. She starred in the national road company of *Hello, Dolly!* Miss Lamour was 81 when she died at a Los Angeles hospital.

Dorothy Lamour

Feature Films

Jungle Princess (Par., 1936), *Swing High, Swing Low* (Par., 1937), *Last Train from Madrid* (Par., 1937), *High, Wide and Handsome* (Par., 1937), *Thrill of a Lifetime* (Par., 1937), *Hurricane* (UA, 1937), *Big Broadcast of 1938* (Par., 1938), *Her*

Jungle Love (Par., 1938), *Spawn of the North* (Par., 1938), *Tropic Holiday* (Par., 1938), *St. Louis Blues* (Par., 1939), *Man About Town* (Par., 1939), *Disputed Passage* (Par., 1939), *Johnny Apollo* (20th, 1940), *Typhoon* (Par., 1940), *Road to Singapore* (Par., 1940), *Moon Over Burma* (Par., 1940), *Chad Hanna* (20th, 1940), *Road to Zanzibar* (Par., 1941), *Caught in the Draft* (Par., 1941), *Aloma of the South Seas* (Par., 1941), *The Fleet's In* (Par., 1942), *Beyond the Blue Horizon* (Par., 1942), *Road to Morocco* (Par., 1942), *Star Spangled Rhythm* (Par., 1942), *They Got Me Covered* (RKO, 1943), *Dixie* (Par., 1943), *Riding High* (Par., 1943), *And the Angels Sing* (Par., 1944), *Rainbow Island* (Par., 1944), *The Road to Utopia* (Par., 1945), *A Medal for Benny* (Par., 1945), *Duffy's Tavern* (Par., 1945), *Masquerade in Mexico* (Par., 1945), *My Favorite Brunette* (Par., 1947), *Road to Rio* (Par., 1947), *Wild Harvest* (Par., 1947), *Variety Girl* (Par., 1947), *On Our Merry Way* (UA, 1948), *Lulu Belle* (Col., 1948), *The Girl from Manhattan* (UA, 1948), *Slightly French* (Col., 1948), *Manhandled* (Par., 1948), *The Lucky Stiff* (UA, 1949), *Road to Bali* (Par., 1952), *The Road to Hong Kong* (UA, 1962), *Donovan's Reef* (Par., 1963), *Pajama Party* (AIP, 1964), *Extraordinary Seaman* (MGM, 1969), *The Phynx* (Cinerama, 1970), *Won Ton, the Dog Who Saved Hollywood* (Par., 1976), *Creep Show 2* (Laurel, 1987)

*Unbilled guest appearance

Burt Lancaster (1913–1994)

Burt Lancaster, the son of a postal worker, was born in New York City. He grew up in the neighborhood around 106th Street and Second Avenue in a flat in a building which his mother inherited. He sang in a church choir and acted in plays at the Union Settlement House while attending DeWitt Clinton High School. He attended New York University on a scholarship for two years. In 1932 Lancaster dropped out and formed an acrobatic team with Nick Cravat, a boyhood friend. They perfected their act and by 1937 they were performing with Ringling and Barnum Circus. A finger injury forced him to give up his acrobatic career in 1939. He held many different jobs from salesman to working in a meat packing plant in Chicago. In 1942 he was drafted and spent three years in the Fifth Army's Special Services Unit, which took him to North Africa. After Lancaster's discharge while in New York, he tried out for a role in the play *The Sound of Hunting* and was cast in it. It had a run of only five weeks but he was offered seven movie contracts by Hollywood producers. He signed with Hal Wallis, who lent him to Mark Hellinger to star in *The Killers*, based on a short story by Ernest Hemingway. The film made him a star. In 1948 he and Harold Hecht formed their own company and produced their own films starring Lancaster. He also did pictures for other producers and Hollywood studios. The early '50s and '60s marked his peak with Academy Award nominations for *From Here to Eternity* (1953), *Birdman of Alcatraz* (1962), and an Oscar for his performance in *Elmer Gantry* (1960). In 1980 he was nominated again for an Oscar for his performance in *Atlantic City*. His first wife was June Ernst, a circus

Top: John Qualen listens to *Elmer Gantry* (played by Burt Lancaster), a traveling salesman giving his sales pitch (United Artists, 1960). *Bottom:* Burt Lancaster and Gary Cooper are two American soldiers-of-fortune who clash during the Mexican revolution of 1866 in *Vera Cruz* (United Artists, 1954).

performer. They married in 1935 and divorced a year later. He married Norma Anderson, a U.S.O. entertainer, in 1946. They had five children and divorced in 1969. In 1990 he married Susan Scherer. He died of a heart attack in his Century City home at the age of 80.

Feature Films

The Killers (Univ., 1946), *Variety Girl* (Par., 1947), *Brute Force* (Univ., 1947), *Desert Fury* (Par., 1947), *I Walk Alone* (Par., 1947), *All My Sons* (Univ., 1948), *Sorry, Wrong Number* (Par., 1948), *Kiss the Blood Off My Hands* (Univ., 1948), *Criss Cross* (Univ., 1949), *Rope of Sand* (Par., 1949), *The Flame and the Arrow* (WB, 1950), *Mr. 880* (20th, 1950), *Vengeance Valley* (MGM, 1951), *Jim Thorpe — All American* (WB, 1951), *Ten Tall Men* (Col., 1951), *The Crimson Pirate* (WB, 1952), *Come Back, Little Sheba* (Par., 1952), *South Sea Woman* (WB, 1953), *From Here to Eternity* (Col., 1953), *His Majesty O'Keefe* (WB, 1953), *Three Sailors and a Girl* (WB, 1953)*, *Apache* (UA, 1954), *Vera Cruz* (UA, 1954), *The Kentuckian* (UA, 1955), *The Rose Tattoo* (Par., 1955), *Trapeze* (UA, 1956), *The Rainmaker* (Par., 1956), *Gunfight at the O.K. Corral* (Par., 1957), *Sweet Smell of Success* (UA, 1957), *The Devil's Disciple*

(UA, 1959), *The Unforgiven* (UA, 1960), *Elmer Gantry* (UA, 1960), *The Young Savages* (UA, 1961), *Judgment at Nuremberg* (UA, 1961), *Birdman of Alcatraz* (UA, 1962), *A Child Is Waiting* (UA, 1961), *The List of Adrian Messenger* (Univ., 1963), *The Leopard* (20th, 1963), *Seven Days in May* (Par., 1964), *The Train* (UA, 1965), *The Hallelujah Trail* (UA, 1965), *The Professionals* (Col., 1966), *The Scalphunters* (UA, 1968), *Castle Keep* (Col., 1968), *The Swimmer* (Col., 1968) *Gypsy Moths* (MGM, 1969), *Airport* (Univ., 1970), *Lawman* (UA, 1971), *Valdez Is Coming* (UA, 1971), *Ulzana's Raid* (Univ., 1972), *Executive Action* (NGP, 1973), *Scorpio* (UA, 1973), *Midnight Man* (Univ., 1974), *Buffalo Bill and the Indians* (UA, 1976), *Conversation Piece* (Italian, 1976), *Moses* (Italian, 1976), *1900* (Italian, 1976), *Cassandra Crossing* (AE, 1977), *The Island of Dr. Moreau* (AIP, 1977), *Twilight's Last Gleaming* (AA, 1977), *Go Tell the Spartans* (AVCO, 1978), *Zulu Dawn* (WB, 1980), *Atlantic City* (Par., 1981), *Cattle Annie and Little Britches* (Univ., 1981), *Local Hero* (WB, 1983), *Osterman Weekend* (20th, 1983), *Little Treasure* (Tri-Star, 1985), *Tough Guys* (Touchstone, 1986), *Il Giorno Prima* (Col., 1987), *Rocket Gibraltar* (Col., 1988), *Field of Dreams* (Univ., 1989)

*Unbilled guest appearance

Myrna Loy (1905–1993)

Myrna Loy was born in Raidersburg, Montana, on a cattle ranch owned by her father, David Williams. He was also a state legislator and her mother Della was a singer. Mr. Williams died in the influenza epidemic of 1918 and Mrs.

Williams moved her daughter and son David to California. Myrna attended Venice High and upon her graduation joined the dancing chorus at Grauman's Chinese Theatre. She came to the attention of Hollywood film studios and

Myrna Loy is the wife of returning war veteran Fredric March. They face his difficult adjustment to civilian life in *Best Years of Our Lives* (RKO, 1946).

signed a five-year contract with Warner Brothers, where she appeared in silent films and talkies. When her contract came to an end, she freelanced for several years. She then signed a contract with MGM, where she became a box-office champion. She was an actress of charm, grace and sophistication, playing both comedy and drama. During World War II she quit movies at the height of her career to devote herself to Red Cross work. After the war she became the U.S. representative to UNESCO and returned occasionally to films. She made her stage debut in *There Must Be a Pony*, which closed on the road in tryout despite Loy's excellent reviews. In summer stock she starred with Claude Dauphin in the comedy *The Marriage Go-Round* and in the long-running national touring company of the comedy *Barefoot in the Park*. She

made her Broadway debut in the revival of Clare Booth Luce's *The Women*. On TV she made her debut on *The Perry Como Show* and later appeared with Melvyn Douglas in *Death Takes a Holiday* and with Henry Fonda in *Summer Solstice*. In 1985, film stars and fans attended a tribute to her at Carnegie Hall. The Academy of Motion Picture Arts and Sciences awarded her an Oscar in 1991 for her lifetime achievements. Loy was married four times — to Arthur Hornblow, Jr., John Hertz, Jr., Gene Markey and Howland Sargeant. Her marriages all ended in divorce. She had no children. For decades she lived in an apartment in upper Manhattan and aided many civic causes. She died in surgery at Lenox Hill Hospital in Manhattan at the age of 88.

William Powell and Myrna Loy as Nick and Nora Charles with Asta, their dog, in the first of *The Thin Man* series which had a total of six films (MGM, 1934).

Sound Feature Films

The Jazz Singer (WB, 1927), *The Desert Song* (WB, 1929), *Black Watch* (Fox, 1929), *The Squall* (WB, 1929), *Hardboiled Rose* (WB, 1929), *Evidence* (WB, 1929), *Show of Shows* (WB, 1929), *The Great Divide* (WB, 1930), *The Jazz Cinderella* (Chesterfield, 1930), *Cameo Kirby* (Fox, 1930), *Isle of Escape* (WB, 1930), *Under a Texas Moon* (WB, 1930), *Cock o' the Walk* (Sono Art-World Wide, 1930), *Bride of the Regiment* (WB, 1930), *The Last of the Duanes* (Fox, 1930), *The Truth About Youth* (WB, 1930), *Renegades* (Fox, 1930), *Rogue of the Rio Grande* (Sono Art-World Wide, 1930), *The Devil to Pay* (UA, 1930), *Naughty Flirt* (WB, 1931), *Body and Soul* (Fox, 1931), *A Connecticut Yankee* (Fox, 1931), *Hush Money* (Fox, 1931), *Transatlantic* (Fox, 1931), *Rebound* (RKO, 1931), *Skyline* (Fox, 1931), *Consolation Marriage* (RKO, 1931)*, *Arrowsmith* (UA, 1931), *Emma* (MGM, 1932), *The Wet Parade* (MGM, 1932), *Vanity Fair* (Hollywood Exchange, 1932), *The Woman in Room 13* (Fox, 1932), *New Morals for Old* (MGM, 1932), *Love Me Tonight* (Par., 1932), *Thirteen Women* (RKO, 1932), *The Mask of Fu Manchu* (MGM, 1932), *The Animal Kingdom* (RKO, 1932), *Topaze* (RKO, 1933), *The Barbarian* (MGM, 1933), *The Prizefighter and the Lady* (MGM, 1933), *When Ladies Meet* (MGM, 1933), *Penthouse* (MGM, 1933), *Night Flight* (MGM, 1933), *Men in White* (MGM, 1934), *Manhattan Melodrama* (MGM, 1934), *The Thin Man* (MGM,

1934), *Stamboul Quest* (MGM, 1934), *Evelyn Prentice* (MGM, 1934), *Broadway Bill* (Col., 1934), *Wings in the Dark* (Par., 1935), *Whipsaw* (MGM, 1935), *Wife vs. Secretary* (MGM, 1936), *Petticoat Fever* (MGM, 1936), *The Great Ziegfeld* (MGM, 1936), *To Mary — With Love* (20th, 1936), *Libeled Lady* (MGM, 1936), *After the Thin Man* (MGM, 1936), *Parnell* (MGM, 1937), *Double Wedding* (MGM, 1937), *Man-Proof* (MGM, 1938), *Test Pilot* (MGM, 1938), *Too Hot to Handle* (MGM, 1938), *Lucky Night* (MGM, 1939), *The Rains Came* (20th, 1939), *Another Thin Man* (MGM, 1939), *I Love You Again* (MGM, 1940), *Third Finger, Left Hand* (MGM, 1940), *Love Crazy* (MGM, 1941), *Shadow of the Thin Man* (MGM, 1941), *The Thin Man Goes Home* (MGM, 1944), *So Goes My Love* (Univ., 1946), *The Best Years of Our Lives* (RKO, 1946), *The Bachelor and the Bobby-Soxer* (RKO, 1947), *Song of the Thin Man* (MGM, 1947), *The Senator Was Indiscreet* (Univ., 1947)*, *Mr. Blandings Builds His Dream House* (RKO, 1948), *The Red Pony* (Rep., 1949), *Cheaper by the Dozen* (20th, 1950), *This Be Sin* (UA, 1950), *Belles on Their Toes* (20th, 1952), *The Ambassador's Daughter* (UA, 1956), *Lonelyhearts* (UA, 1958), *From the Terrace* (20th, 1960), *Midnight Lace* (Univ., 1960), *The April Fools* (1969), *Airport '75* (Univ., 1974), *The End* (UA, 1978), *Just Tell Me What You Want* (WB, 1980)

*Unbilled guest appearance

Ida Lupino (1918–1995)

Ida Lupino was born in London during a German zeppelin bombing. Her paternal forebears were traveling players and puppeteers in Renaissance Italy. Later generations migrated to England. Her father, Stanley Lupino, was a noted comedian and her mother, Connie Emerald, was an actress who came from a theatrical family. At the age of 13 Ida enrolled at the Royal Academy of Dramatic Arts. When she was 15 she made her film debut. She made five more films and then was signed by Paramount Pictures in Hollywood. There for the next five years she played ingenue roles. The turning point in her career came when she was cast as a vengeful prostitute opposite Ronald Colman in *The Light That Failed*. Her portrayal of a demented murderess in *They Drive by Night* won her a long-term contract at Warner Brothers. During the next decade critics hailed Lupino as one of the great film actresses. The New York film critics honored her as the best actress of 1943 for her portrayal of a ruthless woman who propels her younger sister to stardom in Warners' *The Hard Way*. The following year Lupino and her producer-husband Collier Young founded Filmakers, an independent film producing company. She acted in their films as well as directing and writing the scripts. In 1948 she became an American citizen and in 1951 divorced Young. On television she starred in the dramatic anthology *Four Star Playhouse* from 1952 to 1956. She produced and starred in the situation comedy *Mr. Adams and Eve* opposite her husband Howard Duff in 1957 and 1958. She also directed scores of episodes of many long-running television series including *The Untouchables, Have Gun, Will Travel* and *Alfred Hitchcock Presents.*

Ann Sheridan meets Ida Lupino. George Raft is the traffic manager of the trucking firm owned by Lupino's husband in *They Drive By Night* (Warner Bros., 1940).

Lupino wrote short stories and children's books and also composed music. One work, "Aladdin Suite," was performed by the Los Angeles Philharmonic Orchestra. She and Duff had a daughter, Bridget, separated in 1972 and divorced in 1983. She had previously been married to Louis Hayward in 1938 and divorced in 1945. Lupino died at the age of 77 at her Burbank home in California of cancer.

Feature Films

Her First Affaire (Sterling, 1933), *Money for Speed* (UA, 1933), *High Finance* (WB, 1933), *The Ghost Camera* (Radio, 1933), *I Lived with You* (Gaumont-British, 1934), *Prince of Arcadia* (Gaumont-British, 1934), *Search for Beauty* (Par., 1934), *Come On Marines* (Par., 1934), *Ready for Love* (Par., 1934), *Paris in Spring* (Par., 1935), *Smart Girl* (Par., 1935), *Peter Ibbetson* (Par., 1935), *Anything Goes* (Par., 1936), *One Rainy Afternoon* (UA, 1936), *Yours for the Asking* (Par., 1936), *The Gay Desperado* (UA., 1936), *Sea Devils* (RKO, 1937), *Let's Get Married* (Col., 1937), *Artists and Models* (Par., 1937), *Fight for Your Lady* (RKO, 1937), *The Lone Wolf Spy Hunt* (Col., 1939), *The Lady and the Mob* (Col., 1939), *The Adventures of Sherlock Holmes* (20th, 1939), *The Light That Failed* (Par., 1939), *They Drive By*

Night (WB, 1940), *High Sierra* (WB, 1941), *The Sea Wolf* (WB, 1941), *Out of the Fog* (WB, 1941), *Ladies in Retirement* (Col., 1941), *Moontide* (20th, 1942), *The Hard Way* (WB, 1942), *Life Begins at 8:30* (20th, 1942), *Forever and a Day* (RKO, 1943), *Thank Your Lucky Stars* (WB, 1943), *In Our Time* (WB, 1944), *Hollywood Canteen* (WB, 1944), *Pillow to Post* (WB, 1945), *Devotion* (WB, 1946), *The Man I Love* (WB, 1947), *Deep Valley* (WB, 1947), *Escape Me Never* (WB, 1947), *Road House* (20th, 1948), *Lust for Gold* (Col., 1949), *Woman in Hiding* (Univ., 1950), *On Dangerous Ground* (RKO, 1951), *Beware My Lovely* (RKO, 1952), *Jennifer* (AA, 1953), *The Bigamist* (Filmakers, 1953), *Private Hell 36* (Filmakers, 1954), *Women's Prison* (Col., 1955), *The Big Knife* (UA, 1955), *While the City Sleeps* (RKO, 1956), *Strange Intruder* (AA, 1956), *Backtrack* (Univ., 1969), *Deadhead Miles* (Par., 1971), *Junior Bonner* (Cinerama, 1972), *The Devil's Rain* (Bryanston, 1975),

Ida Lupino

Food of the Gods (AIP, 1976), *My Boys Are Good Boys* (Independent Release, 1978)

Joel McCrea (1905–1990)

Son of a Los Angeles Gas and Electric Company executive, McCrea was born in South Pasadena. As a youth he delivered the *Los Angeles Times* to film notables and in the summers he worked for King Cattle Company Ranch in the Tehachapi Mountains. He attended Pomona College and acted at the Pasadena Community Playhouse. From 1922 to 1929 McCrea appeared in films as an extra, stunt man and bit player. In 1929 he acted in the part-talking film *The Jazz Age* and in DeMille's talkie *Dyna-* mite. He signed a contract with RKO and was one of their busiest actors as well as working on loan-out to Paramount and Fox. In 1933 McCrea met actress Frances Dee. After a whirlwind courtship, they entered a marriage that lasted until his death. On the advice of Will Rogers, he purchased his first thousand acres of ranch land, gradually increasing it to 3,000 acres. In 1959 he sold most of it. He also owned 20,000 acres in Nevada. McCrea's career spanned three decades in which he appeared in 86 films. He

Merle Oberon, a teacher in a private girls' school, is in love with the local doctor, Joel McCrea, in *These Three.* Their happiness is shattered by a lie (United Artists, 1936).

appeared opposite such stars as Dorothy Mackaill, Ginger Rogers, Kay Francis, Constance Bennett, Fay Wray, Barbara Stanwyck, Maureen O'Sullivan, Miriam Hopkins, Merle Oberon, Joan Bennett, Sylvia Sidney, Jean Arthur and Shelley Winters. He died at the age of 84 of pulmonary complications with wife Frances at his bedside in Woodland Hills, California.

Sound Feature Films

So This Is College (MGM, 1929), *Dynamite* (Par., 1929), *Lightnin'* (Fox, 1930), *Silver Horde* (RKO, 1930), *Once a Sinner* (Fox, 1931), *Kept Husbands* (RKO, 1931), *Born to Love* (RKO, 1931), *Girls About Town* (Par., 1931), *Business and Pleasure* (Fox, 1932), *Lost Squadron* (RKO, 1932), *Bird of Paradise* (RKO, 1932), *The Most Dangerous Game* (RKO, 1932), *Rockabye*

Criminologist Joel McCrea is hired to track down art thieves and is assisted by Jean Arthur in *Adventure in Manhattan* (Columbia, 1936).

(RKO, 1932), *The Sport Parade* (RKO, 1932), *The Silver Cord* (RKO, 1933), *Bed of Roses* (RKO, 1933), *One Man's Journey* (RKO, 1933), *Chance at Heaven* (RKO, 1933), *Gambling Lady* (WB, 1934), *Half a Sinner* (Univ., 1934), *Richest Girl in the World* (RKO, 1934), *Private Worlds* (Par., 1935), *Splendor* (UA, 1935), *These Three* (UA, 1936), *Two in a Crowd* (Univ., 1936), *Adventure in Manhattan* (Col., 1936), *Come and Get It* (UA, 1936), *Banjo on My Knee* (20th, 1936), *Interns Can't Take Money* (Par., 1937), *Wells Fargo* (Par., 1937), *Woman Chases Man* (UA, 1937), *Dead End* (UA, 1937), *Three Blind Mice* (20th, 1938), *Youth Takes a Fling* (Univ., 1938), *Union Pacific* (Par., 1939), *They Shall Have Music* (UA, 1939), *Espionage Agent* (WB, 1939), *He Married His Wife* (20th, 1940), *Primrose Path* (RKO, 1940), *Foreign Correspondent* (UA, 1940), *Reaching for the Sun* (Par., 1940), *Sullivan's Travels* (Par., 1941), *The Great Man's Lady* (Par., 1942), *The Palm Beach Story* (Par., 1942), *The More the Merrier* (Col., 1943), *Buffalo Bill* (20th, 1944), *The Great Moment* (Par., 1944), *The Unseen* (Par., 1945), *The Virginian* (Par., 1946), *Ramrod* (UA, 1947), *Four Faces West* (UA, 1948), *South of St. Louis* (WB, 1949), *Colorado Territory* (WB, 1949), *Stars in My Crown* (MGM, 1950), *The Outriders* (MGM, 1950), *Saddle Tramp* (Univ., 1950), *Frenchie* (Univ., 1950), *The Hollywood Story* (Univ., 1951)*, *Cattle Drive* (Univ., 1951), *The San Francisco Story* (WB, 1952), *Lone Hand* (Univ., 1953),

Shoot First (UA, 1953), *Border River* (Univ., 1954), *Stranger on Horseback* (UA, 1955), *Wichita* (AA, 1955), The *First Texan* (AA, 1956), *The Oklahoman* (AA, 1957), *Trooper Hook* (UA, 1957), *Gunsight Ridge* (UA, 1957), *The Tall Stranger* (AA, 1957), *Cattle Empire* (20th, 1958), *Fort Massacre* (UA, 1958), *The Gunfight at Dodge City* (UA, 1959), *Ride the High Country* (MGM, 1962), *Cry Blood, Apache* (Golden Eagle, 1970)

*Unbilled guest appearance

Fred MacMurray (1908–1991)

Fred MacMurray was born in Kankakee, Illinois, where his father, a concert violinist, was on tour. When he was five his parents separated. He spent his youth in Beaver Dam, Wisconsin, with his mother and graduated from high school with ten letters in athletics. In high school and for one year at Carroll College in Waukesha, Wisconsin, where he had an American Legion scholarship, he led his own three-piece band, "Mac's Melody Boys." Over the next eight years MacMurray was a saxophonist and vocalist with various dance and vaudeville bands around the country. On Broadway he appeared first in two successful revues, *Three's a Crowd* and *The Third Little Show*, and then in the Jerome Kern musical *Roberta*. MacMurray was signed by Paramount, and in the film *The Gilded Lily* he achieved stardom. He became one of Hollywood's most durable stars, appearing opposite Claudette Colbert, Jean Arthur, Barbara Stanwyck, Katharine Hepburn, Rosalind Russell, Madeleine Carroll, Irene Dunne, Alice Faye, Joan Crawford and Marlene Dietrich. In 1943 his annual salary was $420,000, making him that year's highest-paid American. MacMurray put his finances into the hands of a capable manager who made many profitable investments, and he became one of Los Angeles' richest citizens. In 1960 MacMurray began playing the lead in the hit TV series *My Three Sons*, which ran through 1972, first on ABC and later on CBS. He married Lillian Lamont in 1936. She died in 1953. They had two children, Susan and Robert. In 1954 he married actress June Haver and they had two daughters, Kathryn and Laurie. At the age of 83, MacMurray died of pneumonia in Santa Monica, California.

Feature Films

Friends of Mr. Sweeney (WB, 1934), *Grand Old Girl* (RKO, 1935), *The Gilded Lily* (Par., 1935), *Car 99* (Par., 1935), *Men Without Names* (Par., 1935), *Alice Adams* (RKO, 1935), *Hands Across the Table* (Par., 1935), *The Bride Comes Home* (Par., 1935), *The Trail of the Lonesome Pine* (Par., 1936), *13 Hours by Air* (Par., 1936), *The Princess Comes Across* (Par., 1936), *The Texas Rangers* (Par., 1936), *Maid of Salem* (Par., 1937), *Champagne Waltz* (Par., 1937), *Swing High, Swing Low* (Par., 1937), *Exclusive* (Par., 1937), *True Confession* (Par., 1937), *Cocoanut Grove* (Par., 1938), *Sing, You Sinners* (Par., 1938), *Men with Wings* (Par., 1938), *Cafe Society* (Par., 1939), *Invitation to Happiness* (Par., 1939), *Honeymoon in Bali* (Par., 1939), *Little Old New York* (20th, 1940), *Remember the Night* (Par.,

Marlene Dietrich is a renowned musical star who finds an abandoned baby and Fred MacMurray is the pediatrician who helps her solve her dilemma in *The Lady Is Willing* (Columbia, 1942).

1940), *Too Many Husbands* (Col., 1940), *Rangers of Fortune* (Par., 1940), *Virginia* (Par., 1941), *One Night in Lisbon* (Par., 1941), *New York Town* (Par., 1941), *Dive Bomber* (WB, 1941), *The Lady Is Willing* (Col., 1942), *Take a Letter, Darling* (Par., 1942), *The Forest Rangers* (Par., 1942), *Star Spangled Rhythm* (Par., 1942), *Flight for Freedom* (RKO, 1943), *Above Suspicion* (MGM, 1943), *No Time for Love* (Par., 1943), *And the Angels Sing* (Par., 1944), *Double Indemnity* (Par., 1944), *Murder, He Says* (Par., 1945), *Practically Yours* (Par., 1945), *Where Do We Go from Here?*

Mary Martin meets Fred MacMurray and together they plan for her to find a rich man to marry while taking free samples from Ann Doran in *New York Town* (Paramount, 1941).

(20th, 1945), *Captain Eddie* (20th, 1945), *Pardon My Past* (Col., 1946), *Smoky* (20th, 1946), *Suddenly It's Spring* (Par., 1947), *The Egg and I* (Univ., 1947), *Singapore* (Univ., 1947), *The Miracle of the Bells* (RKO, 1948), *On Our Merry Way* (UA, 1948), *Don't Trust Your Husband* (UA, 1948), *Family Honeymoon* (Univ., 1948), *Father Was a Fullback* (20th, 1949), *Borderline* (Univ., 1950), *Never a Dull Moment* (RKO, 1950), *A Millionaire for Christy* (20th, 1951), *Callaway Went Thataway* (MGM, 1951), *Fair Wind to Java* (Rep., 1953), *The Moonlighter* (WB, 1953), *The Caine Mutiny* (Col., 1954), *Pushover* (Col., 1954), *Woman's World* (20th, 1954), *The Far Horizons* (Par.,

1955), *The Rains of Ranchipur* (20th, 1955), *At Gunpoint* (AA, 1955), *There's Always Tomorrow* (Univ., 1956), *Gun for a Coward* (Univ., 1957), *Quantez* (Univ., 1957), *Day of the Bad Man* (Univ., 1958), *Good Day for a Hanging* (Col., 1958), *The Shaggy Dog* (BV, 1959), *Face of a Fugitive* (Col., 1959), *The Oregon Trail* (20th, 1959), *The Apartment* (UA, 1960), *The Absent-Minded Professor* (BV, 1961), *Bon Voyage* (BV, 1962), *Son of Flubber* (BV, 1963), *Kisses for My President* (WB, 1964), *Follow Me, Boys* (BV, 1966), *The Happiest Millionaire* (BV, 1967), *Charlie and the Angel* (BV, 1973), *The Swarm* (WB, 1978)

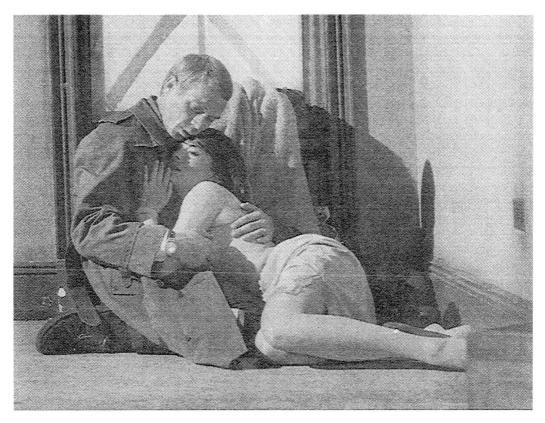

Steve McQueen and Natalie Wood are young lovers who face an unwanted pregnancy in *Love with the Proper Stranger* (Paramount, 1963).

Steve McQueen (1930–1980)

Steve McQueen was born in Beach Grove, Indiana, and lived with his mother's grandparents until he was eleven, when his mother took him to California. At 15 he was sent by the court to Boys' Republic in Chino. When he left there he joined the Merchant Marines, jumped ship in the Dominican Republic and worked his way back to the States doing all sorts of odd jobs. He next joined the Marines and did a three-year hitch. Upon his discharge, he went to New York where he enrolled at the Neighborhood Playhouse and studied acting. In 1952 he appeared in summer stock in *Peg o' My Heart* with Margaret O'Brien and *Member of the Wedding* with

Ethel Waters. Then he toured nationally with Melvyn Douglas in *Time Out for Ginger*. He replaced Ben Gazzara in *A Hatful of Rain*, his only Broadway appearance, which also went on tour. Then came roles in television plays for *Goodyear*, *Playhouse 90*, the *U.S. Steel Hour* and *Studio One*. Next he starred in the TV series *Wanted: Dead or Alive* which ran for three seasons. After signing a Hollywood contract he concentrated on his film career but still appeared occasionally on TV in *Alfred Hitchcock Presents*, *The Dick Powell Theater* and the Perry Como, Bob Hope and Ed Sullivan variety shows. He was married three times. His first wife, Neile

Tuesday Weld and Steve McQueen (as *The Cincinnati Kid*) learn that making the wrong moves at the right time is what gambling is about (MGM, 1965).

Adams, gave him two children but the marriage ended in divorce as did his second marriage to Ali MacGraw. He was married to his third wife, Barbara Minty, when he died of cancer at 50.

Feature Films

Somebody Up There Likes Me (MGM, 1956), *Never Love a Stranger* (AA, 1958), *The Blob* (Par., 1958), *Never So Few* (MGM, 1959), *The Great St. Louis Bank Robbery* (UA, 1959), *The Magnificent Seven* (UA, 1960), *The Honeymoon Machine* (MGM, 1961), *Hell Is for Heroes* (Par., 1961), *The War Lover* (Col., 1962), *The Great Escape* (UA, 1963), *Love with the Proper Stranger* (Par., 1963), *Soldier in the Rain* (AA, 1963), *Baby, the Rain Must Fall* (Col., 1965), *The Cincinnati Kid* (MGM, 1965), *Nevada Smith* (Par., 1966), *The Sand Pebbles* (20th, 1966), *The Thomas Crown Affair* (UA, 1968), *Bullitt* (WB/7 Arts, 1968), *The Reivers* (NGP, 1969), *LeMans* (NGP, 1971), *On Any Sun-*

day (Cinema 5, 1971), *Junior Bonner* (Cinerama, 1972), *The Getaway* (NGP, 1972), *Papillon* (AA, 1973), *The Towering Inferno* (20th-WB, 1974), *An Enemy of the People* (WB, 1977), *Tom Horn* (Col., 1980), *The Hunter* (Par., 1980)

Marjorie Main (1890–1975)

Marjorie Main was born in Action, Indiana. She was the daughter of a minister, the Rev. S.J. Tomlinson, and was christened Mary. Because her father took a dim view of actresses, she took the stage name Marjorie Main after attending drama school. In 1921 she married Dr. Stanley L. Krebs, a psychologist and lecturer who encouraged her to pursue her acting career on the stage and in films until his death in 1935. On Broadway she appeared with W.C. Fields in *The Family Ford* and with John Barrymore in *Cheating Cheaters*. In Sidney Kingsley's *Dead End* she played the mother of a gangster and went to Hollywood to repeat the role. Many successful movie appearances followed. Main's last stage appearance was *The Women on Broadway* in 1936. She then played the same part in the film version. She signed a long-term contract with MGM with whom she had a series of successes opposite Wallace Beery. She was loaned to Universal to play Ma Kettle, the eccentric farmer's wife in *The Egg and I* which starred Claudette Colbert and Fred MacMurray. For her performance she won an Academy nomination in 1947. Ma Kettle became a popular movie character; Percy Kilbride played her husband, Pa Kettle, in a subsequent series of nine highly successful movies. After her retirement from films she spent her time at her homes in Los Angeles and Palm Springs. At the age of 85, Main died in Los Angeles after a long battle with cancer.

Feature Films

A House Divided (Univ., 1932), *Take a Chance* (Par., 1933), *Crime Without Passion* (Par., 1934), *Music in the Air* (Fox, 1934), *Naughty Marietta* (MGM, 1935), *City Girl* (20th, 1937), *Love in a Bungalow* (Univ., 1937), *Dead End* (UA, 1937), *Stella Dallas* (UA, 1937), *The Man Who Cried Wolf* (Univ., 1937), *The Wrong Road* (Rep., 1937), *The Shadow* (Col., 1937), *Boy of the Streets* (Mon., 1937), *Penitentiary* (Col., 1938), *King of the Newsboys* (Rep., 1938), *Test Pilot* (MGM, 1938), *Prison Farm* (Par., 1938), *Romance of the Limberlost* (Mon., 1938), *Little Tough Guy* (Univ., 1938), *Under the Big Top* (Mon., 1938), *Too Hot to Handle* (MGM, 1938), *Girls' School* (Col., 1938), *There Goes My Heart* (UA, 1938), *Three Comrades* (MGM, 1938), *Lucky Night* (MGM, 1939), *They Shall Have Music* (UA, 1939), *Angels Wash Their Faces* (WB, 1939), *The Women* (MGM, 1939), *Another Thin Man* (MGM, 1939), *Two Thoroughbreds* (RKO, 1939), *I Take This Woman* (MGM, 1940), *Women Without Names* (Par., 1940), *Dark Command* (Rep., 1940), *Turnabout* (UA, 1940), *Susan and God* (MGM, 1940), *The Captain Is a Lady* (MGM, 1940), *Wyoming* (MGM, 1940), *The Wild Man of Borneo* (MGM, 1941), *The Trial of Mary Dugan* (MGM, 1941), *A Woman's Face* (MGM, 1941), *Barnacle Bill* (MGM, 1941), *The Shepherd of the Hills* (Par., 1941), *Honky Tonk* (MGM, 1941), *The Bugle Sounds*

Top: Marjorie Main, *The Wistful Widow of Wagon Gap,* comes under the care of Bud Abbott and Lou Costello. Jack Shutta plays a game of cards with them (Universal, 1947). *Bottom:* Percy Kilbride and Marjorie Main are proud but poor parents trying their best to earn enough money at the county fair to send a daughter to college in *Ma and Pa Kettle at the Fair* (Universal, 1952).

(MGM, 1941), *We Were Dancing* (MGM, 1942), *Tennessee Johnson* (MGM, 1942), *The Woman of the Town* (UA, 1943), *Heaven Can Wait* (20th, 1943), *Johnny Come Lately* (UA, 1943), *Rationing* (MGM, 1944), *Gentle Annie* (MGM, 1944), *Meet Me in St. Louis* (MGM, 1944), *Murder, He Says* (Par., 1945), *The Harvey Girls* (MGM, 1946), *Bad Bascomb* (MGM, 1946), *Undercurrent* (MGM, 1946), *The Show-Off* (MGM, 1946), *The Egg and I* (Univ., 1947), *The Wistful Widow of Wagon Gap* (Univ., 1947), *Feudin', Fussin' and Afightin'* (Univ., 1948), *Ma and Pa Kettle* (Univ., 1949), *Big Jack* (MGM, 1949), *Ma and Pa Kettle Go to Town* (Univ., 1950), *Summer Stock* (MGM, 1950), *Mrs. O'Malley and Mr. Malone* (MGM, 1950), *Ma and Pa Kettle Back on the Farm* (Univ., 1951), *The Law and the Lady* (MGM, 1951), *Mr. Imperium* (MGM, 1951), *It's a Big Country* (MGM, 1951), *The Belle of New York* (MGM, 1952), *Ma and Pa Kettle at the Fair* (Univ., 1952), *Ma and Pa Kettle on Vacation* (Univ., 1953), *Fast Company* (MGM, 1953), *The Long, Long Trailer* (MGM, 1954), *Rose Marie* (MGM, 1954), *Ma and Pa Kettle at Home* (Univ., 1954), *Ricochet Romance* (Univ., 1954), *Ma and Pa Kettle at Waikiki* (Univ., 1955), *The Kettles in the Ozarks* (Univ., 1956), *Friendly Persuasion* (AA, 1956), *The Kettles on Old MacDonald's Farm* (Univ., 1957)

Dean Martin (1917–1995)

Dean Martin, the son of an Italian immigrant barber, was born in Stubenville, Ohio, in 1917. As a teenager he began his singing career in a local spaghetti parlor. Later he alternated between singing and working as a croupier in nightclubs. In 1946 he was booked into the 500 Club where Jerry Lewis was on the same bill. They then worked as a team and were booked at the Copacabana in New York for a six-week engagement. It was extended to twelve weeks at a weekly salary of $5,000. Producer Hal Wallis saw them and signed them to a long-term movie contract. From 1949 to 1956 they made 16 films together before they dissolved their relationship and went to work independently. Martin's film career flourished and in 1965 he became a television star with his one-hour variety show, which had a run of eight years. His career with Capitol Records was also very successful.

He had 40 singles on Billboard's charts between 1950 and 1969. For Reprise Records he made 11 "gold" albums. In the '70s and '80s he continued to be a top attraction in nightclubs. Martin was married three times. He had four children by his first wife, Elizabeth Ann McDonald. They were married in 1940 and divorced in 1949. His second marriage to Jeanne Riegger lasted three years and produced three children. His third and last marriage to Catherine Mae Hawn in 1973 ended three years later in divorce. Martin died in his Beverly Hills home of acute respiratory failure at the age of 78.

Feature Films

My Friend Irma (Par., 1949), *My Friend Irma Goes West* (Par., 1950), *At War with the Army* (Par., 1950), *That's My Boy*

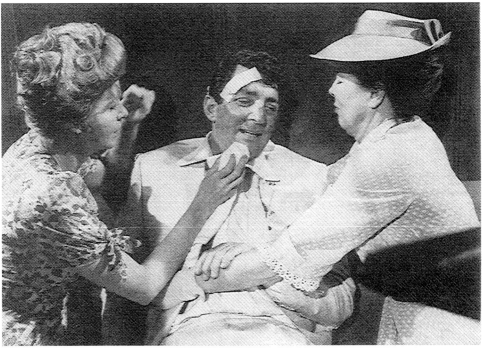

Top: Frank Sinatra is a World War II veteran and a failed writer. He returns to his hometown where Dean Martin, a gambler, is his best friend in *Some Came Running* (MGM, 1959). *Bottom:* Dean Martin is beaten and robbed by thugs and is comforted by his two sisters (Geraldine Page and Wendy Hiller) in Lillian Hellman's *Toys in the Attic* (United Artists, 1963).

(Par., 1951), *Sailor Beware* (Par., 1951), *Jumpin' Jacks* (Par., 1952), *Road to Bali* (Par., 1952)*, *The Stooge* (Par., 1952), *Scared Stiff* (Par., 1953), *The Caddy* (Par., 1953), *Money from Home* (Par., 1953), *Living It Up* (Par., 1954), *Three Ring Circus* (Par., 1954), *You're Never Too Young* (Par., 1955), *Artists and Models* (Par., 1955), *Pardners* (Par., 1956), *Hollywood or Bust* (Par., 1956), *Ten Thousand Bedrooms* (MGM, 1957), *The Young Lions* (20th, 1958), *Some Came Running* (MGM, 1958), *Rio Bravo* (WB, 1959), *Career* (Par., 1959), *Who Was That Lady?* (Col., 1960), *Bells Are Ringing* (MGM, 1960), *Ocean's 11* (WB, 1960), *Pepe* (Col., 1960*, *All in a Night's Work* (Par., 1961), *Ada* (MGM, 1961), *Sergeants 3* (UA, 1962), *Road to Hong Kong* (UA, 1962)*, *Who's Got the Action?* (Par., 1962), *Come Blow Your Horn* (Par., 1963)*, *Toys in the Attic* (UA, 1963), *Who's Been Sleeping in My Bed?* (Par., 1963), *4 for Texas* (WB, 1963), *What a Way to Go!* (20th, 1964), *Robin and the 7 Hoods* (WB, 1964), *Kiss Me, Stupid* (Lopert, 1964), *The Sons of Katie Elder* (Par., 1965), *The Silencers* (Col., 1966), *Texas Across the River* (Univ., 1966), *Murderers' Row* (Col., 1966), *Rough Night in Jericho* (Univ., 1967), *The Ambushers* (Col., 1967), *Bandolero* (20th, 1968), *How to Save a Marriage — and Ruin Your Life* (Col., 1968), *5 Card Stud* (Par., 1968), *The Wrecking Crew* (Columbia, 1969), *Airport* (Univ., 1970), *Something Big* (NGP, 1971), *Showdown* (Univ., 1973), *Mr. Ricco* (MGM/UA, 1976), *The Cannonball Run* (20th, 1981), *Cannonball Run II* (20th, 1984)

*Unbilled guest appearance

Mary Martin (1913–1990)

At the age of five, this Weatherford, Texas, native began singing and dancing in community shows there. At 17 she attended the University of Texas for one year. There she met and married Benjamin Hagman. They had one son, Larry. They were divorced and she left Texas for California to pursue a singing career. In Hollywood she got a job as a dance instructor and singer at the Trocadero. She made her Broadway debut in 1938 singing "My Heart Belongs to Daddy" in Cole Porter's *Leave It to Me* with Victor Moore, William Gaxton and Sophie Tucker. Her success in the show led to a contract with Paramount. In 1940 she married story editor Richard Halliday, who later became her manager. They had a daughter, Heller. Martin returned to the theater in two flop musicals, *Dancing in the Streets* and *Nice Goin'*. They both folded in Boston and never got to New York. Broadway producer Cheryl Crawford signed Martin for the musical *One Touch of Venus* which Marlene Dietrich had turned down. It was a hit show and ran for 567 performances with John Boles and Kenny Baker in the male leads. The show also had a successful tour of the U.S. She next appeared in the national touring company of *Annie Get Your Gun* and then starred with Yul Brynner in *Lute Song* on Broadway. Over the years she was a star of the musical stage, playing opposite Ezio Pinza in *South Pacific*, Charles Boyer in *Kind Sir* (a non-singing role), Cyril Ritchard in *Peter Pan* and Robert Preston in *I Do, I Do*. She won two Tony awards — one for *South Pacific* and the other for *The Sound of Music*. She was also quite successful in television,

Top: Mary Martin is a southern girl who auditions to play the lead in a Broadway musical. Don Ameche is the producer in *Kiss the Boys Goodbye* (Paramount, 1944). *Bottom: The Great Victor Herbert* was a biographical film about the composer of musicals at the turn of the century. Seated at a celebration are Jerome Cowan, Walter Connelly and Judith Barrett. Standing by the table are Mary Martin and Allan Jones as the waiters look on (Paramount, 1939).

appearing in a TV version of *Peter Pan* and the PBS series *Over Easy* (1981–83). She died in Rancho Mirage, California, of cancer at the age of 76.

Feature Films

Rage of Paris (Univ., 1938), *The Great Victor Herbert* (Par., 1939), *Love Thy Neighbor* (Par., 1940), *Rhythm on the River* (Par., 1940), *Birth of the Blues* (Par., 1941), *Kiss the Boys Goodbye* (Par., 1941), *New York Town* (Par., 1941), *Star Spangled Rhythm* (Par., 1942), *Happy Go Lucky* (Par., 1943), *Night and Day* (WB, 1946), *Main Street to Broadway*(MGM, 1953)

Lee Marvin (1924–1987)

Lee Marvin, the son of an advertising executive and a fashion editor, was born in New York City. As a youth he was expelled from exclusive boarding schools for breaking rules. When he was 18 in 1942, he joined the Marines and served in the South Pacific, participating in 21 island landings until he was wounded and hospitalized for 13 months. After his recovery he enrolled at New York's American Theater Wing to study acting. Then he worked in stock, television, Off Broadway, and the cast of *Billy Budd* in 1951. That same year he made his first screen appearance under Henry Hathaway's direction. Many supporting roles followed. In addition to his work in films, he was the star of the TV series *M Squad* for three years and appeared on *Pepsi Cola Playhouse, Kraft Suspense Theatre, The U.S. Steel Hour, G.E. Theatre* and narrated *Lawbreakers*. In 1965 he won an Oscar for *Cat Ballou* in which he played the dual roles of gunfighter Kid Shelton and his evil brother, Tim Straun. He bought a ranch and lived in Tucson, Arizona, but continued acting and commuted for appearances. He died at 63 of a heart attack, leaving his wife, Pamela, a son, and three daughters.

Feature Films

You're in the Navy Now (20th, 1951), *Diplomatic Courier* (20th, 1952), *We're Not Married* (20th, 1952), *The Duel at Silver Creek* (Univ., 1952), *Eight Iron Men* (Col., 1952), *Hangman's Knot* (Col., 1952), *Seminole* (Univ., 1953), *Down Among the Sheltering Palms* (20th, 1953), *The Glory Brigade* (20th, 1953), *The Stranger Wore a Gun* (Col., 1953), *The Big Heat* (Col., 1953), *Gun Fury* (Col., 1953), *The Wild One* (Col., 1954), *Gorilla at Large* (20th, 1954), *The Caine Mutiny* (Col., 1954), *The Raid* (20th, 1954), *Bad Day at Black Rock* (MGM, 1954), *A Life in the Balance* (20th, 1955), *Violent Saturday* (20th, 1955), *Not as a Stranger* (UA, 1955), *Pete Kelly's Blues* (WB, 1955), *I Died a Thousand Times* (WB, 1955), *Shack Out on 101* (AA, 1955), *The Rack* (MGM, 1956), *Seven Men From Now* (WB, 1956), *Pillars of the Sky* (Univ., 1956), *Attack!* (UA, 1956), *Raintree County* (MGM, 1957), *The Missouri Traveler* (BV, 1958), *The Comancheros* (20th, 1961), *The Man Who Shot Liberty Valance* (Par., 1962), *Donovan's Reef* (Par., 1963), *The Killers* (Univ., 1964), *Ship of Fools* (Col., 1965), *Cat Ballou* (Col., 1965), *The Professionals* (Col., 1966), *The Dirty Dozen* (MGM, 1967),

Jane Fonda plays a respectable schoolteacher who turns to crime and Lee Marvin is cast in dual roles as Kid Shelleen and Tim Straum in *Cat Ballou* (Columbia, 1965).

Point Blank (MGM, 1967), *Tonite Let's Make Love in London* (documentary; Lorrimer, 1967), *Sergeant Ryker* (Univ., 1968), *Hell in the Pacific* (Cinerama, 1968), *Paint Your Wagon* (Par., 1969), *Monte Walsh* (NG, 1970), *Pocket Money* (NG, 1972), *Prime Cut* (NG, 1972), *Emperor of the North Pole* (20th, 1973), *The Iceman Cometh* (American Film Theatre, 1973), *The Spikes Gang* (UA, 1974), *The Klansman* (Par., 1974), *Shout at the Devil* (AIP, 1976), *The Great Scout*

Lee Marvin is a failed baseball player and Vivien Leigh is a divorcée who flirts with everyone, leading men on and then shunting them aside in *Ship of Fools* (Columbia, 1965).

and *Cathouse Thursday* (AIP, 1976), *Avalanche Express* (1979), *The Big Red One* (UA, 1980), *Death Hunt* (20th, 1981), *Gorky Park* (Orion, 1983), *Dog Day* (Cinetele, 1983), *The Delta Force* (Cannon, 1986)

James Mason (1909–1984)

Mason was born in the mill town of Huddersfield, Yorkshire, England, and was educated at Marlborough and Cambridge where he received a B.A. degree in architecture in 1931. During his college years he performed in student productions. Upon graduation he answered a newspaper ad and won a role in the touring play *The Rascal*. For the next few years Mason worked with various repertory companies and then made his West End debut in *Gallows Glorious* in 1933. He joined the Old Vic and was also a member of the Dublin Gate Theatre. During this period he also appeared in films. With two friends, Roy and Pamela Kellino, Mason co-scripted the movie *I Met a Murderer* and starred in it opposite

Robert Newton is an eccentric painter who takes a wounded IRA leader (James Mason) to his loft to be the subject of a portrait of death in *Odd Man Out* (GFD–Universal, 1947).

Pamela Kellino, whom he later married after her divorce from her previous husband. Success followed Mason and he became the biggest film draw in England and its highest paid actor. He also continued his stage work in the West End. In 1947 he came to the U.S. He and his wife appeared on Broadway in the failure *Bathsheba* by Jacques Deval. His first Hollywood films were disappointing until he appeared in *The Desert Fox* as Field Marshall Rommel and in Joseph L. Mankiewicz's espionage thriller *Five Fingers*. Refusing to sign long-term contracts, he continued to work in Hollywood, appearing only in roles of his own choice. In 1954 he got rave reviews in Stratford, Ontario, for his appearances in

Measure for Measure and *Oedipus Rex*. He received his only Oscar nomination for Best Actor opposite Judy Garland in *A Star Is Born*. In 1964 he and his first wife were divorced. He married actress Clarissa Kay in 1971. In 1978 he returned to Broadway with his wife in Brian Friel's short-run play *Faith Healer*. Until his death he continued to work in films and television. He died of a heart attack in Lausanne, Switzerland, at the age of 75.

Feature Films

Late Extra (Fox, 1935), *Troubled Waters* (Fox, 1935), *Twice Branded* (George

Cary Grant, a successful advertising executive, is mistaken for a spy by Russian spymaster James Mason in Alfred Hitchcock's thriller *North by Northwest* (MGM, 1959).

Smith, 1936), *The Prison Breakers* (George Smith, 1936), *Blind Man's Bluff* (20th, 1936), *The Secret of Stanboul* (Wainwright, 1936), *The Mill on the Floss* (John Klein, 1936), *The High Command* (Fanfare, 1937), *Catch as Catch Can* (20th, 1937), *Fire Over England* (London Films, 1937), *The Return of the Scarlet Pimpernel* (UA, 1937), *Deadwater* (KMK, 1937), *I Met a Murderer* (Gamma Films, 1939), *Hatter's Castle* (Par., 1941), *The Patient Vanishes* (Associated British Pictures, 1941), *This Man Is Dangerous* (Pathe, 1941), *Secret Mission* (Hellman, 1942), *Thunder Rock* (Charter, 1942), *Alibi* (British Lion, 1943), *Bells Go Down* (Ealing, 1943), *Candlelight in Algeria* (King, 1943), *The Man in Grey* (Gainsborough, 1943), *They Met in the Dark* (Hellman, 1943), *Fanny By Gaslight* (Gainsborough, 1944), *Hotel Reserve* (RKO, 1944), *A Place of One's Own* (Gainsborough, 1945), *The Seventh Veil* (Ortus, 1945), *Odd Man Out* (Rank, 1947), *The Upturned Glass* (Rank, 1947), *Madame Bovary* (MGM, 1949), *The Reckless Moment* (Col., 1949), *East Side, West Side* (MGM, 1949), *One Way Street* (Univ., 1950), *The Desert Fox* (20th, 1951), *Pandora and the Flying Dutchman* (MGM, 1951), *Five Fingers* (20th, 1952), *Lady Possessed* (Rep., 1952), *The Prisoner of Zenda* (MGM, 1952), *Face to Face* (RKO, 1952), *The Story of Three Loves* (MGM, 1953), *The Desert Rate* (20th, 1953), *Julius Caesar* (MGM, 1953), *Botany Bay* (Par., 1953), *The Man Between* (UA, 1953), *Prince Valiant* (20th, 1954), *A Star Is Born* (WB, 1954), *20,000 Leagues Under the Sea* (BV, 1954), *Forever Darling* (MGM, 1956), *Bigger Than Life* (20th, 1956), *Island in the Sun* (20th, 1957), *Cry Terror* (MGM, 1958), *The Decks Ran Red* (MGM, 1958), *North By*

Northwest (MGM, 1959), *Journey to the Center of the Earth* (20th, 1959), *A Touch of Larceny* (Par., 1960), *The Green Carnation* (Warick, 1960), *The Marriage-Go-Round* (20th, 1960), *Escape from Zahrain* (Par., 1962), *Lolita* (MGM, 1962), *Hero's Island* (UA, 1962), *Tiara Tahiti* (Zenith International, 1962), *Torpedo Bay* (AIP, 1964), *The Fall of the Roman Empire* (Par., 1964), *The Pumpkin Eater* (Royal Film International, 1964), *Lord Jim* (Col., 1965), *Genghis Khan* (Col., 1966), *Georgy Girl* (Col., 1966), *The Deadly Affair* (Col., 1967), *Cop Out* (Cinerama, 1968), *Duffy* (Col., 1968), *Mayerling* (MGM, 1968), *The Sea Gull* (WB, 1968), *The Uninhibited* (Tera Explorer, 1968), *Age of Consent* (Col., 1969), *Child's Play* (Par., 1972), *Kill! Kill! Kill!* (Cociner, 1973), *The Last of Sheila* (WB, 1973), *The Mackintosh Man* (WB, 1973), *Cold Sweat* (Emerson, 1974), *The Destructors* (AIP, 1974), *11 Whorehouse* (20th, 1974), *Great Expectations* (Transcontinental, 1975), *Inside Out* (WB, 1975), *Mending* (Par., 1975), *Voyage of the Damned* (AE, 1976), *Cross of Iron* (AE, 1977), *The Boys from Brazil* (20th, 1978), *Heaven Can Wait* (Par., 1978), *Bloodline* (Par., 1979), *Murder by Decree* (Ambassador, 1979), *The Passage* (UA, 1979), *The Water Babies* (Pethurst International, 1979), *Ffolkes* (Univ., 1980), *Evil Under the Sun* (Univ., 1982), *The Verdict* (20th, 1982), *Yellowbeard* (AIP, 1983)

Ethel Merman (1908–1984)

Ethel Merman was born in Astoria, New York. Her father, an accountant for a dry goods firm, encouraged her to pursue her natural vocal abilities and she sang at churches, amateur contests and at Army camp shows during World War I. After graduating from high school, Merman took a job as a stenographer. In her spare time she sang at clubs and social events. She made one short, *The Cave Club*, for Warner Brothers in 1930 and performed in vaudeville and nightclubs around New York. George and Ira Gershwin saw her and cast her in the Broadway musical *Girl Crazy* with Ginger Rogers. She was an immediate success. After signing a Paramount contract she made five shorts at the New York Studio in Astoria while she was the toast of Broadway, appearing in top musicals. She went to Hollywood and appeared in *We're Not Dressing* for Paramount and *Kid Millions* for Samuel Goldwyn opposite Eddie Cantor. Then she returned to Broadway in the hit Cole Porter musical *Anything Goes* and went back again to Hollywood to repeat her role in the film version opposite Bing Crosby. She appeared again with Eddie Cantor in *Strike Me Pink* and stole the picture. Broadway beckoned and Merman returned for *Red, Hot and Blue* opposite Bob Hope and Jimmy Durante. It was a hit in New York and on the road. She signed with 20th Century–Fox but the films were not to her liking. Again she returned to Broadway in *Stars in Your Eyes* with Jimmy Durante before starring in Irving Berlin's blockbuster *Annie Get Your Gun*. Between Broadway triumphs she did film work. On Broadway in *Call Me Madam* she won a Tony Award. Other hit musicals followed: *Happy Hunting, Gypsy,* and a revival of *Hello, Dolly*. Her career continued with more films and television appearances. She was married four times, to William Smith, Robert D. Levitt, Robert F. Six and Ernest Borgnine. Each

Top: On board a liner bound for England, Jerry Tucker bothers fellow travelers Charles Ruggles, Ethel Merman and Bing Crosby in *Anything Goes* (Paramount, 1936). *Bottom:* Tyrone Power, Alice Faye, Ethel Merman and Jack Haley star in *Alexander's Ragtime Band* which included 28 Irving Berlin songs (20th Century–Fox, 1938).

marriage ended in divorce. She died of a brain tumor in 1984. She was 76.

Feature Films

Follow the Leader (Par., 1930), *We're Not Dressing* (Par., 1934), *Kid Millions* (UA, 1934), *Anything Goes* (Par., 1936), *Strike Me Pink* (UA, 1936), *Happy Landing* (20th, 1938), *Alexander's Ragtime Band* (20th, 1938), *Straight, Place and Show* (20th, 1938), *Stage Door Canteen* (UA, 1943), *Call Me Madam* (20th, 1953), *There's No Business Like Show Business* (20th, 1954), *It's a Mad Mad Mad Mad World* (UA, 1963), *The Art of Love* (Univ., 1965), *Journey Back to Oz* (voice only, Filmation, 1974), *Won Ton Ton, the Dog Who Saved Hollywood* (Par., 1976), *Airplane!* (Par., 1980)

Ray Milland (1905–1984)

Ray Milland was born in Neath, Wales, and educated at the University of Wales before serving three years as a Royal Guardsman in London. He became interested in the theater and was cast in *The Woman in Room 13* which brought him to the attention of English film producers. After appearing in minor films in England, he signed a Hollywood contract with MGM. Milland made routine movies with occasional loan-outs to other studios before he clicked opposite Jean Arthur in *Easy Living* on his home lot. He then co-starred opposite Dorothy Lamour, Miriam Hopkins, Sonja Henie, Loretta Young, Claudette Colbert and Ginger Rogers before winning an Oscar for *The Lost Weekend* opposite Jane Wyman. More films of less distinction followed while he was working for Paramount, Warner Brothers, MGM and 20th Century–Fox. In 1953 he appeared in the successful television series *Meet Mr. McNulty* in which he played a college professor. Next he played a private investigator in *Markham*. On Broadway Milland appeared in *Hostile Witness* and later toured with it in Australia. For the remainder of his career he did films, television work and occasional stock. He died of cancer at Torrance Memorial Hospital in California at the age of 79.

Feature Films

The Plaything (British, 1929), *The Flying Scotsman* (British, 1929), *The Lady from the Sea* (Par., 1929), *The Informer* (Warder, 1929), *Way for a Sailor* (MGM, 1930), *Passion Flower* (MGM, 1930), *Bachelor Father* (MGM, 1931), *Just a Gigolo* (MGM, 1931), *Bought* (WB, 1931), *Ambassador Bill* (Fox, 1931), *Blonde Crazy* (WB, 1931), *Polly of the Circus* (MGM, 1932), *The Man Who Played God* (WB, 1932), *Payment Deferred* (MGM, 1932), *But the Flesh Is Weak* (MGM, 1932), *This Is the Life* (British Lion, 1933), *Orders Is Orders* (Gaumont-British, 1933), *Bolero* (Par., 1934), *We're Not Dressing* (Par., 1934), *Many Happy Returns* (Par., 1934), *Menace* (Par., 1934), *Charlie Chan in London* (Fox, 1934), *The Gilded Lily* (Par., 1934), *The Mystery of Mr. X* (MGM, 1934), *One Hour Late* (Par., 1935), *Four Hours to Kill* (Par., 1935), *The Glass Key* (Par., 1935), *Alias Mary Dow* (Univ., 1935), *Next Time We*

Top: Ray Milland plays the successful businessman and Claudette Colbert is his wife. He promises to quit his job to be with her in *Skylark* (Paramount, 1941). *Bottom:* Marlene Dietrich plays a gypsy and Ray Milland is a British agent she helps escape from the Gestapo in *The Golden Earrings* (Paramount, 1947).

Love (Univ., 1936), *The Return of Sophie Lang* (Par., 1936), *The Big Broadcast of 1937* (Par., 1936), *The Jungle Princess* (Par., 1936), *Three Smart Girls* (Univ., 1937), *Wings Over Honolulu* (Univ., 1937), *Easy Living* (Par., 1937), *Ebb Tide* (Par., 1937), *Wise Girl* (RKO, 1937), *Bulldog Drummond Escapes* (Par., 1937), *Her Jungle Love* (Par., 1938), *Tropic Holiday* (Par., 1938), *Men with Wings* (Par., 1938), *Say It in French* (Par., 1938), *Hotel Imperial* (Par., 1939), *Beau Geste* (Par., 1939) *Everything Happens at Night* (20th, 1939), *French Without Tears* (Par., 1940), *Irene* (RKO, 1940), *The Doctor Takes a Wife* (Col., 1940), *Untamed* (Par., 1940), *Arise, My Love* (Par., 1941), *I Wanted Wings* (Par., 1941), *Skylark* (Par., 1941), *The Lady Has Plans* (Par., 1942), *Are Husbands Necessary?* (Par., 1942), *The Major and the Minor* (Par., 1942), *Reap the Wild Wind* (Par., 1942), *Star Spangled Rhythm* (Par., 1942), *Forever and a Day* (RKO, 1943), *The Crystal Ball* (UA, 1943), *The Uninvited* (Par., 1944), *Lady in the Dark* (Par., 1944), *Till We Meet Again* (Par., 1944), *Ministry of Fear* (Par., 1944), *The Lost Weekend* (Par., 1945), *Kitty* (Par., 1945), *The Well-Groomed Bride* (Par., 1946), *California* (Par., 1946), *The Imperfect Lady* (Par., 1947), *The Trouble with Women* (Par., 1947), *Golden Earrings* (Par., 1947), *Variety Girl* (Par., 1947), *The Big Clock* (Par., 1948), *Miss Tatlock's Millions* (Par., 1948), *So Evil My Love* (Par., 1948), *Sealed Verdict* (Par., 1948), *Alias Nick Beal* (Par., 1949), *It Happened Every Spring* (20th, 1949), *A Woman of Distinction* (Col., 1950), *A Life of Her Own* (MGM, 1950), *Copper Canyon* (Par., 1950), *Circle of Danger* (EL, 1951), *Night Into Morning* (MGM, 1951), *Rhubarb* (Par., 1951), *Close to My Heart* (WB, 1951), *Bugles in the Afternoon* (WB, 1952), *Something to Live For* (Par., 1952), *The Thief* (UA, 1952), *Jamaica Run* (Par., 1953), *Let's Do It Again* (Col., 1953), *Dial M for Murder* (WB, 1954), *A Man Alone* (Rep., 1955), *The Girl in the Red Velvet Swing* (20th, 1955), *Lisbon* (Rep., 1956), *Three Brave Men* (20th, 1957), *The River's Edge* (20th, 1957), *The Safecracker* (MGM, 1958), *High Flight* (Col., 1958), *The Premature Burial* (AIP, 1962), *Panic in Year Zero* (AIP, 1962), *The Man with the X-Ray Eyes* (AIP, 1963), *Quick, Let's Get Married* (*The Confession*) (Golden Eagle, 1965), *Hostile Witness* (UA, 1968), *Red Roses for the Fuehrer* (Dino Films, 1968), *Company of Killers* (Univ., 1970), *Love Story* (Par., 1970), *The Big Game* (Comet, 1972), *Embassy* (Hemdale, 1972), *Frogs* (AIP, 1972), *The Thing with Two Heads* (AIP, 1972), *Terror in the Wax Museum* (Cinerama, 1973), *The House in Nightmare Park* (MGM-British, 1973), *Gold* (AA, 1974), *Escape to Witch Mountain* (BV, 1975), *The Last Tycoon* (Par., 1976), *The Swiss Conspiracy* (WB, 1976), *Aces High* (Cine Artists, 1977), *Slavers* (Lord Film, 1977), *The Uncanny* (Cinevideo, 1977), *Blackout* (New World, 1978), *Oliver's Story* (Par., 1978), *The Attic* (Atlantic, 1979), *Battlestar Galactica* (Univ., 1979), *Game for Vultures* (New Line, 1980), *Survival Run* (Ventures International, 1980), *The Sea Serpent* (Calepas, 1986)

David Niven (1911–1983)

Born in Kirriemuir, Scotland, a descendant of two generations of professional soldiers, he attended Sandhurst Military School (1927–29) and served with the Highland Light Infantry at home and in Malta. After resigning his commission in 1932, he became a world drifter. He landed up in Los Angeles where he became an extra in the movies in 1934. Soon he was put under contract to Samuel Goldwyn. Niven's popularity increased with each new role and loan-out and he became a star. With the beginning of World War II, he returned to England and entered service as a lieutenant in the Commandos. He was decorated for valor and discharged as a colonel. During his time in service he was given permission to appear in two British propaganda films — Leslie Howard's *The First of the Few* and Carol Reed's *The Way Ahead*. After the war he returned to movies but made only routine films. He appeared briefly on Broadway opposite Gloria Swanson in *Nina*, then had a hit movie, *The Moon Is Blue*. Together with Charles Boyer and Dick Powell he founded the television production company Four Star, which was enormously successful. He appeared occasionally in some of its productions. He continued his successful career, winning an Oscar as Major Pollock in *Separate Tables* in 1958. He also starred in two television series, *The David Niven Show* and *The Rogues*. He wrote two autobiographies (*The Moon's a Balloon* and *Bring On the Empty Horses*) and a novel, *Round the Rugged Rocks*. They were all best-sellers. He died at the age of 73 in Switzerland from amyotrophic lateral sclerosis with his wife, Hjordis, at his side.

Feature Films

Without Regret (Par., 1935), *A Feather in Her Hat* (Col., 1935), *Mutiny on the Bounty* (MGM, 1935), *Barbary Coast* (UA, 1935), *Splendor* (UA, 1935), *Rose Marie* (MGM, 1936), *Thank You, Jeeves* (20th, 1936), *Palm Springs* (Par., 1936), *The Charge of the Light Brigade* (WB, 1936), *Dodsworth* (UA, 1936), *Beloved Enemy* (UA, 1936), *We Have Our Moments* (Univ., 1937), *Dinner at the Ritz* (20th, 1937), *The Prisoner of Zenda* (UA, 1937), *Four Men and a Prayer* (20th, 1938), *Bluebeard's Eighth Wife* (Par., 1938), *Three Blind Mice* (20th, 1938), *The Dawn Patrol* (WB, 1938), *Wuthering Heights* (UA, 1939), *Bachelor Mother* (RKO, 1939), *The Real Glory* (UA, 1939), *Eternally Yours* (UA, 1939), *Raffles* (UA, 1940), *The First of the Few* (King, 1941), *This Way Ahead* (Rank, 1944), *The Perfect Marriage* (Par., 1946), *The Magnificent Doll* (Univ., 1946), *Stairway to Heaven* (Rank, 1946), *The Other Love* (UA, 1947), *The Bishop's Wife* (RKO, 1947), *Bonnie Prince Charlie* (Korda, 1947), *Enchantment* (RKO, 1948), *The Elusive Pimpernel* (Carrol Pictures, 1948), *A Kiss in the Dark* (WB, 1949), *A Kiss for Corliss* (UA, 1949), *The Toast of New Orleans* (MGM, 1950), *Soldiers Three* (MGM, 1951), *Happy Go Lovely* (MGM, 1951), *The Lady Says No* (UA, 1951), *Island Rescue* (Univ., 1952), *The Moon Is Blue* (UA, 1953), *Love Lottery* (Continental Distributing, 1954), *Tonight's the Night* (AA, 1954), *The King's Thief* (MGM, 1955), *Court-Martial* (Kingsley International, 1955), *The Birds and the Bees* (Par., 1956), *Around the World in 80 Days* (UA, 1956), *Oh, Men! Oh Women!* (20th, 1957), *The Little Hut* (MGM, 1957), *My Man Godfrey* (Univ., 1957), *The Silken Affair* (DCA, 1957),

Ginger Rogers plays a salesgirl in a large department store. She finds a baby and everyone assumes that she is an unwed mother. David Niven is the playboy who falls in love with her in *Bachelor Mother* (RKO, 1939).

Bonjour Tristesse (Col., 1958), *Separate Tables* (UA, 1958), *Ask Any Girl* (MGM, 1959), *Happy Anniversary* (UA, 1959), *Please Don't Eat the Daisies* (MGM, 1960), *The Guns of Navarone* (Col., 1961), *Guns of Darkness* (WB, 1962), *Road to Hong Kong* (UA, 1962)*, *The Best of Enemies* (Col., 1962), *55 Days at Peking* (AA,

David Niven plays Major Pollock, a guest at an inn run by Wendy Hiller. He is arrested for harassing women and exposed as a fraud in *Separate Tables* (United Artists, 1958).

1963), *The Pink Panther* (UA, 1964), *Bedtime Story* (Univ., 1964), *Where the Spies Are* (MGM, 1965), *Lady L* (MGM, 1966), *Casino Royale* (Col., 1967), *Eye of the Devil* (MGM, 1967), *The Extraordinary Seaman* (MGM, 1968), *Prudence and the Pill* (20th, 1968), *The Impossible Years* (MGM, 1968), *Before Winter Comes* (Col., 1969), *The Brain* (Par., 1969), *The Statue* (Cinerama, 1971), *King, Queen, Knave* (AE, 1972), *Old Dracula* (AIP, 1975), *Paper Tiger* (MacLean, 1975), *Murder by Death* (Col., 1976), *No Deposit, No Return* (BV, 1976), *Candleshoe* (BV, 1978), *Death on the Nile* (Par., 1978), *Escape to Athena*

(Grade/AFD, 1979), *A Nightingale Sang in Berkeley Square* (AIP, 1979), *Rough Cut* (Par., 1980), *Sea Wolves* (Par., 1981), *Trail of the Pink Panther* (MGM/UA, 1982), *Better Late Than Never* (WB, 1983), *Curse of the Pink Panther* (MGM, UA, 1983)

*Unbilled guest appearance

Jack Oakie (1903–1978)

Born Lewis Offield in Sedalia, Missouri, and raised in Muskogee, Oklahoma, Oakie went to New York while still a youth. There he attended business college and worked for a brokerage firm. At the annual company benefit show, he was a great success as a comedian and was encouraged to follow a career in show business. His first job was as a chorus boy in George M. Cohan's *Little Nelly Kelly* (1922). Oakie then toured as a comic in vaudeville. In 1928 he was signed to a contract by Paramount. He was at Paramount for nine years and then worked for RKO, 20th Century–Fox and Universal. With wise investments he became one of Hollywood's wealthiest actors. He did not like to appear on television talk shows because they paid only minimum union scale and he believed that was too low for his time and effort. His first marriage to Venita Verdon ended in divorce. His second marriage (to Victoria Horne) lasted for 30 years until his death in 1978 (caused by a stomach ailment). At the time of his death he was writing an autobiography.

Sound Feature Films

Chinatown Nights (Par., 1929), *The Dummy* (Par., 1929), *Wild Party* (Par., 1929), *Close Harmony* (Par., 1929), *The Man I Love* (Par., 1929), *Fast Company* (Par., 1929), *Street Girl* (RKO, 1929), *Hard to Get* (WB, 1929), *Sweetie* (Par., 1929), *Paramount on Parade* (Par., 1930), *Hit the Deck* (RKO, 1930), *Social Lion* (Par., 1930), *Let's Go Native* (Par., 1930), *The Sap from Syracuse* (Par., 1930), *Gang Busters* (Par., 1931), *June Moon* (Par., 1931), *Dude Ranch* (Par., 1932), *Touchdown* (Par., 1931), *Dancers in the Dark* (Par., 1932), *Sky Bride* (Par., 1932), *Make Me a Star* (Par., 1932), *Million Dollar Legs* (Par., 1932), *Once in a Lifetime* (Univ., 1932), *Uptown New York* (Sono Art-World Wide, 1932), *From Hell to Heaven* (Par., 1933), *Sailor Be Good* (Par., 1933), *Eagle and the Hawk* (Par., 1933), *College Humor* (Par., 1933), *Too Much Harmony* (Par., 1933), *Sitting Pretty* (Par., 1933), *Alice in Wonderland* (Par., 1933), *Looking for Trouble* (UA, 1934), *Murder at the Vanities* (Par., 1934), *Shoot the Works* (Par., 1934), *College Rhythm* (Par., 1934), *Call of the Wild* (Fox, 1935), *Big Broadcast of 1936* (Par., 1935), *King of Burlesque* (Fox, 1935), *Collegiate* (Par., 1936), *Colleen* (WB, 1936), *Florida Special* (Par., 1936), *The Texas Rangers* (Par., 1936), *That Girl from Paris* (RKO, 1936), *Champagne Waltz* (RKO, 1937), *Super Sleuth* (RKO, 1937), *The Toast of New York* (RKO, 1937), *Fight for Your Lady* (RKO, 1937), *Hitting a New High* (RKO, 1937), *Radio City Revels* (RKO, 1938), *The Affairs of Annabel* (RKO, 1938), *Annabel Takes a Tour* (RKO, 1938), *Thanks for Everything* (20th, 1938), *Young People* (20th, 1940), *The Great Dictator* (UA, 1940), *Tin Pan Alley* (20th, 1940), *Little Men* (RKO, 1940), *Rise and Shine*

Top: Warner Baxter is the *King of Burlesque* producer who aspires to do a big Broadway musical with Jack Oakie's girlfriend, Arline Judge (20th Century–Fox, 1935). *Bottom:* Charlie Chaplin is *The Great Dictator.* Henry Daniell is his propaganda minister and Jack Oakie is cast as Napolini, the Dictator of Bacteria (United Artists, 1940).

(20th, 1941), *Great American Broadcast* (20th, 1941), *Hello, Frisco, Hello* (20th, 1943), *Wintertime* (20th, 1943), *Something to Shout About* (Col., 1943), *It Happened Tomorrow* (UA, 1944), *The Merry Monahans* (Univ., 1944), *Sweet and Low Down* (20th, 1944), *Bowery to Broadway* (Univ., 1944), *That's the Spirit* (Univ., 1945), *On Stage Everybody* (Univ., 1945), *She Wrote the Book* (Univ., 1946), *Northwest Stampede* (EL, 1948), *When My Baby Smiles at Me* (20th, 1948), *Thieves Highway* (20th, 1949), *Last of the Buccaneers* (Col., 1950), *Tomahawk* (Univ., 1951), *Around the World in 80 Days* (UA, 1956), *The Wonderful Country* (UA, 1959), *The Rat Race* (Par., 1960), *Lover Come Back* (Univ., 1961)

Pat O'Brien (1899–1983)

Born in Milwaukee, Wisconsin, Pat (William Joseph) O'Brien and neighborhood buddy Spencer Tracy enlisted in the navy and served in World War I. After service they returned to Marquette University in Milwaukee to study law but withdrew, went to New York and enrolled in the American Academy of Dramatic Arts. At that time they met James Cagney, a struggling actor. The friendship between the three men lasted until Spencer Tracy's death in 1967. O'Brien gained stage experience in road companies and stock before his first Broadway appearance in 1923. In 1931 he married actress Eloise Taylor. He was appearing on Broadway in *The Front Page* when Howard Hughes signed him to repeat the role of Hildy Johnson in the film. It made him a star and he signed a long-term contract with Warner Brothers where he appeared in many memorable movies. O'Brien also appeared in television movies and was a guest star on many TV shows. He was a lead in the television series *Harrigan and Son* (1960). For many years he and his wife toured in stock and dinner theaters together, appearing last in *On Golden Pond*. At the age of 83 he had a heart attack after minor surgery and died at St. John's Hospital in Santa Monica, California.

Feature Films

Front Page (UA, 1931), *Honor Among Lovers* (Par., 1931), *Personal Maid* (Par., 1931), *Flying High* (MGM, 1931), *Consolation Marriage* (RKO, 1931), *Final Edition* (Col., 1932), *Hell's House* (Capitol Film Exchange, 1932), *Strange Case of Clara Deane* (Par., 1932), *Scandal for Sale* (Univ., 1932), *American Madness* (Col., 1932), *Hollywood Speaks* (Col., 1932), *Virtue* (Col., 1932), *Air Mail* (Univ., 1932), *Laughter in Hell* (Univ., 1932), *Destination Unknown* (Univ., 1933), *World Gone Mad* (Majestic, 1933), *Bureau of Missing Persons* (WB, 1933), *Bombshell* (MGM, 1933), *College Coach* (WB, 1933), *Flaming Gold* (RKO, 1934), *Gambling Lady* (WB, 1934), *I've Got Your Number* (WB, 1934), *20 Million Sweethearts* (WB, 1934), *Here Comes the Navy* (WB, 1934), *Personality Kid* (WB, 1934), *I Sell Anything* (WB, 1934), *Flirtation Walk* (WB, 1934), *Devil Dogs of the Air* (WB, 1935), *In Caliente* (WB, 1935), *Oil for the Lamps of China* (WB, 1935), *Page Miss Glory* (WB, 1935), *The Irish in Us* (WB, 1935), *Stars Over Broadway* (WB, 1935), *Ceiling Zero* (WB, 1935), *I Married a Doctor* (WB, 1936), *Public Enemy's Wife* (WB, 1936), *China Clipper* (WB, 1936), *The Great O'Malley* (WB, 1937), *Slim*

Top: Pat O'Brien, a detective, and Spencer Tracy, a reformed alcoholic attorney, John Hodiak and Yvette Duguay attempt to solve a murder in *The People Against O'Hara* (MGM, 1951). *Bottom:* Robert Ryan portrays Father Tim Donovan, friend and former teammate of Pat O'Brien who is cast as Frank Cavanaugh, the legendary football coach of Dartmouth, Boston College and Fordham in *The Iron Major* (RKO, 1943).

(WB, 1937), *San Quentin* (WB, 1937), *Back in Circulation* (WB, 1937), *Submarine D-1* (WB, 1937), *Women Are Like That* (WB, 1938), *The Cowboy from Brooklyn* (WB, 1938), *Boy Meets Girl* (WB, 1938), *Garden of the Moon* (WB, 1938), *Angels with Dirty Faces* (WB, 1938), *Off the Record* (WB, 1939), *The Kid from Kokomo* (WB, 1939), *Indianapolis Speedway* (WB, 1939), *The Night of Nights* (Par., 1939), *The Fighting 69th* (WB, 1940), *Slightly Honorable* (UA, 1940), *Castle on the Hudson* (WB, 1940), *Till We Meet Again* (WB, 1940), *Torrid Zone* (WB, 1940), *Flowing Gold* (WB, 1940), *Knute Rockne — All American* (WB, 1940), *Submarine Zone* (Col., 1941), *Two Yanks in Trinidad* (Col., 1942), *Broadway* (Univ., 1942), *Flight Lieutenant* (Col., 1942), *The Navy Comes Through* (RKO, 1942), *Bombardier* (RKO, 1943), *The Iron Major* (RKO, 1943), *His Butler's Sister* (Univ., 1943), *Secret Command* (Col., 1944), *Marine Raiders* (RKO, 1944), *Having Wonderful Crime* (RKO, 1945), *Man Alive* (RKO, 1945), *Perilous Holiday* (Col., 1946), *Riffraff* (RKO, 1947), *Fighting Father Dunne* (RKO, 1948), *The Boy with Green Hair* (RKO, 1948), *A Dangerous Profession* (RKO, 1949), *Johnny One-Eye* (UA, 1950), *The Fireball* (20th, 1950), *The People Against O'Hara* (MGM, 1951), *Criminal Lawyer* (Col., 1951), *Okinawa* (Col., 1952), *Jubilee Trail* (Rep., 1954), *Ring of Fear* (WB, 1954), *Inside Detroit* (Col., 1955), *Kill Me Tomorrow* (Tudor Pictures, 1957), *The Last Hurrah* (Col., 1958), *Some Like It Hot* (UA, 1959), *Town Tamer* (Par., 1965), *The Phynx* (Cinema, 1970), *Billy Jack Goes to Washington* (Taylor-Laughlin, 1977), *The End* (UA, 1978), *Ragtime* (Par., 1981)

Laurence Olivier (1907–1989)

Born in Dorking, Surrey, Laurence Olivier was the son of a clergyman. He made his stage debut at 15 in the Shakespeare Festival Theatre while he was a student at St. Edward's School. After his schooling he joined the Birmingham Repertory for two years. He then appeared in a number of plays in London's West End and did some film work. Olivier went to New York and while appearing with Noël Coward in *Private Lives* he was signed by RKO. There he played opposite Lili Damita, Elissa Landi and Ann Harding. He returned to England, signed a movie contract with Alexander Korda and made films opposite Gloria Swanson, Gertrude Lawrence, Merle Oberon, Elisabeth Bergner and Vivien Leigh. While making films, he joined the Old Vic and appeared to critical acclaim in many Shakespearean plays. He returned to the American screen in Samuel Goldwyn's *Wuthering Heights* and was on the New York stage opposite Katherine Cornell in *No Time for Comedy*. Next he appeared in the film *Rebecca* opposite Joan Fontaine under the masterful direction of Alfred Hitchcock. He starred in MGM's *Pride and Prejudice* opposite Greer Garson. His first marriage to Jill Esmond ended in divorce. His next marriage to Vivien Leigh endured for 20 years. In 1941 he joined the Fleet Air arm of the Royal Navy and served until his discharge in 1944. He returned to Old Vic as co-director of that venerable institution and continued making such distinguished films as *Henry V* which won

Top: Wuthering Heights is a mysterious house where Heathcliff (Laurence Olivier) and Cathy (Merle Oberon) are the tragic lovers (United Artists, 1939). *Bottom: Hamlet* (Laurence Olivier) swears revenge for his father's murder in Shakespeare's tragedy. Eileen Herlie, Terence Morgan and Basil Sydney suffer because of his vengeance (Rank, 1948).

Laurence Olivier is the manager of a swank Chicago restaurant. He falls in love with *Carrie* (Jennifer Jones) and steals ten thousand dollars from his employer so that they can go off together (Paramount, 1952).

worldwide acclaim and numerous awards. In 1963 he was knighted and appointed artistic director of the National Theatre. Taking his seat in the House of Lords, he was the only actor to obtain this honor. He continued with his stage roles, films and television, won Oscars, was honored by the Film Society of Lincoln Center, and was guest of honor at the White House in Washington. His wife since 1961, Joan Plowright, was at his side when he died at the age of 82.

Feature Films

The Temporary Widow (UFA, 1930), *Too Many Crooks* (Fox, 1930), *The Yellow Ticket* (Fox, 1931), *Friends and Lovers* (RKO, 1931), *Potiphar's Wife* (Elvey, 1931), *Westward Passage* (RKO, 1932), *The Perfect Understanding* (UA, 1933), *No Funny Business* (Principal, 1934), *Moscow Nights* (Lenauer, 1935), *As You Like It* (20th, 1936), *Fire Over England* (UA, 1937), *The Divorce of Lady X* (UA, 1938), *Conquest of the Air* (Shaw, 1938), *Twenty-One Days* (London, 1938), *Wuthering Heights* (UA, 1939), *Q Planes* (Col., 1939), *Rebecca* (UA, 1940), *Pride and Prejudice* (MGM, 1940), *The Invaders* (*The 49th Parallel*) (Ortus, 1941), *That Hamilton Woman* (*Lady Hamilton*) (Korda, 1941), *The Demi-Paradise* (Two Cities, 1942), *Henry V* (UA, 1946), *Hamlet* (Rank, 1948), *Carrie* (Par., 1952), *The Magic Box* (Rank, 1952), *The Beggar's Opera* (WB, 1953), *Richard III* (Lopert, 1953), *The Prince and the Showgirl* (WB, 1957), *The Devil's Disciple* (UA, 1959), *Spartacus* (Univ., 1960), *The Entertainer* (Continental Distributing, 1960), *Term of Trial* (WB, 1962), *Bunny Lake Is Missing* (Col., 1965), *Othello* (WB, 1965), *Khartoum* (UA, 1966), *Shoes of the Fisherman* (MGM, 1968), *Romeo and Juliet* (voice only; Par., 1968), *Oh! What a Lovely War* (Par., 1968), *Battle of Britain* (UA, 1969), *Three Sisters* (AFT, 1970), *Nicholas and Alexandra* (Col., 1971), *Dance of Death* (Par., 1971), *Lady Caroline Lamb* (UA, 1971), *Sleuth* (20th, 1972), *The Seven-Percent Solution* (Univ., 1976), *Marathon Man* (Par., 1976), *A Bridge Too Far* (UA, 1976), *The Betsy* (AA, 1978), *The Boys from Brazil* (20th, 1978), *A Little Romance* (WB, 1979), *Dracula* (Univ., 1979), *Inchon* (MGM/UA, 1980), *The Jazz Singer* (Associated, 1980), *Clash of the Titans* (MGM, 1981), *The Bounty* (Orion, 1984), *Wild Geese II* (Univ., 1985), *Jigsaw Man* (United Films, 1985), *War Requiem* (ABF, 1989)

Paul Newman takes up with a fading motion picture actress (Geraldine Page) and takes her to his hometown where tragedy awaits him in *Sweet Bird of Youth* (MGM, 1962).

Geraldine Page (1924–1987)

Born the daughter of a physician in Kirksville, Missouri, Geraldine Page was educated in Chicago and first acted with a church group. She studied theater at Goodman school from 1942 to 1945 and did stock work at various theaters in the Midwest before moving to New York in 1950. While seeking acting jobs, she was a hat-check girl, factory worker and lingerie model. Her big break came in 1952 with the starring role in *Summer and Smoke* directed by Jose Quintero at the Circle-in-the-Square. In 1953 she appeared on Broadway in Vina Delmar's *Midsummer*, and during the run the producers placed Page's name in light above

the title of the play. For her role in the film *Hondo* opposite John Wayne, she received her first Oscar nomination. She returned to Broadway to appear opposite Louis Jourdan and James Dean in *The Immoralist* and Darren McGavin in *The Rainmaker*. Both were hits. She continued working in the theater in a revival of Eugene O'Neill's *Anna Christie, The Innkeepers* and opposite Eric Portman in *Separate Tables*. In 1959 she appeared opposite Paul Newman in *Sweet Bird of Youth* before going to Hollywood. She refused to sign a long-term contract and accepted only films of her own choosing. She returned to theater work and also

Geraldine Page

appeared on television, winning two Emmys. Now and then she did a film. Eight times she was nominated for an Oscar before winning one for *A Trip to*

Bountiful. She died of a heart attack at the age of 62.

Feature Films

Out of the Night (Moody Bible Institute, 1947), *Taxi* (20th, 1953), *Hondo* (WB, 1953), *Summer and Smoke* (Par., 1961), *Sweet Bird of Youth* (MGM, 1962), *Toys in the Attic* (UA, 1963), *Dear Heart* (WB, 1964), *You're a Big Boy Now* (7 Arts, 1966), *The Happiest Millionaire* (BV, 1967), *Monday's Child* (DuRoda Productions, 1968), *Whatever Happened to Aunt Alice?* (Cinerama, 1969), *The Beguiled* (Univ., 1971), *J.W. Coop* (Col., 1971), *Pete 'n' Tillie* (Univ., 1972), *The Day of the Locust* (Par., 1975), *Nasty Habits* (Brute, 1976), *Interiors* (UA, 1978), *Honky Tonk Freeway* (Univ., 1981), *I'm Dancing as Fast as I Can* (Par., 1982), *The Pope of Greenwich Village* (Orion, 1984), *White Nights* (Col., 1985), *The Trip to Bountiful* (Island, 1985)

Lilli Palmer (1914–1986)

Lilli Palmer, the daughter of a surgeon and an actress, was born in Posen, Germany. She studied at the Ilka Gruneng School of Acting in Berlin. At 18 she made her stage debut and then appeared in German repertory theater. She went to Paris for further theater work and then to London to appear in English films and stage productions. In 1943 she married Rex Harrison. They both came to Hollywood in 1945 with studio contracts. After making films, Palmer went on Broadway to appear opposite Jean-Pierre Aumont in *My*

Name Is Aquilon and Sir Cedric Hardwicke in George Bernard Shaw's *Caesar and Cleopatra*. Palmer and husband Harrison appeared together in such Broadway hits as *Bell, Book, and Candle*, *Venus Observed* and *Love of Four Colonels*. In 1948 she divorced Harrison. Later she married Carlos Thompson. She made films in Hollywood, France, Germany, Austria and Italy and also worked in television. She was the author of three bestsellers and a successful painter with a London exhibit of her paintings. She died of cancer at the age of 71.

Rex Harrison and Lilli Palmer star in the two-character film *The Four Poster* which tells of the ups and downs of a married couple over many years (Columbia, 1952).

English-Language Feature Films

Crime Unlimited (WB, 1934), *Bad Blood* (Gainsborough, 1935), *First Offense* (Gainsborough, 1935), *Secret Agent* (Gaumont-British, 1936), *Wolf's Clothing* (Gaumont-British, 1936), *The Great Barrier* (Gaumont-British, 1937), *Sunset in Vienna* (Wilcox, 1937), *Where There's a Will* (Gaumont-British, 1937), *Command Performance* (Grosvenor, 1937), *Crackerjack* (Gaumont-British, 1938), *Man with a Hundred Faces* (Gaumont-British, 1938), *A Girl Must Live* (Gainsborough, 1938), *Blind Folly* (Gainsborough, 1940), *Chamber of*

Charles Ruggles, Tab Hunter, Debbie Reynolds, Lilli Palmer, Fred Astaire and Gary Merrill in the screen adaptation of the hit Broadway comedy *The Pleasure of His Company* (Paramount, 1961).

Horrors (The Door with Seven Locks) (Monogram, 1940), *Thunder Rock* (Charter, 1942), *The Gentle Sex* (Two Cities, 1943), *English with Tears* (Two Cities, 1943), *Beware of Pity* (Two Cities, 1945), *Notorious Gentleman* (Univ., 1946), *Cloak and Dagger* (WB, 1946), *Body and Soul* (UA, 1947), *My Girl Tisa* (WB, 1948), *No Minor Vices* (MGM, 1948), *Her Man Gilbey* (Univ., 1949), *The Wicked City* (UA, 1951), *The Long, Dark Hall* (EL, 1951), *The Four Poster* (Col., 1952), *Main Street to Broadway* (MGM, 1953), *But Not for Me* (Par., 1959), *Conspiracy of Hearts* (Par., 1960), *Conspiracy of Hearts* (Par., 1960), *The Pleasure of His Company* (Par., 1961), *The Counterfeit Traitor* (Par., 1962), *The Miracle of the White Stallions* (BV, 1963), *Torpedo Bay* (AIP, 1964), *Operation Crossbow* (MGM, 1965), *The Amorous Adventures of Moll Flanders* (Par., 1965), *Jack of Diamonds* (MGM, 1967), *Sebastian* (Par., 1968), *Nobody Runs Forever* (Rank, 1968), *The High Commissioner* (American Broadcasting Co., 1968), *Oedipus* (Univ., 1968), *Hard Contract* (20th, 1969), *The House That Screamed* (AIP, 1970), *Murders in the Rue Morgue* (AIP, 1971), *Night Hair Child* (BIP, 1971), *The Boys from Brazil* (20th, 1978)

Three songsmiths (Elisha Cook, Jr., Jack Oakie and John Payne) try to interest singer Alice Faye in one of their songs in *Tin Pan Alley* (20th Century–Fox, 1940).

John Payne (1912–1989)

John Payne was born in Roanoke, Virginia, and attended Roanoke College. He studied acting and singing at Columbia University in New York. Professionally he began as a band vocalist and then acted in stock before going to Hollywood to appear in films. Payne first signed with Warner Brothers and then moved to 20th Century–Fox where he appeared opposite Betty Grable, Alice Faye, Sonja Henie and June Haver in musicals and opposite Maureen O'Hara, Anne Baxter, Linda Darnell and Claudette Colbert in straight roles. After his contract expired, he starred in westerns and outdoor films. For television he produced and starred in the series *Restless Gun* which ran from

1959 until 1963. In 1973 he starred with Alice Faye in a revival of the stage musical *Good News* which played to packed houses. Payne's first two marriages to Anne Shirley and Gloria DeHaven ended in divorce. He then married Alexandria Curtis in 1953 and that union lasted until his death of heart failure in 1989.

Feature Films

Dodsworth (UA, 1936), *Hats Off* (GN, 1936), *Fair Warning* (20th, 1937), *Love on Toast* (Par., 1938), *College Swing* (Par., 1938), *Garden of the Moon* (WB, 1938), *Bad Lands* (RKO, 1939), *Wings of the*

June Haver has faith that a missing-in-action sailor (John Payne) is still alive. She is reunited with him in *Wake Up and Dream* (20th Century–Fox, 1946).

Navy (WB, 1939), *Indianapolis Speedway* (WB, 1939), *Kid Knightingale* (WB, 1939), *Stardust* (20th, 1940), *Maryland* (20th, 1940), *The Great Profile* (20th, 1940), *King of the Lumberjacks* (WB, 1940), *Tear Gas Squad* (WB, 1940), *The*

Great American Broadcast (20th, 1941), *Week-End in Havana* (20th, 1941), *Remember the Day* (20th, 1941), *Sun Valley Serenade* (20th, 1941), *Iceland* (20th, 1942), *Springtime in the Rockies* (20th, 1942), *To the Shores of Tripoli* (20th,

1942), *Hello, Frisco, Hello* (20th, 1943), *The Dolly Sisters* (20th, 1945), *Sentimental Journey* (20th, 1946), *The Razor's Edge* (20th, 1946), *Wake Up and Dream* (20th, 1946), *Miracle on 34th Street* (20th, 1947), *Larceny* (Univ., 1948), *The Saxon Charm* (Univ., 1948), *El Paso* (Par., 1949), *The Crooked Way* (UA, 1949), *Captain China* (Par., 1949), *The Eagle and the Hawk* (Par., 1950), *Tripoli* (Par., 1950), *Passage West* (Par., 1951), *Crosswinds* (Par., 1951), *Caribbean* (Par., 1952), *The Blazing Forest* (Par., 1952), *Kansas City Confidential* (UA, 1952), *Raiders of the Seven Seas* (UA, 1953), *The Vanquished* (Par., 1953), *99 River Street* (UA, 1953), *Rails into Laramie* (Univ., 1954), *Silver Lode* (RKO, 1954), *Santa Fe Passage* (Rep., 1955), *Hell's Island* (Par., 1955), *The Road to Denver* (Rep., 1955), *Tennessee's Partner* (RKO, 1955), *Slightly Scarlet* (RKO, 1956), *Rebel in Town* (UA, 1956), *Hold Back the Night* (AA, 1956), *The Boss* (UA, 1956), *Bailout at 43,000* (UA, 1957), *Hidden Fear* (UA, 1957), *Gift of the Nile* (PRO, 1968), *They Ran for Their Lives* (Color Vision, 1968), *The Savage Wild* (AIP, 1970)

Walter Pidgeon (1897–1984)

Walter Pidgeon was born in East St. John, New Brunswick, Canada, and attended the University of New Brunswick before enlisting in the Canadian army in World War I. A serious injury received during his training hospitalized him for 17 months and he was discharged. In 1922 he went to Boston where he worked in a bank and married his childhood sweetheart. She died two years later in childbirth. Pidgeon studied voice at the New England Conservatory of Music and then joined E.E. Clive's Copley Players, making his stage debut in Boston. Under the name of Walter Verne, he toured as a baritone with Elsie Janis in the U.S. and England. He played in numerous silent films and with the advent of sound he appeared in musicals. In 1930 he married Edna Aikens and the union lasted the rest of his life. Pidgeon appeared on Broadway opposite Tallulah Bankhead before signing an MGM contract. He was cast only in routine films until he was loaned to other studios where he appeared in top productions. His performance in John Ford's Oscar-winning *How Green Was My Valley* made him a star. He returned to MGM and co-starred with Greer Garson in many films. In 1943 Pidgeon became a U.S. citizen and toured for the U.S.O. He became a member of the SAG board in 1941 and served as its president from 1952 until 1956. He returned to Broadway for a successful run in *The Happiest Millionaire* and next appeared with Jackie Gleason in the hit musical *Take Me Along*. He continued his stage and film career and also made television appearances. At 87 he died of complications from a series of strokes.

Sound Feature Films

Melody of Love (Univ., 1928), *Her Private Life* (WB, 1929), *A Most Immoral Lady* (WB, 1929), *Bride of the Regiment* (WB, 1930), *Viennese Nights* (WB, 1930), *Sweet Little Bellaire* (WB, 1930), *Going Wild* (WB, 1931), *The Gorilla* (WB, 1931), *Kiss Me Again* (WB, 1931), *Hot Heiress* (WB, 1931), *Rockabye* (RKO, 1932), *The Kiss*

Top: Greer Garson and Walter Pidgeon were teamed again in the sequel *The Miniver Story* with Brian Roper (center) (MGM, 1950). *Bottom:* Walter Pidgeon, a studio chief, pours a champagne toast to the seated guests (Sammy White, Paul Stewart, Lana Turner and Gilbert Roland) as other guests look on in *The Bad and the Beautiful* (MGM, 1952).

Before the Mirror (Univ., 1933), *Journal of a Crime* (WB, 1934), *Fatal Lady* (Par., 1936), *Big Brown Eyes* (Par., 1936), *Girl Overboard* (Univ., 1937), *She's Dangerous* (Univ., 1937), *As Good as Married* (Univ., 1937), *Saratoga* (MGM, 1937), *My Dear Miss Aldrich* (MGM, 1937), *A Girl with Ideas* (Univ., 1937), *Man-Proof* (MGM, 1938), *The Girl of the Golden West* (MGM, 1938), *The Shopworn Angel* (MGM, 1938), *Listen Darling* (MGM, 1938), *Too Hot to Handle* (MGM, 1938), *Society Lawyer* (MGM, 1939), *6,000 Enemies* (MGM, 1939), *Stronger Than Desire* (MGM, 1939), *Nick Carter, Master Detective* (MGM, 1939), *It's a Date* (Univ., 1940), *Dark Command* (Rep., 1940), *The House Across the Bay* (UA, 1940), *Sky Murder* (MGM, 1940), *Flight Command* (MGM, 1940), *Man Hunt* (20th, 1941), *How Green Was My Valley* (20th, 1941), *Blossoms in the Dust* (MGM, 1941), *Design for Scandal* (MGM, 1941), *Mrs. Miniver* (MGM, 1942), *White Cargo* (MGM, 1942), *Madame Curie* (MGM, 1943), *The Youngest Profession* (MGM, 1943), *Mrs. Parkington* (MGM, 1944), *Week-end at the Waldorf* (MGM, 1945), *Holiday in Mexico* (MGM, 1946), *The Secret Heart* (MGM, 1946), *If Winter Comes* (MGM, 1947), *Cass Timberlane* (MGM, 1947)*, *Julia Misbehaves* (MGM, 1948), *Command Decision* (MGM, 1948), *The Red Danube* (MGM, 1949), *That Forsyte Woman* (MGM, 1949), *The Miniver Story* (MGM, 1950), *Soldiers Three* (MGM, 1951), *Calling Bulldog Drummond* (MGM, 1951), *The Unknown Man* (MGM, 1951), *The Sellout* (MGM, 1951), *Million Dollar Mermaid* (MGM, 1952), *The Bad and the Beautiful* (MGM, 1952), *Scandal at Scourie* (MGM, 1953), *Dream Wife* (MGM, 1953), *Executive Suite* (MGM, 1954), *Men of the Fighting Lady* (MGM, 1954), *The Last Time I Saw Paris* (MGM, 1954), *Keep in My Heart* (MGM, 1954), *Hit the Deck* (MGM, 1955), *Forbidden Planet* (MGM, 1956), *The Rack* (MGM, 1956), *Voyage to the Bottom of the Sea* (20th, 1961), *Big Red* (BV, 1962), *Advise and Consent* (Col., 1962), *Warning Shot* (Par., 1967), *Two Colonels* (Comet, 1967), *Funny Girl* (Col., 1968), *Rascal* (BV, 1969), *Skyjacked* (MGM, 1972), *Harry in Your Pocket* (UA, 1973), *Neptune Factor* (Canadian, 1973), *Two Minute Warning* (Univ., 1976), *Won Ton Ton, the Dog Who Saved Hollywood* (Par., 1976), *Sextette* (Crown International, 1978)

*Unbilled guest appearance

Robert Preston (1918–1987)

Born in Newton Highlands, Massachusetts, Preston moved to California as a child. After high school he appeared in many plays before being signed to a movie contract with Paramount at the age of 19. While under contract he first appeared in routine films, then notable hits such as *Union Pacific* and *Beau Geste* before World War II service in the Army Air Force. After the war Preston finished out his contract with Paramount. Then he freelanced, appearing opposite Joan Bennett, Susan Hayward and Barbara Stanwyck in hit films. He came to Broadway as a replacement for Jose Ferrer, in *Twentieth Century*. He was so successful that he appeared in many more hit plays before he accepted the lead in *The Music Man*. He was awarded a Tony for his performance and stayed

As a con man, Robert Preston tells the citizens of River City, Iowa, that he is a music teacher and sells band instruments to them for their children. He is reformed by the love of the local librarian in *The Music Man* (Warner Bros., 1962).

with the musical on Broadway for over two years, giving 1,375 performances.

Other Broadway productions followed. Preston won his second Tony award for his role in *I Do, I Do*. When *The Music Man* was made into a film, he recreated the lead role. After many screen roles, he returned to the theater and did a television series, *The Chisholms*, for CBS. (It was first a miniseries in 1979; the following year it became a regular series.) Other television work followed. Preston appeared in the TV movies *Finnegan Begins Again* opposite Mary Tyler Moore and *Rehearsal for Murder* opposite Lynn Redgrave. He married actress Catharine Craig in 1940. Their marriage lasted until his death of lung cancer in 1987.

Feature Films

King of Alcatraz (Par., 1937), *Illegal Traffic* (Par., 1938), *Disbarred* (Par., 1939), *Union Pacific* (Par., 1939), *Beau Geste* (Par., 1939) *Typhoon* (Par., 1940), *North West Mounted Police* (Par., 1940), *Moon Over Burma* (Par., 1940), *The Lady from Cheyenne* (Univ., 1941), *Parachute Battalion* (RKO, 1941), *New York Town* (Par., 1941), *Night of January 16th* (Par., 1941), *Star Spangled Rhythm* (Par., 1942), *Reap the Wild Wind* (Par., 1942), *This Gun for Hire* (Par., 1942), *Wake Island* (Par., 1942), *Pacific Blackout* (Par., 1942), *Night Plane from Chungking* (Par., 1943), *Wild Harvest* (Par., 1947), *The Macomber Affair* (UA, 1947), *Variety Girl* (Par., 1947), *Whispering Smith* (Par., 1948), *The Big City* (MGM, 1948), *Blood on the Moon* (RKO, 1948), *Tulsa* (EL, 1949), *The*

Civil War comrades Robert Preston and Joel McCrea are on opposite sides during the building of the *Union Pacific* railroad (Paramount, 1939).

Lady Gambles (Univ., 1949), *The Sundowners* (EL, 1950), *My Outlaw Brother* (EL, 1951), *When I Grow Up* (EL, 1951), *Best of the Bad Men* (RKO, 1951), *Cloudburst* (UA, 1952), *Face to Face* (RKO, 1952), *The Last Frontier* (Col., 1955), *The Dark at the Top of the Stairs* (WB, 1960), *The Music Man* (WB, 1962), *How the West Was Won* (MGM, 1962), *Island of Love* (WB, 1963), *All the Way Home* (Par., 1963), *Child's Play* (Par., 1972), *Junior Bonner* (Cinerama, 1972), *Mame* (WB, 1974), *SemiTough* (UA, 1977), *S.O.B.* (Par., 1981), *Victor/Victoria* (MGM/UA, 1982), *The Last Starfighter* (Univ., 1984)

Vincent Price (1911–1993)

Price was born in St. Louis where his father was the president of a candy-manufacturing company. He attended private schools and as a teenager made the grand tour of Europe. At Yale and the University of London he earned degrees in art history. While in London he became interested in the theater, took up acting, and scored as Prince Albert in *Victoria Regina*. He repeated the role

Vincent Price and Judith Anderson are prime suspects in the killing of *Laura*. Dana Andrews is the detective investigating her murder as Dorothy Adams (the maid) listens (20th Century–Fox, 1944).

opposite Helen Hayes on Broadway for 18 months and on tour in the U.S. He appeared opposite Elissa Landi in *The Lady Has a Heart* and Judith Evelyn in *Angel Street* on Broadway and also did summer stock. He made his film debut opposite Constance Bennett in the comedy *Service Deluxe*. In subsequent films he frequently played historical figures and supporting roles in distinguished vehicles. At Warners he played the lead in the three-dimensional thriller *House of Wax* as a cruelly betrayed wax sculptor who becomes demented after being scarred in a fire. That film helped begin a major revival of horror movies in which he played a succession of macabre characters.

Price was a noted art connoisseur and collector. He lectured on art at colleges and clubs and with his expertise in art he tied for top prize on *The $64,000 Challenge* TV quiz show in 1956. For many years he wrote a syndicated newspaper column on art and authored several popular books on fine art. He was also an accomplished chef and co-wrote some best-selling cookbooks. He appeared on more than 2,000 television shows.

Price's third wife, actress Carol Brown, whom he married in 1974, died in 1991. He was previously married to actress Edith Barrett from 1938 to 1948 and to designer Mary Grant from 1949 to 1973. He died of lung cancer in Thousand Oaks, California, at the age of 82.

Vincent Price plays a Dutchman who lives on a huge feudal estate in New York's Hudson Valley in 1840. Gene Tierney is cast as his second wife in *Dragonwyck*, based on a novel by Anya Seton (20th Century–Fox, 1946).

English-Language Feature Films

Service Deluxe (Univ., 1938), *The Private Lives of Elizabeth and Essex* (WB, 1939), *Tower of London* (Univ., 1939), *Green Hell* (Univ., 1940), *The House of the Seven Gables* (Univ., 1940), *The Invisible Man Returns* (Univ., 1940), *Brigham Young* (20th, 1940), *Hudson's Bay* (20th, 1940), *The Song of Bernadette* (20th, 1943), *The Eve of St. Mark* (20th, 1944), *Wilson* (20th, 1944), *Laura* (20th, 1944), *The Keys of the Kingdom* (20th, 1944), *Leave Her to Heaven* (20th, 1945), *A Royal Scandal* (20th, 1945), *Dragonwyck* (20th, 1946), *Shock* (20th, 1946), *The Long Night* (RKO, 1947), *Moss Rose* (20th, 1947), *The Web* (Univ., 1947), *Up in Central Park* (Univ., 1948), *Abbott and Costello Meet Frankenstein* (voice only; Univ., 1948), *The Three Musketeers* (MGM, 1948), *Rogues' Regiment* (Univ., 1948), *Bagdad* (Univ., 1949), *The Bribe* (MGM, 1949), *The Baron of Arizona* (Lip., 1950), *Champagne for Caesar* (UA, 1950), *Curtain Call at Cactus Creek* (Univ., 1950), *His Kind of Woman* (RKO, 1951), *Adventures of Captain Fabian* (Rep., 1951), *The Las Vegas Story* (RKO, 1952), *House of Wax* (WB, 1953), *Cassanova's Big Night* (Par., 1954), *Dangerous Mission* (RKO, 1954), *The Mad Magician* (Col., 1954), *Son of Sinbad* (RKO, 1955), *Serenade* (WB, 1956), *While the City Sleeps* (RKO, 1956), *The Ten Commandments* (Par., 1956), *The Story of Mankind* (WB, 1957), *The Fly* (20th, 1958), *House on Haunted Hill* (AA, 1958), *Return of the Fly* (20th, 1959), *The Bat*

(AA, 1959), *The Big Circus* (AA, 1959), *The Tingler* (Col., 1959), *House of Usher* (AIP, 1960), *Master of the World* (AIP, 1961), *Pit and the Pendulum* (AIP, 1961), *Tales of Terror* (AIP, 1962), *Convicts 4* (AA, 1962), *Confessions of an Opium Eater* (AA, 1962), *Tower of London* (UA, 1962), *The Raven* (AIP, 1963), *The Haunted Palace* (AIP, 1963), *Twice-Told Tales* (AIP, 1963), *The Comedy of Terrors* (AIP, 1963), *The Masque of the Red Death* (AIP, 1964), *The Last Man on Earth* (AIP, 1964), *The Tomb of Ligeia* (AIP, 1965), *War-Gods of the Deep* (AIP, 1965), *Taboos of the World* (narrator; AIP, 1965), *Dr. Goldfoot and the Bikini Machine* (AIP, 1965), *Dr. Goldfoot and the Girl Bombs* (AIP, 1966), *House of a Thousand Dolls* (AIP, 1968), *Conqueror Worm* (AIP, 1968), *More Dead Than Alive* (UA, 1968), *The Oblong Box* (AIP, 1969), *The Trouble with Girls* (MGM, 1969), *Spirits of the Dead* (voice only; AIP, 1969), *Cry of the Banshee* (AIP, 1970), *Scream and Scream Again* (AIP, 1970), *The Abominable Dr. Phibes* (AIP, 1971), *Dr. Phibes Rises Again* (AIP, 1972), *Theater of Blood* (UA, 1973), *Journey Into Feat* (Sterling Gold, 1976), *It's Not the Size That Counts* (Box/Thomes, 1970), *Scavenger Hunt* (20th, 1979), *The Monster Club* (Independent, 1981), *House of the Long Shadows* (Cannon, 1984), *Bloodbath at the House of Death* (Goldfarb Distributors, 1984), *The Great Mouse Detective* (voice only; BV, 1986), *Escapes* (Visual, 1987), *The Offspring* (Conquest, 1987), *The Whales of August* (Alive, 1987), *Dead Heat* (New World, 1988), *Edward Scissorhands* (20th, 1990), *Backtrack* (Vestron, 1993), *Arabian Knight* (voice only; Miramax, 1995)

George Raft (1903–1980)

George Raft was born in New York City and grew up in the area known as Hell's Kitchen. As a youth he did some boxing and earned a living as a dance hall gigolo. He became the dance partner of Elsie Pilcer, dancing in clubs in New York and London. Then he appeared as a dancer in Broadway musicals. Texas Guinan got him cast in her film *Queen of the Night Clubs* which began his Hollywood career. Raft was under contract to Paramount from 1932 to 1939. Then he moved to Warner Brothers where he stayed until 1943. He was dissatisfied with his film roles and bought his contract out to become a freelance player. He became a host of gambling clubs in London and Havana. His life story was filmed with Ray Danton playing Raft. He died penniless at the age of 77.

Feature Films

Queen of the Night Clubs (WB, 1929), *Quick Millions* (Fox, 1931), *Hush Money* (Fox, 1931), *Palmy Days* (UA, 1931), *Taxi* (WB, 1932), *Scarface* (UA, 1932), *Dancers in the Dark* (Par., 1932), *Madame Racketeer* (Par., 1932), *Night After Night* (Par., 1932), *If I Had a Million* (Par., 1932), *Undercover Man* (Par., 1932), *Pick-up* (Par., 1933), *The Midnight Club* (Par., 1933), *The Bowery* (UA, 1933), *Bolero* (Par., 1934), *All of Me* (Par., 1934), *The Trumpet Blows* (Par., 1934), *Limehouse Blues* (Par., 1934), *Rumba* (Par., 1935), *Stolen Harmony* (Par., 1935), *The Glass Key* (Par., 1935), *Every Night at Eight* (Par., 1935), *She Couldn't Take It* (Col., 1935), *It Had to Happen* (20th, 1936), *Souls at Sea* (Par., 1937), *You and Me*

Top: Mae West plays George Raft's uncouth old flame. She upsets high society in *Night After Night* (Paramount, 1932). *Bottom:* Humphrey Bogart and George Raft are brothers and independent truckers who pick up hitchhiker Ann Sheridan in *They Drive By Night* (Warner Bros., 1938).

Par., 1938), *The Lady's from Kentucky* (Par., 1939), *Each Dawn I Die* (WB, 1939), *I Stole a Million* (Univ., 1939), *They Drive By Night* (WB, 1940), *Invisible Stripes* (WB, 1940), *House Across the Bay* (UA, 1940), *Manpower* (WB, 1941), *Broadway* (Univ., 1942), *Stage Door Canteen* (UA, 1943), *Background to Danger* (WB, 1943), *Follow the Boys* (Univ., 1944), *Johnny Angel* (RKO, 1945), *Nocturne* (RKO, 1946), *Mr. Ace* (UA, 1946), *Whistle Stop* (UA, 1946), *Christmas Eve* (UA, 1947), *Intrigue* (UA, 1947), *Race Street* (RKO, 1948), *Johnny Allegro* (Col., 1949), *A Dangerous Profession* (RKO, 1949), *Outpost in Morocco* (UA, 1949), *Red Light* (UA, 1949), *Lucky Nick Cain* (20th, 1951), *Loan Shark* (Lip., 1952), *I'll Get You* (Lip., 1953), *Man from Cairo* (Lip., 1953), *Rogue Cop* (MGM, 1954), *Black Widow* (20th, 1954), *A Bullet for Joey* (UA, 1955), *Around the World in 80 Days* (UA, 1956), *Jet Over the Atlantic* (Intercontinent Releasing, 1959), *Some Like It Hot* (UA, 1959), *Ocean's 11* (WB, 1960)*, *The Ladies' Man* (Par., 1961), *For Those Who Think Young* (UA, 1964), *The Patsy* (Par., 1964)*, *Casino Royale* (Col., 1967)*, *The Silent Treatment* (Ralph Andrews, 1967), *Five Golden Dragons* (Blanc Films, 1967), *The Upper Hand* (*Du Rififi a Paname*) (1967), *Madigan's Millions* (1968)*, *Skidoo* (Par., 1968), *Deadhead Miles* (Par., 1971), *Hammersmith Is Out* (UA, 1972), *Sextette* (1978)*, *The Man with Bogart's Face* (1980)

*Unbilled guest appearance

Martha Raye (1916–1994)

Martha Raye's real name was Margie Yvonne Reed. She was born into a show business family in the charity ward of a hospital in Butte, Montana. Her mother and father were Irish immigrants whose song-and-dance routines took them to carnivals and vaudeville houses throughout the United States. At the age of three, Martha joined her parents' act. She was taught to read and write by her mother and from time to time she attended public schools in Montana, Chicago and New York. At 15 she was dancing and clowning in a children's act. She picked the name Martha Raye from a phone book and was billed by that name from then on. She became a member of the Benny Davis revue. Then she joined the Ben Blue company on the Loew's vaudeville circuit as well as being a member of the Will Morrisey act. Raye was a featured performer in *Earl Carroll's Sketchbook* and the Broadway musical comedy *Calling All Stars.* In Hollywood she was a guest performer at the Trocadero nightclub. Producer Norman Taurog saw her act and persuaded Paramount to sign her. In 1936 she was cast with Bing Crosby in the film *Rhythm on the Range.* In it her slapstick comedy and singing rendition of "Mr. Paganini" made her an overnight star. She appeared in many more Hollywood films. In 1940 she starred opposite Al Jolson on Broadway in *Hold onto Your Hats.* She did guest appearances on the Eddie Cantor and Bob Hope radio shows. During World War II Raye began entertaining American troops overseas. The film *Four Jills in a Jeep* was based on a U.S.O. tour of bases in England and Africa in the company of Kay Francis, Carole Landis and Mitzi Mayfair. She also entertained the troops in Korea and Vietnam. Her most notable

Two guests talk to Martha Raye, who has just married *Monsieur Verdoux* (Charlie Chaplin). He preys on rich widows by using lovelorn columns (United Artists, 1947).

movie role was in *Monsieur Verdoux* with Charlie Chaplin in 1947. She had her own variety series on television (*The Martha Raye Show* on NBC) and appeared on the nightclub circuit. In 1958 she returned to Broadway in a revival of *Annie Get Your Gun* followed by summer stock appearances. She took over from Ginger Rogers in *Hello, Dolly!* (1967) and also played the lead in *No, No Nanette*. Further television work in *McMillan* and *McMillan and Wife* followed. She received the Jean Hersholt Humanitarian Award from the Academy of Motion Picture Arts and Sciences in 1969 for her charity work. President Clinton awarded her the Presidential Medal of Freedom in 1993. She was married seven times and had a daughter, Melody, by husband Nick Condos. She was in poor health for many years and died at Cedars-Sinai Medical Center in Los Angeles at the age of 78.

Feature Films

Rhythm on the Range (Par., 1936), *The Big Broadcast of 1937* (Par., 1936), *College Holiday* (Par., 1936), *Hideaway Girl* (Par., 1937), *Waikiki Wedding* (Par., 1937), *Mountain Music* (Par., 1937), *Double or Nothing* (Par., 1937), *Artists and Models* (Par., 1937), *The Big Broadcast of 1938* (Par., 1938), *College Swing* (Par., 1938), *Give Me a Sailor* (Par., 1938), *Tropic*

Martha Raye and Jimmy Durante star in the musical *Jumbo*. They attempt to salvage a circus (MGM, 1962).

Holiday (Par., 1938), *Never Say Die* (Par., 1939), *$1,000 a Touchdown* (Par., 1939), *The Farmer's Daughter* (Par., 1940), *The Boys from Syracuse* (Univ., 1940), *Navy Blues* (WB, 1941), *Keep 'Em Flying* (Univ., 1941), *Hellzapoppin* (Univ., 1941), *Four Jills in a Jeep* (20th, 1944), *Pin-Up Girl* (20th, 1944), *Monsieur Verdoux* (UA, 1947), *Billy Rose's Jumbo* (MGM, 1962), *The Phynx* (WB, 1970), *Pufnstuf* (Univ., 1970), *The Concorde: Airport '79* (Univ., 1979)

An Army officer is accused of killing a man who beat and raped his wife (Lee Remick). James Stewart is her husband's attorney in *Anatomy of a Murder* (Columbia, 1959).

Lee Remick (1935–1991)

Lee Remick was born in Quincy, Massachusetts, in 1935. Her father was a department store owner and her mother a stage actress. As a child she studied dancing and at the age of 16 began acting with a summer stock company in Cape Cod. While attending the fashionable Miss Hewitt's School in Boston and studying theater, Remick was encouraged to try out for a Broadway play entitled *Act Your Age*. Even though the play failed, she received good reviews, which

Lee Remick is the wife of Steven McQueen, a singer and composer on parole. He reverts to violence in *Baby, the Rain Must Fall* (Columbia, 1965).

led to a summer stock engagement with Rudy Vallee. She returned to New York to enroll at Barnard College. Then she toured with Lillian and Dorothy Gish in *The Chalk Garden*. Next she appeared on television in *Playhouse 90*, *Philco Playhouse*, and *Robert Montgomery Presents*. Elia Kazan cast her as the seductive cheerleader in the movie *A Face in the Crowd* opposite Andy Griffith. Her performance led to a seven-year contract with 20th Century–Fox. Many outstanding films followed and she was nominated for an Oscar for her performance in *Days of Wine and Roses* in 1962. Remick returned to Broadway in 1966 in the successful thriller *Wait Until Dark*. Next came the unsuccessful musical *Anyone Can Whistle* by Arthur Laurents and Stephen Sondheim. Her first marriage in 1957 was to television producer-director William Colleran, with whom she had a daughter, Kate, and a son, Matthew. They divorced in 1968. In 1970 she married William ("Kip") Gowans, an English producer and director, and went to live in England where she continued her career in films and television. Her greatest television triumph was in *Jennie* in which she played Winston Churchill's free-spirited, American-born mother. She died at her home in Los Angeles of cancer at the age of 55.

Feature Films

A Face in the Crowd (WB, 1957), *The Long, Hot Summer* (20th, 1958), *These Thousand Hills* (20th, 1959), *Anatomy of* a *Murder* (Col., 1959), *Wild River* (20th, 1960), *Sanctuary* (20th, 1961), *Experiment in Terror* (Col., 1962), *Days of Wine and Roses* (WB, 1962), *The Running Man* (Col., 1963), *The Wheeler Dealers* (MGM, 1963), *Baby, the Rain Must Fall* (Col., 1965), *The Hallelujah Trail* (UA, 1965), *No Way to Treat a Lady* (Par., 1968), *The Detective* (20th, 1968), *Hard Contract* (20th, 1969), *Loot* (Performing Arts, 1971), *Severed Head* (Col., 1971), *Sometimes a Great Notion* (Univ., 1971), *Delicate Balance* (American Film Theatre, 1973), *Touch Me Not* (Atlas, 1974), *Hennessy* (AIP, 1975), *The Omen* (20th, 1976), *Telefon* (MGM/UA, 1977), *Medusa Touch* (WB, 1978), *The Europeans* (Levitt-Pickman, 1979), *The Competition* (Col., 1980), *Tribute* (20th, 1980), *It's My Party* (UA, 1986)

Paul Robeson (1898–1976)

Paul Robeson was born in Princeton, New Jersey. His father was a former slave who became a minister and his mother was a teacher who died when he was nine. Robeson won a scholarship to Rutgers University and graduated with honors. Then he studied law at Columbia and was admitted to the New York bar. He was also an excellent athlete and an all–American football player. He married in 1921 and his wife Eslanda directed his career until her death in 1965. His first stage appearance (1920) was in *Simon the Cyrenian* at Harlem's YMCA. His performance led to an offer to appear in Eugene O'Neill's *Emperor Jones* with the Provincetown Players, but he turned it down and Charles S. Gilpin was cast. Robeson played the famed Cotton Club in Harlem where he first gained notice for his outstanding singing voice. Then he went to England to appear in the play *Taboo*. When he returned to New York, he was cast in Eugene O'Neill's *All God's Chillun Got Wings* and a revival of *Emperor Jones*. He did concert work and then went back to England to appear in *Emperor Jones*, *Porgy*, *Othello*, *The Hairy Ape*, *Stevedore*, *Black Boy*, *John Henry* and *Show Boat*. He also did some film work in England. In 1939 Robeson returned to Broadway in *John Henry*. Concerts, recordings and film appearances followed. In 1943 he starred in the Theatre Guild's record-breaking *Othello* with Jose Ferrer, Uta Hagen and Margaret Webster. Because of bad press starting in 1949, Robeson's political affiliations were questioned; when he won the Stalin Peace Prize in 1952, his passport was cancelled. He took his case to the Supreme Court and won. He went back to England to live and appeared with the Royal Shakespeare Company in *Othello* in 1958. Because of ill health in 1963 he returned to New York, where he lived in seclusion and did not even attend a Carnegie Hall concert in his honor (1973). He moved to Philadelphia where he died in 1976 of complications following a stroke. He was 77.

Feature Sound Films

Emperor Jones (UA, 1933), *Sanders of the River* (UA., 1935), *Show Boat* (Univ., 1936), *Big Fella* (Lion-Beaconsfield, 1937), *King Solomon's Mines* (Gaumont, 1937), *Dark Sands* (Buckingham, 1938), *Song of Freedom* (Hammer-Trio, 1938), *The Proud Valley* (Ealing-Capad, 1941), *Native Land* (narrator; Frontier, 1942)

Ethel Waters and Paul Robeson are two poor sharecroppers who find a coat stuffed with money. They take it to their minister (played by Eddie "Rochester" Anderson) in *Tales of Manhattan* (20th Century–Fox, 1942). ***Bottom:*** Paul Robeson as Brutus Jones, a former railroad porter who kills a man and becomes a fugitive in Haiti. There he keeps the natives in line for a brutal trader who holds them in virtual slavery in Eugene O'Neill's *Emperor Jones* (United Artists, 1933).

Ginger Rogers and Fred Astaire appeared as a team in nine black-and-white musicals from 1933 to 1939 at RKO. They were reunited at MGM in 1949 in the technicolor musical *The Barkleys of Broadway* (MGM, 1949).

Ginger Rogers (1911–1995)

Ginger Rogers was born Virginia Katherine in Independence, Missouri, and nicknamed "Ginger." Her mother, Lela Rogers, had theatrical ambitions for her daughter and propelled her into vaudeville early on. At 17 she was married briefly to Jack Pepper with whom she toured in an act called Ginger and Pepper. At 18 she appeared on Broadway in the hit musical *Top Speed*, which led to film work in New York with Paramount. Her next Broadway appearance was in George Gershwin's hit musical *Girl Crazy* with Ethel Merman. Rogers

signed a Hollywood contract which led to second-string work until Mervyn LeRoy cast her in *42nd Street*. In 1933 she signed with RKO. She and Fred Astaire were cast in secondary roles in *Flying Down to Rio*. It was her twentieth film and Astaire's second. The two dancers clicked together. In the next six years, RKO created eight profitable musicals starring Rogers and Astaire. Both became first-rank Hollywood stars and as a team were among the top ten money makers at the box office. On her own between musicals, she did mostly

Adolphe Menjou is a stage producer, Ginger Rogers is a sarcastic struggling entertainer and Katharine Hepburn (sitting) is a wealthy debutante seeking a theatrical career in *Stage Door* (RKO, 1937).

comedies. She was cast in the dramatic film *Kitty Foyle* based on Christopher Morley's novel and her performance earned her an Academy Award in 1940. Her film career continued to flourish

through 1965. She appeared on Broadway in 1951 in the ill-fated *Love and Let Love*. In stock she starred in *Bell, Book and Candle* and *The Unsinkable Molly Brown*. On Broadway she took over the star role

Ginger Rogers hosts showings of old movies on her television show. Clifton Webb is her former co-star who finds this embarrassing as he is now a university professor in *Dream Boat* (20th Century–Fox, 1952).

of Dolly Levi from Carol Channing in *Hello, Dolly!* and in London she starred in the musical *Mame.* She did television work and in the late '70s appeared in a highly successful nightclub act which played London and U.S. cities. Rogers was married and divorced five times. Her husbands were Jack Pepper, actor Lew Ayres, Marine private Jack Briggs, Paris attorney-turned-actor Jacques Bergerac and actor-director-producer William Marshall. In 1991 she wrote her autobiography *Ginger: My Story.* She died at her home in Rancho Mirage at the age of 83 of natural causes.

Feature Films

Young Man of Manhattan (Par., 1930), *Queen High* (Par., 1930), *The Sap from Syracuse* (Par., 1930), *Follow the Leader* (Par., 1930), *Honor Among Lovers* (Par., 1931), *The Tip-Off* (Pathé, 1931), *Suicide Fleet* (Pathé, 1931), *Carnival Boat* (RKO, 1932), *The Tenderfoot* (WB, 1932), *The Thirteenth Guest* (Mon., 1932), *Hat Check Girl* (Fox, 1932), *You Said a Mouthful* (WB, 1932), *42nd Street* (WB, 1933), *Broadway Bad* (Fox, 1933), *Gold Diggers of 1933* (WB, 1933), *Professional Sweet-heart* (RKO, 1933), *A Shriek in the Night* (Allied, 1933), *Don't Bet on Love* (Univ.,

1933), *Sitting Pretty* (Par., 1933), *Flying Down to Rio* (RKO, 1933), *Chance at Heaven* (RKO, 1933), *Rafter Romance* (RKO, 1934), *Finishing School* (RKO, 1934), *20 Million Sweethearts* (WB, 1934), *Change of Heart* (Fox, 1934), *Upper World* (WB, 1934), *The Gay Divorcee* (RKO, 1934), *Romance in Manhattan* (RKO, 1934), *Roberta* (RKO, 1935), *Star of Midnight* (RKO, 1935), *Top Hat* (RKO, 1935), *In Person* (RKO, 1935), *Follow the Fleet* (RKO, 1936), *Swing Time* (RKO, 1936), *Shall We Dance* (RKO, 1937), *Stage Door* (RKO, 1937), *Having Wonder Time* (RKO, 1938), *Vivacious Lady* (RKO, 1938), *Carefree* (RKO, 1938) *The Story of Vernon and Irene Castle* (RKO, 1939), *Bachelor Mother* (RKO, 1939), *Fifth Avenue Girl* (RKO, 1939), *Primrose Path* (RKO, 1940), *Lucky Partners* (RKO, 1940), *Kitty Foyle* (RKO, 1940), *Tom, Dick and Harry* (RKO, 1941), *Roxie Hart* (20th, 1942), *Tales of Manhattan* (20th, 1942), *The Major and the Minor* (Par., 1942), *Once Upon a Honeymoon* (RKO, 1942), *Tender Comrade* (RKO, 1943), *Lady in the Dark* (Par., 1944), *I'll Be Seeing You* (Selznick-UA, 1944), *Week-End at the Waldorf* (MGM, 1945), *Heartbeat* (RKO, 1946), *Magnificent Doll* (Univ., 1946), *It Had to Be You* (Col., 1947), *The Barkleys of Broadway* (MGM, 1949), *Perfect Strangers* (WB, 1950), *Storm Warning* (WB, 1950), *The Groom Wore Spurs* (Univ., 1951), *We're Not Married* (20th, 1952), *Monkey Business* (20th, 1952), *Dreamboat* (20th, 1952), *Forever Female* (Par., 1953), *Black Widow* (20th, 1954), *Twist of Fate* (UA, 1954), *Tight Spot* (Col., 1955), *The First Traveling Saleslady* (RKO, 1956), *Teenage Rebel* (20th, 1956), *Oh, Men! Oh, Women!* (20th, 1957), *Quick, Let's Get Married* (*The Confession*) (Golden Eagle, 1965), *Harlow* (Magna, 1965)

Robert Ryan (1909–1973)

Robert Ryan, the son of a construction firm executive, was born in Chicago. He studied at Chicago's Loyola Academy and then at Dartmouth, where he excelled in sports. For four years he held the college's heavyweight boxing championship. After graduating from college, Ryan worked at a variety of odd jobs including ranch hand, ship stoker, male model, salesman and debt collector. He trained for the stage at the Max Reinhardt Theatre Workshop in Hollywood. His performance in summer stock led to a Paramount contract. After making three films there, he went to New York and appeared opposite Tallulah Bankhead in Clifford Odets' *Clash By Night*. With this recognition he returned to Hollywood with an RKO contract and appeared in several films before serving with the Marines in World War II. Upon his return from the service, his film career flourished. He played opposite Joan Bennett in Jean Renoir's *The Woman on the Beach*, as an anti–Semitic murderer in Edward Dmytryk's *Crossfire* and in Fred Zinnemann's *Act of Violence* and Robert Wise's *The Set-Up*. After his RKO contract ended in 1952, he freelanced. His income from movies permitted him to return to the theater — Off Broadway in *Coriolanus* and *Long Day's Journey Into Night*— and as *Othello* in England. In 1960 he appeared opposite Katharine Hepburn in *Antony and Cleopatra* at the American Shakespeare

Joan Fontaine is the heartless Christabel in *Born to Be Bad* and Robert Ryan is the moody novelist who refuses to play the witch's game (RKO, 1950).

Festival in Stratford, Connecticut. Between films he appeared in the Irving Berlin musical *Mr. President* and a revival of *The Front Page*. He married Jessica Cadwalader in 1939 and they had three children — Timothy, Cheney and Lisa. She died of cancer in 1972. Ryan died of lymph cancer in 1973 in New York Hospital.

Barbara Stanwyck, a married woman, begins a secret affair with cynical Robert Ryan only to find tragedy in *Clash by Night* (RKO, 1952).

Feature Films

Golden Gloves (Par., 1940), *Queen of the Mob* (Par., 1940), *North West Mounted Police* (Par., 1940), *Bombardier* (RKO, 1943), *The Sky's the Limit* (RKO, 1943), *Behind the Rising Sun* (RKO, 1943), *Gangway for Tomorrow* (RKO, 1943), *The Iron Major* (RKO, 1943), *Tender Comrade* (RKO, 1943), *Marine Raiders* (RKO, 1944), *Trail Street* (RKO, 1947), *The Woman on the Beach* (RKO, 1947), *Crossfire* (RKO, 1947), *Berlin Express* (RKO, 1948), *Return of the Bad Men* (RKO, 1948), *Act of Violence* (MGM, 1948), *The Boy with Green Hair* (RKO, 1948), *Caught* (MGM, 1949), *The Set-Up* (RKO, 1949), *I Married a Communist* (RKO, 1949), *The Secret Fury* (RKO, 1950), *Born to Be Bad* (RKO, 1950), *Best of the Bad Men* (RKO, 1951), *Flying Leathernecks* (RKO, 1951), *The Racket* (RKO, 1951), *On Dangerous Ground* (RKO, 1951), *Clash by Night* (RKO, 1952), *Beware My Lovely* (RKO, 1952), *Horizons West* (Univ., 1952), *City Beneath the Sea* (Univ., 1953), *The Naked Spur* (MGM, 1953), *Inferno* (20th, 1953), *Alaska Seas* (Par., 1954), *About Mrs. Leslie* (Par., 1954), *Her Twelve Men* (MGM, 1954), *Bad Day at Black Rock* (MGM, 1954), *Escape to Burma* (RKO, 1955), *House of Bamboo* (20th, 1955), *The Tall Men* (20th, 1955), *The Proud Ones* (20th, 1956), *Back from Eternity* (RKO, 1956), *Men in War* (UA, 1957),

God's Little Acre (UA, 1958), *Lonelyhearts* (UA, 1958), *Day of the Outlaw* (UA, 1959), *Odds Against Tomorrow* (UA, 1959), *Ice Palace* (WB, 1960), *The Canadians* (20th, 1961), *King of Kings* (MGM, 1961), *Billy Budd* (AA, 1962), *The Longest Day* (20th, 1962), *The Inheritance* (narrator; Shochiku Films of America, 1964), *Battle of the Bulge* (WB, 1965), *Crooked Road* (7 Arts, 1965), *The Dirty Game* (AIP, 1965), *The Professionals* (Col., 1966), *The Busy Body* (Par., 1967), *Custer of the West* (Cinerama, 1967), *Hour of the Gun* (UA, 1967), *The Prodigal Gun* (Cinerama, 1968), *Anzio* (Col., 1968), *A Minute to Pray, a Second to Die* (Cinerama, 1968), *Captain Nemo and the Underwater City* (MGM, 1969), *The Wild Bunch* (WB, 1969), *Lawman* (UA, 1971), *The Love Machine* (Col., 1971), *And Hope to Die* (20th, 1972), *The Iceman Cometh* (American Film Theater, 1973), *The Lolly-Madonna XXX* (MGM, 1973), *The Outfit* (MGM, 1973), *Executive Action* (NGP, 1973)

George Sanders (1906–1972)

Born in St. Petersburg, Russia, of British parents, Sanders' family fled back to England during the Russian Revolution. He was educated at Brighton College and Manchester Technical College and then went into the textile business. Then he went to South America and worked in the tobacco business. Upon his return to England, he began acting on the stage and after a short while in British films. In 1937 he went to Hollywood, where he was cast in *Lloyds of London*. His performance led to a 20th Century–Fox contract. RKO borrowed him for the lead in two detective series—*The Saint* and *The Falcon*. Always in demand, Sanders continued his film career and in 1950 he won an Oscar for his portrayal of the cynical drama critic in *All About Eve*. He did more movies and the television series *The George Sanders Mystery Theatre*. His wives were Susan Larsen, Zsa Zsa Gabor, Benita Hume and Magda Gabor. He committed suicide at 66 by taking an overdose of sleeping pills in Barcelona, Spain.

Feature Films

Strange Cargo (British & Dominion, 1936), *The Man Who Could Work Miracles* (UA, 1936), *Dishonor Bright* (British & Dominion, 1936), *Things to Come* (UA, 1936), *Lloyds of London* (20th, 1936), *Find the Lady* (20th, 1936), *Love Is News* (20th, 1937), *Slave Ship* (20th, 1937), *The Lady Escapes* (20th, 1937), *Lancer Spy* (20th, 1937), *International Settlement* (20th, 1938), *Four Men and a Prayer* (20th, 1938), *Mr. Motto's Last Warning* (20th, 1939), *The Saint Strikes Back* (RKO, 1939), *Confessions of a Nazi Spy* (WB, 1939), *The Saint in London* (RKO, 1939), *Allegheny Uprising* (RKO, 1939), *Nurse Edith Cavell* (RKO, 1939), *The Outsider* (Alliance, 1939), *Green Hell* (Univ., 1940), *Rebecca* (UA, 1940), *The Saint's Double Trouble* (RKO, 1940), *The House of the Seven Gables* (Univ., 1940), *The Saint Takes Over* (RKO, 1940), *So This Is London* (20th, 1940), *Foreign Correspondent* (UA, 1940), *Bitter Sweet* (MGM, 1940), *The Son of Monte Cristo* (UA, 1940), *Rage in Heaven* (MGM, 1941), *The Saint in Palm Springs* (RKO,

George Sanders

1941), *Man Hunt* (20th, 1941), *The Gay Falcon* (RKO, 1941), *A Date with the Falcon* (RKO, 1941), *Sundown* (UA, 1941), *Son of Fury* (20th, 1942), *The Falcon Takes Over* (TKO, 1942), *Her Cardboard Lover* (MGM, 1942), *Tales of Manhattan* (20th, 1942), *The Moon and Sixpence* (UA, 1942), *The Falcon's Brother* (RKO, 1942), *The Black Swan* (20th, 1942), *Quiet Please — Murder* (20th, 1942), *This Land Is Mine* (RKO, 1943), *They Came to Blow Up America* (20th, 1943), *Appointment in*

Robert Montgomery escapes from a mental hospital in France and returns to England where he plans the murder of his friend (George Sanders) because of his unfounded jealousy toward his wife (Ingrid Bergman) in *Rage in Heaven* (MGM, 1941).

Berlin (Col., 1943), *Paris After Dark* (20th, 1943), *Action in Arabia* (RKO, 1944), *The Lodger* (20th, 1944), *Summer Storm* (UA, 1944), *The Picture of Dorian Gray* (MGM, 1945), *Hangover Square* (20th, 1945), *The Strange Affair of Uncle Harry* (Univ., 1945), *A Scandal in Paris* (UA, 1946), *The Strange Woman* (UA, 1946), *The Private Affairs of Bel Ami* (UA, 1947), *The Ghost and Mrs. Muir* (20th, 1947), *Lured* (UA, 1947), *Forever Amber* (20th, 1947), *The Fan* (20th, 1949), *Samson and Delilah* (Par., 1949), *All About Eve* (20th, 1950), *I Can Get It for You Wholesale* (20th, 1951), *The Light Touch* (MGM, 1951), *Ivanhoe* (MGM, 1952), *Captain Blackjack* (Classic, 1952), *Assign-ment Paris* (Col., 1952), *Call Me Madam* (20th, 1953), *Witness to Murder* (UA, 1954), *King Richard and the Crusaders* (WB, 1954), *Moonfleet* (MGM, 1955), *The Scarlet Coat* (MGM, 1955), *Jupiter's Darling* (MGM, 1955), *The King's Thief* (MGM, 1955), *Never Say Goodbye* (Univ., 1956), *While the City Sleeps* (RKO, 1956), *That Certain Feeling* (Par., 1956), *Death of a Scoundrel* (RKO, 1956), *The Seventh Sin* (MGM, 1957), *The Whole Truth* (Col., 1958), *From the Earth to the Moon* (WB, 1958), *That Kind of Woman* (Par., 1959), *Solomon and Sheba* (UA, 1959), *A Touch of Larceny* (Par., 1960), *The Last Voyage* (MGM, 1960), *Bluebeard's Ten Honeymoons* (AA, 1960), *Village of the*

Damned (MGM, 1960), *Call Me Genius* (Continental Distributing, 1961), *Five Golden Hours* (Col., 1961), *Trouble in the Sky* (Univ., 1961), *Operation Snatch* (Continental Distributing, 1962), *In Search of the Castaways* (BV, 1962), *The Cracksman* (Associated British Pathe, 1963), *Cairo* (MGM, 1963), *Dark Purpose* (Univ., 1964), *A Shot in the Dark* (UA, 1964), *The Amorous Adventures of Moll Flanders* (Par., 1965), *Ecco* (narrator; Cresa Roma, 1965), *Trunk to Cairo* (AIP, 1966), *The Quiller Memorandum* (20th, 1966), *Warning Shot* (Par., 1967), *Good Times* (Col., 1967), *The Jungle Book* (voice only; BV, 1967), *King of Africa* (NTA, 1968), *Best House in London* (MGM, 1969), *Body Stealers* (AA, 1969), *Candy Man* (AA, 1969), *One Step to Hell* (BIP, 1969), *The Kremlin Letter* (20th, 1970), *Endless Night* (AA, 1971), *Doomwatch* (AA, 1972), *Psychomania* (Scotia International, 1972)

Simone Signoret (1921–1985)

Signoret was born Simone Kaminker in 1921 to French parents in Weisbaden, Germany, where her father, a soldier of a Jewish family, was a member of the French occupation army in Germany following World War I. When she was two years old, her parents moved to Paris where she was educated. When France signed an armistice with Nazi Germany in 1940, her father fled to Britain and joined the Free French Forces. Simone took her mother's name to escape being sent to a concentration camp and worked as a secretary before she became interested in a film career. During the Nazi occupation, she met some screenwriters and film directors and began to work in movies. She married film director Yves Allegret and continued her film career in France. In 1952 she achieved stardom when she played in Jacques Becker's *Casque d'Or*. After divorcing Allegret, she married singer-actor Yves Montand and continued her French film work. She gained international recognition when she appeared in the English film *Room at the Top*, for which she won an Oscar in 1959. On the Paris stage Signoret appeared in *The Crucible* and *The Little Foxes*. She played Lady Macbeth in a revival of the Royal Court Theatre in London, receiving rave notices in 1966. Between film work she wrote two volumes of memoirs and a novel. She died of cancer at her country home in Normandy at the age of 64.

Feature Films

The Living Corpse (Alliance-Juno, 1940), *Against the Wind* (GFD, 1948), *Dedee* (Discina International Films, 1949), *The Cheat* (Discina International Films, 1950), *Four Days' Leave* (Film Classics, 1950), *Casque d'Or* (Speva-Paris, 1951), *La Ronde* (Discina International Films, 1954), *Diabolique* (Vera Films, 1955), *The Adultress* (Times Film Corp., 1959), *Room at the Top* (Romulus, 1959), *Gina* (Dismage Prod., 1961), *Back Streets of Paris* (President, 1962), *Term of Trial* (WB, 1962), *The Day and the Hour* (MGM, 1963), *Naked Autumn* (United, 1963), *Love a la Carte* (Zebra, 1965), *Ship of Fools* (Col., 1965), *Is Paris Burning?* Par., 1966), *The Sleeping Car Murder* (Seven Arts, 1966), *The Deadly Affair*

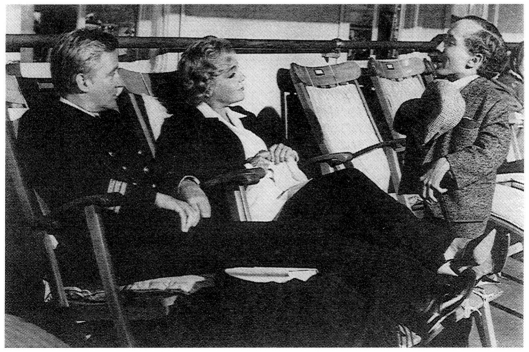

Top: As gratitude for his hospitality, house guest Simone Signoret offers her host, James Caan, a valuable hand-engraved dueling pistol in *Games* (Universal, 1967). *Bottom:* Oscar Werner is the ship's doctor. Simone Signoret and Michael Dunn are two of the doomed passengers in *Ship of Fools* (Columbia, 1965).

(Col., 1967), *Games* (Univ., 1967), *The Sea Gull* (WB, 1968), *The Confession* (Corona, 1970), *Mister Freedom* (Les Films, 1970), *The Cat* (Joseph Green Pictures, 1975), *Police Python 357* (Albania, 1976), *Death in the Garden* (Bauer International, 1977), *Madame Rose* (Lira Films, 1977), *The Adolescent* (Carthago, 1978), *The Case Against Ferro* (Specialty, 1980), *I Sent a Letter to My Love* (Atlantic, 1981), *The North Star* (Sara-Antenne, 1982)

Barbara Stanwyck (1907–1990)

Born Ruby Stevens in Brooklyn, New York, Barbara Stanwyck was orphaned at an early age and raised by her older sister. At age 15 she worked in a Brooklyn department store while training as a dancer. She appeared in the Ziegfeld Follies and other stage revues on Broadway, then made her screen debut in a minor role in a silent film. In 1926 Stanwyck played the lead in the play, *The Noose*. Her next Broadway appearance in *Burlesque* made her a star. She married comic Frank Fay in 1928 and when he went to Hollywood under contract to Warner Brothers, she went with him. With Fay's help she was signed by Columbia and Warner Brothers, making films on both lots. She returned to the theater with Fay in the musical *Tattle Tales*. In 1935 she divorced Fay and returned to Hollywood to resume her film career as a freelance actress, working at all the Hollywood studios. In 1939 she married actor Robert Taylor and their marriage lasted until 1952. Stanwyck was Oscar-nominated four times, and in 1982 she received an honorary Oscar. On TV she appeared in *The Barbara Stanwyck Theatre* and three television movies of ABC. For her starring role in TV's *The Big Valley*, which ran for four years, she won two Emmies. Her appearance in the 1983 miniseries *The Thorn Birds* won her another Emmy. She was also honored by the Film Society of Lincoln Center in 1982 and received the American Film Institute's Life Achievement Award in 1987. At the age of 82, she died of congestive heart disease in Santa Monica, California.

Feature Films

The Locked Door (UA, 1930), *Mexicali Rose* (Col., 1930), *Ladies of Leisure* (Col., 1930), *Ten Cents a Dance* (Col., 1931), *Illicit* (WB, 1931), *Miracle Woman* (Col., 1931), *Night Nurse* (WB, 1931), *Forbidden* (Col., 1932), *Shopworn* (Col., 1932), *So Big* (WB, 1932), *The Purchase Price* (WB, 1932), *The Bitter Tea of General Yen* (Col., 1933), *Ladies They Talk About* (WB, 1933), *Baby Face* (WB, 1933), *Ever in My Heart* (WB, 1933), *A Lost Lady* (WB, 1934), *Gambling Lady* (WB, 1934), *The Secret Bride* (WB, 1935), *The Woman in Red* (WB, 1935), *Red Salute* (UA, 1935), *Annie Oakley* (RKO, 1935), *A Message to Garcia* (20th, 1936), *The Bride Walks Out* (RKO, 1936), *His Brother's Wife* (MGM, 1936), *Banjo on My Knee* (20th, 1936), *The Plough and the Stars* (RKO, 1936), *Interns Can't Take Money* (Par., 1937), *This Is My Affair* (20th, 1937), *Stella Dallas* (UA, 1937), *Breakfast for Two* (RKO, 1937), *The Mad Miss Manton* (RKO, 1938), *Always Goodbye* (20th, 1938), *Union Pacific* (Par., 1939), *Golden Boy* (Col., 1939), *Remember the Night* (Par., 1940), *The Lady Eve* (Par.,

Barbara Stanwyck as Dixie Daisy, the burlesque star in *Lady of Burlesque,* based on Gypsy Rose Lee's mystery novel *The G-String Murders* (United Artists, 1943).

1941), *Meet John Doe* (WB, 1941), *You Belong to Me* (Col., 1941), *Ball of Fire* (RKO, 1941), *The Great Man's Lady* (Par., 1942), *The Gay Sisters* (WB, 1942), *Lady of Burlesque* (UA, 1943), *Flesh and Fantasy* (Univ., 1943), *Double Indemnity* (Par., 1944), *Hollywood Canteen* (WB, 1944), *Christmas in Connecticut* (WB,

Barbara Stanwyck as a newspaper columnist and Clark Gable as a race car driver clash and make up in *To Please a Lady* (MGM, 1950).

1945), *My Reputation* (WB, 1946), *The Bride Wore Boots* (Par., 1946), *The Strange Love of Martha Ivers* (Par., 1946), *California* (Par., 1946), *Variety Girls* (Par., 1947), *The Other Love* (UA, 1947), *The Two Mrs. Carrolls* (WB, 1947), *Cry Wolf* (WB, 1947), *B.F.'s Daughter* (MGM, 1948), *Sorry, Wrong Number* (Par., 1948), *The Lady Gambles* (Univ., 1949), *East Side, West Side* (MGM, 1949), *Thelma Jordon* (Par., 1949), *No Man of Her Own* (Par., 1950), *The Furies* (Par., 1950), *To Please a Lady* (MGM, 1950), *The Man with a Cloak* (MGM, 1951), *Clash By Night* (RKO, 1952), *Jeopardy* (MGM, 1953), *Titanic* (20th, 1953), *All I Desire* (Univ., 1953), *The Moonlighter* (WB, 1953), *Blowing Wild* (WB, 1953), *Executive Suite* (MGM, 1954), *Witness to Murder* (UA, 1954), *Cattle Queen of Montana* (RKO, 1954), *The Violent Men* (Col., 1955), *Escape to Burma* (RKO, 1955), *There's Always Tomorrow* (Univ., 1956), *The Maverick Queen* (Rep., 1956), *These Wilder Years* (MGM, 1956), *Crime of Passion* (UA, 1957), *Trooper Hook* (UA, 1957), *Forty Guns* (20th, 1957), *Walk on the Wild Side* (Col., 1962), *Roustabout* (Par., 1964), *The Night Walker* (Univ., 1965)

Jessica Tandy, a Southern matron, and her chauffeur, Morgan Freeman, stop for a break on their trip to Mobile in *Driving Miss Daisy* (Warner Bros., 1989).

Jessica Tandy (1909–1994)

Jessica Tandy was born in London and began studying acting at the Ben Greet Academy of Acting. She joined the Birmingham Repertory Company and made her London debut in 1929 in *The Rumour*, followed by the critically acclaimed *Children in Uniform*. In 1932 she made her film debut in *The Indiscretions of Eve*. Returning to the theater, Tandy received acclaim in Shakespearean roles opposite Laurence Olivier in *Twelfth Night* and *Henry V*. She played opposite John Gielgud in *Hamlet, King Lear* and *The Tempest*. In 1940 she divorced actor Jack Hawkins and came to the United States to pursue her acting career. She married Hume Cronyn in 1942 and they moved to California. He was placed under contract with MGM and she signed with 20th Century–Fox. She appeared in a few films (mostly loanouts to other studios). Under Cronyn's direction she appeared in Los Angeles at the Las Palmas Theatre in several one-act plays by Tennessee Williams. She won critical approval, which resulted in her being signed to play Blanche Dubois in the legendary play *A Streetcar Named Desire*, directed by Elia Kazan, with Marlon Brando, Kim Hunter and Karl Malden. The production ran two years on Broadway and then went on tour. For her performance Tandy received her first Tony in 1948. Next Cronyn directed her on Broadway in Samson Raphaelson's *Hilda Crane*. Then Tandy and Cronyn appeared together on the stage in *The Four Poster, The Honeys, A Day by the Sea, Triple Play, The Physicists* and Edward Albee's *A Delicate Balance*. She returned now and then to inferior film work. In 1978 she received her second Tony for the role opposite her husband in *The Gin Game* directed by Mike Nichols. A third Tony was won in 1983 for her performance in *Foxfire*. Director Ron Howard cast Tandy and Cronyn in the highly successful film *Cocoon* and its sequel. Her next film, *Driving Miss Daisy*, won her an Oscar. More successful film work followed. In 1944 both she and Cronyn were awarded the first Tony Lifetime Achievement Awards. She died at her Connecticut home of ovarian cancer at the age of 85.

Feature Films

Indiscretions of Eve (BIP, 1932), *Murder in the Family* (20th, 1938), *The Seventh Cross* (MGM, 1944), *The Valley of Decision* (MGM, 1945), *Dragonwyck* (20th, 1946), *The Green Years* (MGM, 1946), *Forever Amber* (20th, 1947), *A Woman's Vengeance* (Univ., 1947), *September Affair* (Par., 1950), *The Desert Fox* (20th, 1951), *The Light in the Forest* (BV, 1958), *Hemingway's Adventures of a Young Man* (20th, 1962), *The Birds* (Univ., 1963), *Butley* (American Film Theater, 1974), *Honky Tonk Freeway* (Univ., 1981), *Best Friends* (WB, 1982), *Still of the Night* (MGM/UA, 1982), *The World According to Garp* (WB, 1982), *Cocoon* (20th, 1985), **batteries not included* (Univ., 1987), *The House on Carroll Street* (Orion, 1988), *Cocoon: The Return* (20th, 1988), *Driving Miss Daisy* (WB, 1989), *Fried Green Tomatoes* (Univ., 1991), *Used People* (20th, 1992), *Camilla* (Miramax, 1994), *Nobody's Fool* (Par., 1994)

Hume Cronyn rants in *The World According to Garp* as his wife, Jessica Tandy, stands behind him (Warner Bros., 1982).

Gene Tierney (1920–1991)

Born in Brooklyn, the daughter of Howard S. Tierney, a successful Manhattan insurance broker, Gene Tierney attended private schools in Connecticut and Switzerland. Despite family disapproval she made her Broadway debut in 1939 in *Mrs. O'Brien Entertains*. Her appearance in the hit play *The Male Animal* brought her a contract with 20th Century–Fox. Under the guidance of Darryl F. Zanuck, Tierney became a star and was nominated for an Academy Award in 1945 for her role in *Leave Her to Heaven*. In 1941 she married designer Oleg Cassini and they had two daughters, Daria and Christina. Daria was born severely retarded because Tierney had contracted German measles during her pregnancy. Returning to the screen in 1944, she made the romantic suspense classic *Laura* opposite Dana Andrews, Vincent Price and Clifton Webb. Tierney was divorced from Cassini in 1952. In 1955 she suffered bouts with manic depression and became a patient at the Menninger Clinic, where she underwent

Top: Don Ameche as the dashing young swain who steals the heart of Gene Tierney from his cousin in Ernst Lubitsch's production *Heaven Can Wait* (20th Century–Fox, 1943). *Bottom:* In a courtroom surrounded by spectators Gene Tierney and Dana Andrews ask Canadian authorities for asylum. They have defected from the Soviets in *The Iron Curtain* (20th Century–Fox, 1948).

lengthy hospitalizations until 1959. In 1960 she married Houston oilman W. Howard Lee. She returned to Hollywood for three more films and appeared in the television movie *Daughter of the Mind* (1969). The following year she appeared on TV's *The FBI*. Her last television appearance was in *Scruples* (1980). Her husband died in 1982 and she retired, living in Houston until her death of emphysema at the age of 70.

Feature Films

The Return of Frank James (20th, 1940), *Hudson's Bay* (20th, 1940), *Tobacco Road* (20th, 1941), *Son of Fury* (20th, 1942), *Rings on Her Fingers* (20th, 1942), *Thunder Birds* (20th, 1942), *Thunder Birds* (20th, 1942), *China Girl* (20th, 1942), *Heaven Can Wait* (20th, 1943), *Laura* (20th, 1944), *A Bell for Adano* (20th, 1945), *Leave Her to Heaven* (20th, 1945), *Dragonwyck* (20th, 1946), *The Razor's Edge* (20th, 1946), *The Ghost and Mrs. Muir* (20th, 1947), *The Iron Curtain* (20th, 1948), *That Wonderful Urge* (20th, 1948), *Whirlpool* (20th, 1949), *Night and the City* (20th, 1950), *Where the Sidewalk Ends* (20th, 1950), *The Mating Season* (Par., 1951), *Close to My Heart* (WB, 1951), *Way of a Gaucho* (20th, 1952), *Plymouth Adventure* (MGM, 1952), *Never Let Me Go* (MGM, 1953), *Personal Affair* (UA, 1954), *Black Widow* (20th, 1954), *The Egyptian* (20th, 1954), *The Left Hand of God* (20th, 1955), *Advise and Consent* (Col., 1962), *Toys in the Attic* (UA, 1963), *The Pleasure Seekers* (20th, 1964)

Lana Turner (1920–1995)

Lana Turner was born in Wallace, Idaho. After her father's murder in 1930 over a gambling debt, she and her mother relocated to San Francisco. In 1936 they moved to the Los Angeles area where she attended Hollywood High School. Across the street from the school was the Top Hat Cafe where she was discovered at the soda fountain by publisher W.R. Wilkerson of *The Hollywood Reporter*. This led to representation by a talent agency run by Zeppo Marx and a movie contract. When Mervyn LeRoy cast her in *They Won't Forget* as a flirtatious student in a tight sweater, the studio publicity machine dubbed her the "sweater girl." Minor roles followed but when LeRoy went to MGM, she also went. Her first picture there was *Love Finds Andy Hardy* in 1938. MGM groomed her and by 1942 she was playing opposite top stars Robert Taylor, Clark Gable and Spencer Tracy. She became one of Hollywood's most popular romantic heroines and MGM's most publicized star. She remained at Metro for 18 years before leaving the studio in 1956 to work independently. In 1957 at 20th Century–Fox she made *Peyton Place* (based on Grace Metalious' best-seller), which led to an Academy Award nomination as Best Actress. In 1958 Turner had a quarrel with her male companion Johnny Stompanto. Cheryl, her daughter by husband Stephen Crane, fearing for her mother's life, stabbed Stompanto in the abdomen, killing him. She was exonerated of murder on grounds of justifiable homicide. Turner's film career continued and in 1976 she made her last movie. On television she appeared regularly on *The Survivors* and the successful *Falcon Crest*.

Clark Gable is an intelligence chief during World War II who recruits Lana Turner, a woman of dubious background, as a spy in *Betrayed* (MGM, 1954).

She also toured in several plays including *Forty Carats*. In 1982 she wrote her memoir *Lana: The Lady, the Legend, the Truth*. Turner was married to and divorced from bandleader Artie Shaw, actor Stephen Crane (they were married and divorced twice), sportsman "Bob" Topping, actor Lex Barker, rancher Fred May, businessman Robert P. Eaton and nightclub hypnotist Ronald Dante. She died at her home of throat cancer at the age of 75 with daughter Cheryl at her side.

Feature Films

A Star Is Born (UA, 1937), *They Won't Forget* (WB, 1937), *The Great Garrick*

John Garfield is a drifter who falls for Lana Turner, a bored housewife with murder on her mind in *The Postman Always Rings Twice* (MGM, 1946).

(WB, 1937), *The Adventures of Marco Polo* (UA, 1938), *Four's a Crowd* (WB, 1938) *Love Finds Andy Hardy* (MGM, 1938), *The Chaser* (MGM, 1938), *Rich Man, Poor Girl* (MGM, 1938), *Dramatic School* (MGM, 1938), *Calling Dr. Kildare* (MGM, 1939), *These Glamour Girls* (MGM, 1939), *Dancing Co-Ed* (MGM, 1939), *Two Girls on Broadway* (MGM, 1940), *We Who Are Young* (MGM, 1940), *Ziegfeld Girl* (MGM, 1941), *Dr. Jekyll and Mr. Hyde* (MGM, 1941), *Honky Tonk*

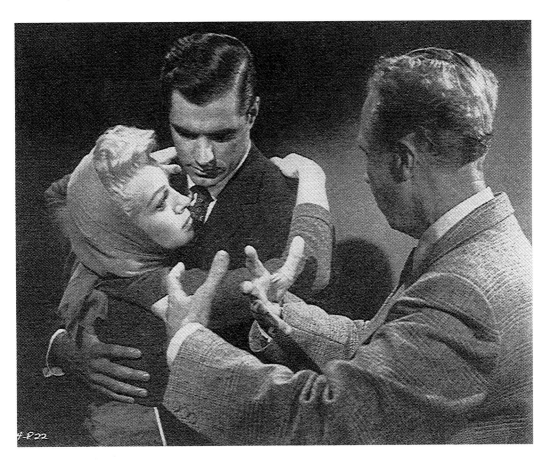

Lana Turner is a successful stage actress who is romantically involved with John Gavin. Here she gets pointers from a photographer (Lee Goodman) in *Imitation of Life* (Univ., 1959).

(MGM, 1941), *Johnny Eager* (MGM, 1941), *Somewhere I'll Find You* (MGM, 1942), *The Youngest Profession* (MGM, 1943), *Slightly Dangerous* (MGM, 1943), *DuBarry Was a Lady* (MGM, 1943)*, *Marriage Is a Private Affair* (MGM, 1944), *Keep Your Powder Dry* (MGM, 1945), *Week-End at the Waldorf* (MGM, 1945), *The Postman Always Rings Twice* (MGM, 1946), *Green Dolphin Street* (MGM, 1947), *Cass Timberlane* (MGM, 1947), *Homecoming* (MGM, 1948), *The Three Musketeers* (MGM, 1948), *A Life of Her Own* (MGM, 1950), *Mr. Imperium* (MGM, 1951), *The Merry Widow* (MGM, 1952), *The Bad and the Beautiful* (MGM, 1952), *Latin Lovers* (MGM, 1953), *Flame and the Flesh* (MGM, 1954), *Betrayed* (MGM, 1954), *The Prodigal* (MGM, 1955), *The Sea Chase* (WB, 1955), *The Rains of Ranchipur* (20th, 1955), *Diane* (MGM, 1955), *Peyton Place* (20th, 1957), *The Lady Takes a Flyer* (Univ., 1958), *Another Time, Another Place* (Par., 1958), *Imitation of Life* (Univ., 1959), *Portrait in Black* (Univ., 1960), *By Love Possessed* (UA, 1961), *Bachelor in Paradise* (MGM, 1961), *Who's Got the Action* (Par., 1962), *Love Has Many Faces* (Col., 1965), *Madame X* (Univ., 1966), *The Big Cube* (WB, 1969), *Persecution* (Fanfare, 1974), *Bittersweet Love* (AE, 1976)

*Unbilled guest appearance

Vera-Ellen and Cesar Romero are Latins whose marriage has been prearranged by their parents. They don't love each other and have different mates in mind in *Carnival in Costa Rica* (20th Century–Fox, 1947).

Vera-Ellen (1926–1981)

Born Vera-Ellen Westmayr Rohe in Cincinnati, she began dancing professionally at the age of 10. She appeared on the Major Bowes radio show, toured with Ted Lewis and his band, and was also a Rockette at the famed Radio City Music Hall. Billy Rose featured her at his Casa Manna Club. This led to other nightclub engagements before she made her Broadway debut in the Jerome Kern-Oscar Hammerstein musical *Very Warm for May*. She then appeared in two Richard Rodgers-Lorenz Hart hits—*Higher and Higher* and *By Jupiter*— and Cole Porter's *Panama Hattie*. While appearing in Rodgers and Hart's *A Connecticut Yankee*, Samuel Goldwyn signed her to a Hollywood contract and she acted in two Danny Kaye films on the Goldwyn lot. She worked next in musicals at 20th Century–Fox and MGM, appearing opposite Gene Kelly, Frank Sinatra, Fred Astaire and Bing Crosby. As well as being an accomplished singer and dancer, Vera-Ellen acted in comedy and drama with David Niven, Edward G. Robinson and the Marx Brothers. She made numerous appearances in Las Vegas and occasional ones on TV. She died of cancer at the UCLA Medical Center in Los Angeles.

Vera-Ellen uses her inheritance to visit Scotland and while going through customs she meets Tony Martin, an American salesman, who wins her heart in *Let's Be Happy* (Allied Artists, 1957).

Feature Films

Wonder Man (RKO, 1945), *The Kid from Brooklyn* (RKO, 1946), *Three Little Girls in Blue* (20th, 1946), *Carnival in Costa Rica* (20th, 1947), *Words and Music* (MGM, 1948), *Love Happy* (UA, 1949), *On the Town* (MGM, 1949), *Three Little Words* (MGM, 1950), *Happy Go Lovely* (RKO, 1951), *The Belle of New York* (MGM, 1952), *Call Me Madam* (20th, 1953), *The Big Leaguer* (MGM, 1953), *White Christmas* (Par., 1954), *Let's Be Happy* (AA, 1957), *That's Entertainment III* (MGM/UA, 1994)

Johnny Weissmuller (1907–1984)

Weissmuller was born in Winder, Pennsylvania, where he took up swimming as a child to overcome polio. He attended the University of Chicago and under the auspices of the Illinois Athletic Club became a renowned swimmer. At the 1924 Olympic Games in Paris, he broke three swimming records. He also set world records at the 1928 Olympic Games in Amsterdam. He retired undefeated in 1928 from competitive swimming and turned professional in 1929. He became an advertising model for BVD underwear and appeared in the

Johnny Weissmuller and Maureen O'Sullivan go in search of their kidnapped son in *Tarzan's New York Adventure* with Virginia Grey and Milton Kibbes (MGM, 1942).

film *Glorifying the American Girl.* MGM signed him and cast him opposite Maureen O'Sullivan in *Tarzan the Ape Man.* It was such a success that many Tarzan films followed. He appeared with his second wife, Lupe Velez, in vaudeville and with Eleanor Holm in *Billy Rose's Aquacade* at Cleveland's Great Lakes Exposition and at the San Francisco Fair of 1940. On television he was in the successful series *Jungle Jim,* a spinoff from his Columbia film series of the same name. Weissmuller was vice-president of a swimming pool company in Florida and then was a host and greeter at Caesar's Palace in Las Vegas for four years. In 1983 he was inducted into the U.S. Olympic Hall of Fame. He died in his sleep at his home in Acapulco, Mexico.

Feature Films

Glorifying the American Girl (Par., 1930), *Tarzan, the Ape Man* (MGM, 1932), *Tarzan and His Mate* (MGM, 1934), *Tarzan Escapes* (MGM, 1936), *Tarzan Finds a Son!* (MGM, 1939), *Tarzan's Secret Treasure* (MGM, 1941), *Tarzan's New York Adventure* (MGM, 1942), *Tarzan Triumphs* (RKO, 1943), *Stage Door Canteen* (UA, 1943), *Tarzan's Desert Mystery* (RKO, 1943), *Tarzan and the Amazons* (RKO, 1945), *Tarzan and the Leopard Women* (RKO, 1946), *Swamp Fire* (Par., 1946), *Tarzan and the Huntress* (RKO, 1947), *Tarzan and the Mermaids* (RKO, 1948), *Jungle Jim* (Col., 1948), *The Lost Tribe* (Col, 1949), *Captive Girl* (Col., 1950), *Mark of the Gorilla* (Col., 1950),

Tarzan and His Mate was the MGM sequel to *Tarzan the Ape Man* with Johnny Weissmuller as Tarzan and Maureen O'Sullivan as Jane (MGM, 1934).

Pygmy Island (Col., 1950), *Fury of the Congo* (Col., 1951), *Jungle Manhunt* (Col., 1951), *Jungle Jim in the Forbidden Land* (Col., 1952), *Voodoo Tiger* (Col., 1952), *Savage Mutiny* (Col., 1953), *Valley of Head Hunters* (Col., 1953), *Killer Ape* (Col., 1953), *Jungle Man-Eaters* (Col., 1954), *Cannibal Attack* (Col., 1954), *Jungle Moon Men* (Col., 1955), *Devil Goddess* (Col., 1955), *The Phynx* (Cinema, 1970), *Won Ton Ton, the Dog Who Saved Hollywood* (Par., 1976)

Everett Sloan holds a trophy presented to *Citizen Kane* (Orson Welles) as Joseph Cotten looks over his shoulder. They are surrounded by employees of the *New York Enquirer*, which Kane has taken over to run for the fun of it (RKO, 1941).

Orson Welles (1915–1985)

Orson Welles was born in Kenosha, Wisconsin. His father was Head Welles, an inventor and manufacturer, and his mother was Beatrice Ives, a talented pianist. When Welles was 11 he was enrolled at Todd School for Boys in Woodstock, Illinois, where he concentrated on his theater interests. During vacations he travelled to Europe and the Orient until his father's death in 1930. The following year he went on a trip to Ireland and auditioned at the Gate Theatre in Dublin. He made his professional acting debut there in *Jew Suss* and

appeared in six more Gate productions. When he returned to the U.S., he went back to the Todd School and then to New York where he appeared with Katharine Cornell in three successful plays on Broadway and on tour. He became director of the Negro People's Theatre and then was appointed director of the New York Federal Theatre. He directed hit plays for both companies. With John Houseman he founded the Mercury Theatre in 1937 and produced brilliant plays on Broadway. Then he gained national attention with radio productions for the

Mercury Theatre. More publicity came with his radio presentation of H.G. Wells' *The War of the Worlds*, which told of the invasion of the U.S. by martians. Many listeners took it for the real thing and there was a mass panic. He secured a contract with RKO and went to Hollywood where his first film with the Mercury Players was *Citizen Kane*, a very controversial piece based on the life of publisher William Randolph Hearst. Welles also co-wrote and directed two other RKO films, *The Magnificent Ambersons* and *Journey Into Fear*. At this point Welles had lost artistic control over his films and both were edited without his participation. They were not successful at the box office. He then acted and directed at other Hollywood studios before moving to Europe, where he continued his work. In later years Welles received an honorary Oscar (1970), the French Legion of Honor (1982) and the Directors Guild of America's D.W. Griffith Award (1984). In his last years he became well known for his TV appearances. He died at 70 of a heart attack. His first marriage to Virginia Nicholson in 1934 ended in divorce in 1940. In 1943 he married Rita Hayworth. They were divorced in 1947. His third wife (married 1956) was the Countess de Girafalco, an Italian actress whose stage name was Paola Mori. Their marriage lasted until his death.

Feature Films

Swiss Family Robinson (narrator; RKO, 1940), *Citizen Kane* (RKO, 1941), *The Magnificent Ambersons* (narrator; RKO, 1942), *Journey into Fear* (RKO, 1942), *Jane Eyre* (20th, 1944), *Follow the Boys* (Univ., 1944), *Tomorrow Is Forever* (RKO, 1946), *The Stranger* (RKO, 1946), *Duel in the Sun* (narrator; Selznick, 1946), *The Lady from Shanghai* (Col., 1948), *Macbeth* (Rep., 1948), *The Third Man* (Selznick, 1949), *Black Magic* (UA, 1949), *Prince of Foxes* (20th, 1949), *The Black Rose* (20th, 1950), *Trent's Last Case* (Rep., 1953), *Trouble in the Glen* (Rep., 1954), *Confidential Report* (WB, 1955), *Three Cases of Murder* (Associated Artists, 1955), *Othello* (UA, 1955), *Moby Dick* (WB, 1956), *Man in the Shadow* (Univ., 1957), *Touch of Evil* (Univ., 1958), *The Vikings* (narrator; 1958), *The Long, Hot Summer* (20th, 1958), *The Roots of Heaven* (20th, 1958), *High Journey* (narrator; Baylis, 1959), *South Seas Adventure* (narrator; Dudley, 1959), *Ferry to Hong Kong* (20th, 1959), *Compulsion* (20th, 1959), *A Crack in the Mirror* (20th, 1960), *Masters of the Congo Jungle* (narrator; 20th, 1960), *King of Kings* (narrator; MGM, 1961), *The Trial* (Gibralter, 1962), *The V.I.P.'s* (MGM, 1963), *The Finest Hours* (narrator; Col., 1964), *Falstaff* (Counor, 1965), *Is Paris Burning?* (Par., 1966), *A Man for All Seasons* (Col., 1966), *Marco the Magnificent* (MGM, 1966), *Casino Royale* (Col., 1967), *The Sailor from Gibralter* (Lippert, 1967), *I'll Never Forget What's 'Is Name* (Rank, 1968), *House of Cards* (Univ., 1968), *Oedipus* (Univ., 1968), *Fight for Rome* (Constantin, 1969), *Immortal Story* (Altura, 1969), *Southern Star* (Col., 1969), *Catch 22* (Par., 1970), *The Kremlin Letter* (20th, 1970), *Start the Revolution Without Me* (WB, 1970), *Twelve Plus One* (CEF, 1970), *Waterloo* (Par., 1970), *The Battle of the Neretva* (AIP, 1971), *A Safe Place* (Col., 1971), *Get to Know Your Rabbit* (WB, 1972), *Malpertius* (UA, 1972), *Necromancy* (Cinerama, 1972), *Ten Days' Wonder* (Les Films, 1972), *Treasure Island* (Mass Films, 1972), *Bugs Bunny, Superstar* (voice only; WB, 1975), *Ten Little Indians* (voice only; Corona, 1975), *Voyage of the Damned* (Associates General, 1976), *Hot Tomorrows* (voice only;

Joan Fontaine as *Jane Eyre,* the governess heroine of Charlotte Bronte's Victorian novel. Orson Welles is Edward Rochester, master of ill-fated Thornffeld Hall (20th Century–Fox, 1944).

American, 1978), *The Muppet Movie* (Entertainment, 1979), *The Double McGuffin* (voice only; Mulberry, 1979), *History of the World — Part 1* (narrator; 20th, 1981), *Butterfly* (Analysis, 1982), *Where Is Parsifal?* (EMI, 1984), *Transformers* (voice only; Sunbow, 1986), *Someone to Love* (International Rainbow, 1987)

Cornel Wilde is the manager of a *Road House* and Ida Lupino sings and plays the piano in the joint (20th Century–Fox, 1948).

Cornel Wilde (1915–1989)

Cornel Wilde was born in New York to Hungarian-Czech parents. He spent part of his childhood and adolescence in Europe where his father traveled extensively, representing a cosmetic firm. In 1932 he enrolled at New York City College as a pre-med student. Wilde earned his tuition by working as a salesman, commercial artist, and in advertising for a French newspaper. He won a scholarship to Columbia University's College of Physicians and Surgeons in 1935. His fencing abilities won him a place on the U.S. Olympic Team in 1936. He dropped out of school to pursue a career in the theater, appearing on Broadway and on the road. While appearing in Hollywood, he was hired as a fencing instructor and actor in Laurence Olivier and Vivien Leigh's stage production of *Romeo and Juliet*. Soon afterward he was signed by Warner Brothers and appeared in several films. He moved to 20th Century–Fox where he became a star, appearing opposite Sonja Henie, Gene Tierney, Linda Darnell and Ida Lupino. He was loaned to Columbia for *A Song to Remember*, a film in which he portrayed Chopin. His performance won him an Oscar nomination. In 1955 he formed his own film company, Theodora, with Jean Wallace, his second wife. Together they produced many successful films in which he was both actor and director. Wilde also appeared as guest star on many television shows and in the television movie *Gargoyles*. He divorced Wallace in 1981 and died in 1989.

Sonja Henie stops at a run-down hotel and meets Cornel Wilde in *Wintertime* (20th Century–Fox, 1943).

Feature Films

The Lady with Red Hair (WB, 1940), *Kisses for Breakfast* (WB, 1941), *High Sierra* (WB, 1941), *Right to the Heart* (WB, 1941), *The Perfect Snob* (20th, 1942), *Life Begins at 8:30* (20th, 1942), *Manila Calling* (20th, 1942), *Wintertime* (20th, 1943), *Guest in the House* (UA, 1944), *A Thousand and One Nights* (Col., 1945), *A Song to Remember* (Col., 1945), *Leave Her to Heaven* (20th, 1945), *The Bandit of Sherwood Forest* (Col., 1946), *Centennial Summer* (20th, 1946), *The Homestretch* (20th, 1947), *Forever Amber* (20th, 1947), *It Had to Be You* (Col., 1947), *Roadhouse* (20th, 1948), *The Walls of Jericho* (20th, 1948), *Four Days Leave* (Film Classics, 1950), *Two Flags West* (20th, 1950), *At Sword's Point* (RKO, 1952), *The Greatest Show on Earth* (Par., 1952), *California Conquest* (Col., 1952), *The Treasure of the Golden Condor* (20th, 1953), *Main Street to Broadway* (MGM, 1953), *Saadia* (MGM, 1953), *Passion* (RKO, 1954), *Woman's World* (20th, 1954), *The Scarlet Coat* (MGM, 1955), *Storm Fear* (UA, 1955), *The Big Combo* (AA, 1955), *Star of India* (UA, 1956), *Hot Blood* (Col., 1956), *The Devil's Hairpin* (Par., 1957), *Omar Khayyam* (Par., 1957), *Beyond Mombasa* (Col., 1957), *Maracaibo* (Par., 1958), *Edge of Eternity* (Col., 1959), *Constantine and the Cross* (Embassy, 1962), *Sword of Lancelot* (Univ., 1963), *The Naked Prey* (Par., 1966), *Beach Red* (UA, 1967), *The Comic* (Col., 1969), *No Blade of Grass* (MGM, 1970), *Shark's Treasure* (UA, 1975), *The Norseman* (AIP, 1978), *The Fifth Musketeer* (Col., 1979)

Natalie Wood and James Dean star in *Rebel Without a Cause,* a powerful study of juvenile violence in which each is seeking identity and love (Warner Bros., 1955).

Natalie Wood (1938–1981)

Born Natasha Gurdin, the daughter of a San Francisco architect, she changed her name to Natalie Wood when she entered films. As an extra in the movie, *Happy Land* she was spotted by director Irving Pichel, who gave her a featured role in *Tomorrow Is Forever.* Her career as a child performer continued and she made an easy transition to teenage and later ingenue roles. Wood was honored twice (1947 and 1950) as child star of the year. She was nominated three times for the Academy Award for her roles in *Rebel Without a Cause, Splendor in the Grass* and *Love with the Proper Stranger.* She received an Emmy nomination in Sir Laurence Olivier's production of *Cat on a Hot Tin Roof* and won the Golden Globe award for her television performance in *From Here to Eternity.* In 1957 she married actor Robert Wagner. They were divorced in 1962. She then wed executive Richard Gregson but the marriage failed. In 1972 she remarried Wagner. She drowned off the coast of Catalina Island where the Wagners' yacht, the *Splendor,* was anchored.

Although stranded, Natalie Wood, Rosalind Russell and Karl Malden still see the bright side by singing in *Gypsy* (Warner Bros., 1962).

Feature Films

as **Natasha Gurdin:** *Happy Land* (20th, 1943)

as **Natalie Wood:** *Tomorrow Is Forever* (RKO, 1946), *The Bride Wore Boots* (Par., 1946), *Miracle on 34th Street* (Par., 1947), *The Ghost and Mrs. Muir* (20th, 1947), *Driftwood* (Rep., 1947), *Scudda Hoo! Scudda Hay!* (20th, 1948), *Chicken Every Sunday* (20th, 1948), *The Green Promise* (RKO, 1949), *Father Was a Fullback* (20th, 1949), *Our Very Own* (RKO, 1950), *No Sad Songs for Me* (Col., 1950), *The Jackpot* (20th, 1950), *Never a Dull Moment* (RKO, 1950), *Dear Brat* (Par., 1951), *The Blue Veil* (RKO, 1951), *Just for You* (Par., 1952), *The Rose Bowl Story* (Mon., 1952), *The Star* (20th, 1953), *The Silver Chalice* (WB, 1954), *One Desire* (Univ., 1955), *Rebel Without a Cause* (WB, 1955), *The Searchers* (WB, 1956), *The Burning Hills* (WB, 1956), A *Cry in the Night* (WB, 1956), *The Girl He Left Behind* (WB, 1956), *Bombers B-52* (WB, 1957), *Marjorie Morningstar* (WB, 1958), *Kings Go Forth* (UA, 1958), *Cash McCall* (WB, 1959), *All the Fine Young Cannibals* (MGM, 1960), *Splendor in the Grass* (WB, 1961), *West Side Story* (UA, 1961), *Gypsy* (WB, 1962), *Love with the Proper Stranger* (Par., 1963), *Sex and the Single Girl* (WB, 1964), *The Great Race* (WB, 1965), *Inside Daisy Glover* (WB, 1965), *This Property Is Condemned* (Par., 1966), *Penelope* (MGM, 1966), *Bob & Carol & Ted & Alice* (Col., 1969), *Peeper* (20th, 1975), *Meteor* (AIF, 1978), *The Last Married Couple in America* (Univ., 1979), *Brainstorm* (MGM, 1983)

Index